...an international forum for innovative research and applications

THE JOURNAL OF

Visualization AND
Computer
Animation

EDITORS
Nadia Magnenat Thalmann, *University of Geneva, Switzerland*
Daniel Thalmann, *Swiss Federal Institute of Technology, Switzerland*
E. Catmull, *Pixar, USA*
T. L. Kunii, *University of Aizu, Japan*

Most of the phenomena which may be represented on the screen of a workstation are typically time-dependent. In order to visualize these phenomena at any given time, it is necessary to know the appearance of the scene at this time, then computer graphics techniques can be used to build and display the scene according to viewing and lighting parameters. The problems to solve are how to express time dependence in the scene and how to make it evolve over time: this is the main challenge of computer animation. With visualization scientists can turn mountains of numbers into animation sequences and display measurements of physical variables in space and time.

Using new technologies, animators and scientists can immerse themselves in these computer-generated worlds, or can at least communicate with them using specific devices. With the existence of graphics workstations able to display complex scenes and with the advent of very new 3-D interactive devices for Virtual Reality, it is possible to create applications based on a full 3-D interaction metaphor in which the specifications of deformations or motion are given in real-time. These new concepts provoke drastic changes in methods of designing animation sequences.

The field of Computer Animation is interdisciplinary and attracts those working in the sciences and arts applying animation techniques. The range of topics covered in the journal includes all theoretical concepts, practical techniques and applications in animation and visualization.

ISSN 1049-8907   **Published Quarterly**

Further details and subscription information from:

Dept AC, John Wiley & Sons Ltd, Baffins Lane, Chichester, West Sussex PO19 1UD, UK

Subscriptions Dept C, John Wiley & Sons Inc, 605 Third Avenue, New York, NY 10158, USA

Artificial Life
and Virtual Reality

Artificial Life and Virtual Reality

Edited by

Nadia Magnenat Thalmann
University of Geneva, Switzerland

and

Daniel Thalmann
Swiss Federal Institute of Technology, Switzerland

JOHN WILEY & SONS
Chichester · New York · Brisbane · Toronto · Singapore

Other Wiley Editorial Offices

John Wiley & Sons, Inc., 605 Third Avenue,
New York, NY 10158-0012, USA

Jacaranda Wiley Ltd, 33 Park Road, Milton,
Queensland 4064, Australia

John Wiley & Sons (Canada) Ltd, 22 Worcester Road,
Rexdale, Ontario M9W 1L1, Canada

John Wiley & Sons (SEA) Pte Ltd, 37 Jalan Pemimpin #05-04,
Block B, Union Industrial Building, Singapore 2057

Library of Congress Cataloging-in-Publication Data

Artificial life and virtual reality / edited by Nadia Magnenat
   Thalmann and Daniel Thalmann
      p. cm.
   Includes bibliographical references and index.
   ISBN 0 471 95146 3
   1. Human-computer interaction. 2. Virtual reality. I. Magnenat
-Thalmann, Nadia. II. Thalmann, Daniel.
QA76.9.H85A785 1994
006—dc20   94-12672
                                                          CIP

British Library Cataloguing in Publication Data

A catalogue record for this book is available from the British Library

ISBN 0 471 95146 3

Produced from camera-ready copy supplied by the editors
Printed and bound in Great Britain by Bookcraft (Bath) Ltd

Contents

9. Body Centered Interaction in Immersive Virtual Environments
Mel Slater and Martin Usoh

10. Manipulation and Exploration of Virtual Objects
Massimo Bergamasco

14. Shared Objects in Private Workspaces: Cooperative Work in Virtual Worlds

Gurminder Singh and Luis Serra

Preface

Artificial Life (AL) refers to all the techniques that try to recreate living organisms and creatures by computer. Originally introduced to recreate, by computer, biological phenomena, artificial life includes today the simulation of behavior processes which result from consciousness and emotions. We can now speak of behavioral artificial life.

Virtual Reality (VR) means the immersion of real humans in virtual worlds, worlds that are completely created by computer. This means interaction with objects from the virtual world, their manipulation, and the feeling that the human user is a real participant in the virtual world.

Actually, artificial life and virtual reality are associated; most virtual worlds will become inhabited by virtual living creatures and users. Real persons, through VR will be able to communicate and interact with these synthetic living beings. Application areas of such systems are simulation, entertainment, and multimedia.

In conclusion, this book is a first attempt to show artificial life in virtual reality. The specificity of simulating artifical life in VR are to visualize life. That means, mainly the behavior, which is a consequence of biological life. In virtual worlds, little has been done to attempt to reproduce biological processes. People interacting with VR, as in real life, expect to be able to interact with plants, animals, and humans as a whole, just as if they were real living beings.

Most of the texts are results of presentations during the workshop "Artificial Life and Virtual Reality" held in November 1993 at the University of Geneva. This workshop was sponsored by the "Troisieme Cycle Romand d'Informatique" and allowed participants to discuss the state of research in these areas. We would like to thank the "Troisieme Cycle Romand d'Informatique" for their generous support in offering all workshop participants a copy of this book, so nicely edited by John Wiley and Sons. Finally, we would like to thank Gaynor Redvers-Mutton for her active collaboration in the making of this book.

Nadia Magnenat Thalmann
Daniel Thalmann

List of Contributors

Igor Aleksander
Department of Electrical and Electronic
Engineering
Imperial College
University of London,
Exhibition Road
London SW7 2BT
UK

Peter Astheimer
Fraunhofer Institute - IGD
Wilhelminenstr. 7
D-64283 Darmstadt,
Germany

Massimo Bargamasco
ARTS Lab
Scuola Superiore S. Anna
Via Carducci 40
6100 Pisa,
Italy

Ulrich Broeckl
Institut für Betriebs- und Dialogsysteme
Abteilung für Dialogsysteme und
Graphisch Datenverarbeitung
Postfach 6980
Am Fasanengarten 5
D-76128 Karlsruhe,
Germany

Michèle Courant
Institut d'Informatique
Université de Fribourg
3 chemin du Musée
CH-1700 Fribourg
Switzerland

Fan Dai
Fraunhofer Institute - IGD
Wilhelminenstr. 7
D-64283 Darmstadt,
Germany

Jean Françon
Department of Computer Science,
Louis-Pasteur University,
CNRS,
7, rue René Descartes
Strasbourg
France

Philippe Gaussier
Laboratoire de Microinformatique
Swiss Federal Institute of Technology,
CH 1015 Lausanne,
Switzerland

Martin Göbel
Fraunhofer Institute - IGD
Wilhelminenstr. 7
D-64283 Darmstadt
Germany

Beat Hirsbrunner
Institut d'Informatique
Université de Fribourg,
3 chemin du Musée,
CH-1700 Fribourg
Switzerland

L. Kettner
Institut für Betriebs- und Dialogsysteme
Abteilung für Dialogsysteme und
Graphisch Datenverarbeitung
Postfach 6980
Am Fasanengarten 5
D-76128 Karlsruhe,
Germany

Guy Kirsch
Séminaire de Finances Publiques
Université de Fribourg, ISES
CH-1700 Fribourg
Switzerland

A.Klingert
Institut für Betriebs- und Dialogsysteme
Abteilung für Dialogsysteme und
Graphisch Datenverarbeitung
Postfach 6980
Am Fasanengarten 5
D-76128 Karlsruhe,
Germany

L. Kobbelt
Institut für Betriebs- und Dialogsysteme
Abteilung für Dialogsysteme und
Graphisch Datenverarbeitung
Postfach 6980
Am Fasanengarten 5
D-76128 Karlsruhe,
Germany

Rolf Kruse
Fraunhofer Institute - IGD
Wilhelminenstr. 7
D-64283 Darmstadt,
Germany

Hilmar Lehnert
Lehrstuhl für Akustik
IC1-132
Ruhruniversität Bochum
D-44780 Bochum
Germany

Pascal Lienhardt
Department of Computer Science
Louis-Pasteur University
CNRS
7, rue René Descartes,
Strasbourg
France

Nadia Magnenat Thalmann
MIRALab-CUI,
University of Geneva
24 rue du Général-Dufour,
CH-1204 Geneva
Switzerland

Daniel Mange
Logic Systems Laboratory
Computer Engineering Department,
Swiss Federal Institute of Technology
CH 1015 Lausanne
Switzerland

Stefan Müller
Fraunhofer Institute - IGD
Wilhelminenstr. 7
D-64283 Darmstadt,
Germany

Hansrudi Noser
Computer Graphics Lab
Swiss Federal Institute of Technology
CH 1015 Lausanne,
Switzerland

Luis Serra
Institute of System Sciences
National University of Singapore
Heng Mui Kent Terrace
Kent Ridge,
Singapore 0511
Republic of Singapore

Gurminder Singh
Institute of System Sciences
National University of Singapore
Heng Mui Kent Terrace
Kent Ridge,
Singapore 0511
Republic of Singapore

Mel Slater
Department of Computer Science
Queen Mary and Westfield College
University of London,
Mile End Road
London E1 4NS
UK

André Stauffer
Logic Systems Laboratory, Computer
Engineering Department, Swiss Federal
Institute of Technology, CH 1015
Lausanne, Switzerland

Beat Stoffel
Institut d'Informatique, Université de
Fribourg, 3 chemin du Musée, CH-1700
Fribourg

Daniel Thalmann
Computer Graphics Lab, Swiss Federal
Institute of Technology, CH 1015
Lausanne, Switzerland

Martin Usoh
Department of Computer Science, Queen
Mary and Westfield College, University
of London, Mile End Road, London E1
4NS, UK

Gabriel Zachmann
Fraunhofer Institute - IGD,
Wilhelminenstr. 7, D-64283 Darmstadt,
Germany

Stéphane Zrehen
Laboratoire de Microinformatique, Swiss
Federal Institute of Technology, CH
1015 Lausanne, Switzerland

Introduction: Creating Artificial Life in Virtual Reality

Nadia Magnenat Thalmann
MIRALab, University of Geneva, Switzerland

Daniel Thalmann
Computer Graphics Lab, Swiss Federal Institute of Technology, Lausanne, Switzerland

I.1. Virtual Worlds

For about 20 years, computer-generated images have been created for films, generics and advertising. At the same time, scientific researchers, medical people, architects discovered the great potential of these images and used them to visualize the invisible or simulate the non-existing. It was the genesis of Virtual Worlds. However, these virtual worlds had two severe limitations:

- There was very little visual representation of living organisms or only very simple creatures in them
- Nobody could really enter into these worlds: the access to the virtual worlds was looking on 2D screens and 2D interaction.

Today, new interfaces and 3D devices allow us a complete immersion into these virtual worlds or at least a direct and real-time communication with them. This new way of immersion into the virtual worlds is called *Virtual Reality*. At the same time, researchers have been able to create plants, trees, and animals. Research in human animation has led to the creation of synthetic actors with complex motion. Moreover, a new field based on biology has tried to recreate the life with a bottom approach, the so-called *Artificial Life* approach. Now all these various approaches should be integrated in order to create truly Virtual Worlds with autonomous living beings, plants, animals and humans with their own behavior and real people should be able to enter into these worlds and meet their inhabitants.

Artificial Life and and Virtual Reality Edited by Nadia Magnenat Thalmann and Daniel Thalmann
© 1994 John Wiley and Sons Ltd

In this introductory chapter, we try to identify the key parameters for creating Artificial Life in Virtual Reality, by referring mainly other chapters of this book. Artificial Life is concerned with biological aspects like *Embryonics* (Mange and Stauffer 1994), a basis of natural mechanism of development of living multicellular beings. Artificial Life also includes living organisms created by rule-based languages (Noser and Thalmann 1994) and topology methods (Françon and Lienhardt 1994) or control of mobile robots (Gaussier and Zrehen 1994). However, this introductory chapter emphasizes the Artificial Life of Virtual Humans (Magnenat Thalmann and Thalmann 1993) in Virtual Reality.

I.2. Artificial Life of Virtual Humans

I.2.1. Why Virtual Humans ?

The fast development of multimedia communication systems will give a considerable impact to virtual worlds by allowing millions of people to enter into these worlds using TV networks. Among the applications of such virtual worlds with virtual humans, we can just mention:

- computer games involving people rather than cartoon-type characters
- computer-generated films which involve simulated people in simulated 3D worlds
- game simulations such as football games which show simulated people rather than cartoon-type characters.
- interactive drama titles in which the user can interact with simulated characters and hence be involved in a scenario rather than simply watching it.
- simulation based learning and training.
- virtual reality worlds which are populated by simulated people.

These applications will require:

- realistic modeling of people's behavior, including interactions with each other and with the human user.
- realistic modeling of people's visual appearance, including clothes and hair

For the modeling of *behaviors*, the ultimate objective is to build *intelligent autonomous* virtual humans with *adaptation, perception* and *memory*. These virtual humans should be able to act *freely* and *emotionally*. They should be *conscious* and *unpredictable*, Finally, they should reinforce the concept of *presence*. But can we expect in the near future to represent in the computer the concepts of behavior, intelligence, autonomy, adaptation, perception, memory, freedom, emotion, consciousness, unpredictability, and presence ? In this introductory part, we will try to define these terms and already identify research aspects in these concepts.

In summary, virtual humans should have a certain number of qualities that are represented in Figure I.1

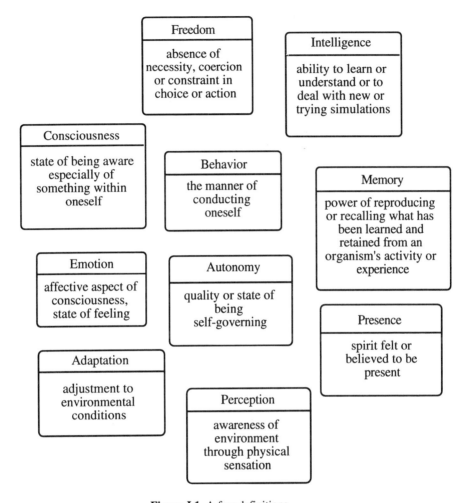

Figure I.1. A few definitions.

Based on classical definitions (Merriam-Webster 1989), we will try first to identify which mechanisms should be simulated in order to implement truly virtual humans or actors.

I.2.2. Behavior

First, virtual humans should be able to have a behavior, which means they must have a manner of conducting themselves. Behavior is often defined as the way in which animals and humans act, and is usually described in natural language terms which have social, psychological or physiological significance, but which are not necessarily easily reducible to the movement of one or two muscles, joints or end effectors. Behavior is also the response of an individual, group, or species to its environment. Based on this definition, Reynolds (1987) introduced the term and the concept of behavioral animation in order to describe the automating of such higher level animation. Behavior is not only reacting to the environment but should also include the flow of information by which the environment acts on the living creature as well as the way the creature codes and uses this information. Reynolds studied in detail the problem of group trajectories: bird flocks, herds of land animals and fish schools.

I.2.3. Intelligence

The classical definition of intelligence is the ability to learn or understand or to deal with new or trying situations. This is also the ability to apply knowledge to manipulate one's environment or to think abstractly as measured by objective criteria. Implement intelligence in virtual humans means to create artificial intelligence, an area that has always grown for many years, even if there are still considerable limitations, due mainly to a purely logical approach.

I.2.4. Autonomy

Autonomy is generally defined as the quality or state of being self-governing. Rodriguez et al. (1994) introduced the concept of autonomous system: a system that is able to give to itself its proper laws, its conduct, opposite to the heteronomous systems which are driven by the outside. Bourgine (1994) defines an autonomous system as a system which has the abdictive capacity to guess viable actions. As stated by Courant et al. (1994), in cybernetics as well as in cognitive psychology, autonomy has always been strongly connected with self-organization. Hence, computer scientists sometimes prefer to take the following definition of autonomy *"the capacity of a system to maintain its viability in various and changing environments"*.

The need to have autonomous behaviour for virtual humans arises from two considerations:

- in computer-generated films, the more autonomous behaviour that is built into the virtual humans, the less extra work there is to be done by the designer to create complete scenarios
- in interactive games, autonomous human-like behaviour is necessary in order to maintain the illusion in the user that the Virtual Humans are real ones.

I.2.5. Adaptation

As defined by Wilson (1991) and Guillot and Meyer (1994), the behavior of an artificial organism, called animat, is adaptive as long as it allows it to "survive" in more or less unpredictable and dangerous environments. For virtual humans, we may consider the general definition of adjustment to environmental conditions and use methods similar to these described by Gaussier and Zrehen (1994) to design control architectures for autonomous robots capable of adapting to an unknown world or the vision-based approach described by Renault et al. (1991).

I.2.6. Perception

Perception is defined as the awareness of the elements of environment through physical sensation. In order to implement perception, virtual humans should be equipped with visual, tactile and auditory sensors. These sensors should be used as a basis for implementing everyday human behaviour such as visually directed locomotion, handling objects, and responding to sounds and utterances. A simulation of the touching system should consist in detecting contacts between the virtual human and the environment. The most important perceptual subsystem is the vision system. A vision based approach for virtual humans is a very important perceptual subsystem and is for example essential for navigation in virtual worlds. It is an ideal approach for modeling a behavioral animation and offers a universal approach to pass the necessary information from the environment to the virtual human in the problems of path searching, obstacle avoidance, and internal knowledge representation with learning and forgetting characteristics. Vision-based behavioral models have been already described by Renault et al. (1991) and Reynolds (1993).

In (Renault et al. 1991), each pixel of the vision input has the semantic information giving the object projected on this pixel, and numerical information giving the distance to this object. So, it is easy to know, for example, that there is a table just in front at 3 meters. With this information, we can directly deal with the problematic question: "what do I do with such information in a navigation system?"

In the context of Virtual Reality, there is an interaction between a virtual human and a real one. In this case, there is no possibility of transferring data structures, and real recognition methods (for example: image understanding) are required to provide the virtual human with a perception of the real human's behaviour. Auditory aspects are also important in this case (Lehnert 1994).

I.2.7. Memory

Memory is generally defined as the power or process of reproducing or recalling what has been learned and retained especially through associative mechanisms. This is also the store of things learned and retained from an organism's activity or experience as evidenced by modification of structure or behavior or by recall and recognition

To implement a concept of memory into a virtual human is not very complex, as already the memory is a key concept in Computer Science. For example, Noser and Thalmann (1994) propose a dynamic occupancy octree grid to serve as a global 3D visual memory and to allow an actor to memorize the environment that he sees and to adapt it to a changing and dynamic environment. His reasoning process allows him to find 3D paths based on his visual memory by avoiding impasses and circuits. The global behavior of the actor is based on a navigation automata, representing the automata of an actor, who has to go from his current position to different places, memorized in a list of destinations. He can displace himself in known or unknown environments.

I.2.8. Emotion

Emotion may be defined as the affective aspect of consciousness; this is a state of feeling, a psychic and physical reaction (as anger or fear) subjectively experienced as strong feeling and physiologically involving changes that prepare the body for immediate vigorous action virtual humans should be capable of responding emotionally to their situation as well as acting physically within it. Apart from making the virtual humans more realistic, visible emotions on the part of the virtual humans could provide designers with a direct way of affecting the user's own emotional state. Virtual humans will therefore be equipped with a simple computational model of emotional behaviour, to which emotionally related behaviour such as facial expressions and posture can be coupled, and which can be used to influence their actions. To render emotions, most facial animation systems are based on the Facial Action Coding System (FACS) developed by Ekman and Friesen (1975). Kalra and Magnenat Thalmann (1993) redefine emotion as a function of two signals in time, one for its intensity and the other for the color. They propose a model of vascular expressions in facial animation (Kalra and Magnenat Thalmann 1994).

I.2.9. Consciousness

Consciousness may be defined as the quality or state of being aware especially of something within oneself or the state of being characterized by sensation, emotion, volition, and thought. Aleksander (1994) discusses the recent renewal of interest in the question of whether an explanation of consciousness can (Dennett 1991) or cannot (Penrose 1989) be captured by some formal theory. He presents a theory of consciousness centered on the concept of a neural state machine. The theory is based on the conditions that may be necessary to synthesize consciousness in constructed artifact. This is given the name "artificial consciousness".

I.2.10. Freedom and Unpredictability

Freedom is the absence of necessity, coercion, or constraint in choice or action; this is also the power or condition of acting without compulsion In terms of Virtual Actors, Kirsch (1994) proposes to say that an actor is free, when and to the extent that his future behaviour is unpredictable to somebody; this somebody may be the actor himself or somebody else.

I.2.11. Presence and Immersion

Presence is the fact or condition of being present and it is something (as a spirit) felt or believed to be present. This spirit is essential in Virtual Reality. As stated by Slater and

Usoh (1994), immersion may lead to a sense of presence. This is an emergent psychological property of an immersive system, and refers to the participant's sense of "being there" in the world created by the Virtual environment system. Astheimer et al. (1994) define an immersive system as follows: if the user cannot tell, which reality is "real", and which one is "virtual", then the computer generated one is immersive.

I.3. Communicating with Virtual Humans in Virtual Reality

Two different kinds of interactivity could be addressed: interaction between virtual humans, and interaction between virtual humans and real ones, a Virtual Reality situation. The first is required for computer-generated films, and the second for games, although in either case both kinds of interaction may be needed. These two kinds of interaction are sufficiently different to require quite different technical solutions. A pair of virtual humans interacting is a closed system that can implemented on different machines as proposed by Singh and Serra (1994) which can be developed by equipping the virtual humans with complementary behaviours, whereas the system consisting of a virtual human interacting with a real human is only partially under control of the designer. In order to support interaction and communication, virtual humans should be equipped with the ability to "recognise" other virtual humans and "perceive" their facial expressions, gestures and postures. There is no need for real recognition or perception, of course, because information from the data structures that define these behaviors in one virtual humans can be passed directly to a second humanoid.

In the context of Virtual Reality, there is an interaction between a virtual human and a real one. As already mentioned, there is no possibility of transferring data structures, and real recognition methods are required to provide the virtual human with a perception of the real human's behaviour. True interaction between the Virtual and the real humans requires a two-way communication between them at the geometric level, at the physical level, and at the behavioral level, as described by Magnenat Thalmann and Thalmann (1991). Consider first a classical example of bi-directional communication: human-machine speech communication. The operator speaks using a microphone, the phonemes and words are recognized by a speech recognizer program that forms sentences. On the basis of these sentences, answers or new sentences are composed. A speech synthesizer generates the corresponding sounds which are amplified and may be heard by the operator.

At the geometric level, 3D devices allow the animator to communicate any geometric information to the actor. For example, the animator may use a SpaceBall to define a trajectory to be followed by the actor. He may use a DataGlove for defining a certain number of hand positions. This possibility may be exploited to create dialogue based on hand gestures (Broeckl-Fox et al. 1994) such as a dialogue between a deaf animator and a deaf synthetic actor using American Sign Language. The animator signs using two DataGloves, and the coordinates are transmitted to the computer. Then a sign-language recognition program interprets these coordinates in order to recognize gestures. A dialogue coordination program then generates an answer or a new sentence. The sentences are then translated into the hand signs and given to a hand animation program which generates the appropriate hand positions.

At the physical level, using a force transducer, a force or a torque may be communicated to an actor who can himself apply a force that may be felt by the animator using a force feedback device (Bergamasco 1994). It is for example possible to simulate the scene of virtual reality where the animator and the actor tug on the two ends of a rope.

At the behavioral level, we consider emotional communication between the actor and the animator (see Figure I.2, Color Section). We may restrict emotions to a few, such as happiness, anger, sadness and consider only the facial expressions as manifestations of these emotions. In such a behavioral communication system or, more accurately in this case, *an emotional communication system*, the animator may smile, his face is recorded in real-time using a device like the living video digitizer and the emotion is detected using an image processing program. The dialog coordinator decides which emotion should be generated in response to the received emotion. This emotion is translated into facial expressions to be generated by the facial animation system. Consider the example where Marilyn smiles when the animator smiles. The difficulty in such a process is to decide whether the animator is smiling based on the analysis of the image captured by the living video digitizer. At present only small images with a rather limited processing is possible with the actual hardware; this implies that the detection of subtleties of the face is not yet feasible.

Magnenat Thalmann et al. (1993) have described such an approach, consisting of recording a real human face using a video input like the Live Video Digitizer and extracting from the image the information necessary to generate similar facial expressions on a synthetic face. The recognition method is based on snakes as introduced by Terzopoulos and Waters (1991). A snake is a dynamic deformable 2D contour in the x-y plane. A discrete snake is a set of nodes with time varying positions. The nodes are coupled by internal forces making the snake acting like a series of springs resisting compression and a thin wire resisting bending. To create an interactive discrete snake, nodal masses are set to zero and the expression forces are introduced into the equations of motion for dynamic node/spring system. Terzopoulos and Waters make it responsive to a force field derived from the image. They express the force field which influences the snake's shape and motion through a time-varying potential function. To compute the potential, they apply a discrete smoothing filter consisting of 4-neighbor local averaging of the pixel intensities allowed by the application of a discrete approximation.

Our approach is different from Terzopoulos-Waters approach because we need to analyze the emotion in real-time. Instead of using a filter which globally transforms the image into a planar force field, we apply the filter in the neighborhood of the nodes of the snake. We only use a snake for the mouth; the rest of the information (jaw, eyebrows, eyes) is obtained by fast image-processing techniques.

I.4. Conclusion

Artificial Life refers to all the techniques that try to recreate living organisms and creatures by computer, including the simulation of behavior processes which result from consciousness and emotions. Virtual Reality means the immersion of real humans in virtual worlds, worlds that are completely created by computer. This means interaction with objects from the virtual world, their manipulation, and the feeling that the human user is a real participant in the virtual world. In the future, most virtual worlds will become inhabited by virtual living creatures and users. Figure I.3 and I.4 (Color Section) shows examples of virtual actors.

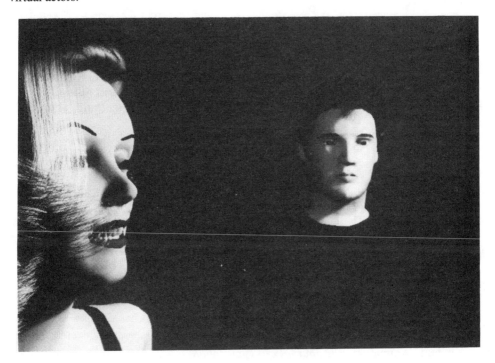

Figure I.3. Virtual Actors.

References

Aleksander I (1994) Artificial Consciousness, in: *This Volume.*

Astheimer P, Dai, Göbel M, Kruse R, Müller S, Zachmann G (1994) Realism in Virtual Reality, in: *This Volume.*

Bergamasco M (1994) Manipulation and Exploration of Virtual Objects, in: *This Volume.*

Bourgine P (1994) Autonomy, Abduction, Adaptation, in: (Magnenat Thalmann N, Thalmann D, eds), *Proc. Computer Animation '94,* IEEE Computer Society Press.

Broeckl-Fox U, Kettner L, Klingert A, Kobbelt L (1994) Using Three-Dimensional Hand-Gesture Recognition as a New 3D Input Technique, in: *This Volume.*

Courant M, Beat Hirsbrunner B, Stoffel B (1994) Managing Entities for an Autonomous Behaviour, in: *This Volume.*

Dennett, DC (1991) *Consciousness explained,* London: Allan Lane/Penguin.

Ekman and Friesen (1975) *Unmasking the Face: A Guide to Recognizing Emotions from Facial Clues,* Prentice Hall.

Françon J, Lienhardt P (1994)   Basic Principles of Topology-Based Methods for Simulating Metamorphoses of Natural Objects, in: *This Volume.*

Gaussier P, Zrehen S (1994)   A Constructivist Approach for Autonomous Agents, in: *This Volume.*

Guillot A and Meyer JA (1994) Computer Simulations of Adaptive Behavior in Animats, in: (Magnenat Thalmann N, Thalmann D, eds) *Proc. Computer Animation '94*, IEEE Computer Society Press.

Kalra P, Magnenat Thalmann N (1993) Simulation of Facial Skin using Texture Mapping and Coloration, Proc. ICCG '93, Bombay, India, in: (Mudur SP, Pattanaik SN, eds) *Graphics, Design and Visualization*, North Holland, pp.365-374.

Kalra P, Magnenat Thalmann N (1994), in: (Magnenat Thalmann N, Thalmann D, eds) Modeling of Vascular Expressions in Facial Animation, in: (Magnenat Thalmann N, Thalmann D, eds) *Proc. Computer Animation '94*, IEEE Computer Society Press.

Kirsch G (1994) Unpredictability - another word for freedom...And if machines were free?, in: *This Volume.*

Lehnert H (1994) Fundamentals of Auditory Virtual Environment, in: *This Volume.*

Magnenat Thalmann N, Cazedevals A, Thalmann D (1993) Modelling Facial Communication Between an Animator and a Synthetic Actor in Real Time, *Proc. IFIP Conf. on Modeling in Computer Graphics*, Genova, 1993, pp.387-396.

Magnenat Thalmann N, Thalmann D (1991) Complex Models for Animating Synthetic Actors, *IEEE Computer Graphics and Applications*, Vol.11, No5, pp.32-44.

Magnenat Thalmann N, Thalmann D (1993) The Artificial Life of Synthetic Actors, *IEICE Transactions*, Japan, invited paper, Vol. J76-D-II, No.8, pp.1506-1514.

Mange D, Stauffer A (1994) Introduction to Embryonics: Towards Self-Repairing and Self-reproducing Hardware Based on Biological-like Properties, in: *This Volume.*

Merriam-Webster (1989) *Webster Ninth New Collegiate Dictionary*

Noser H, Thalmann D (1994) Simulating the Life of Virtual Plants, Fishes and Butterflies, in: *This Volume.*

Penrose R (1989) *The emperor's new mind.* London: Vintage.

Renault O, Magnenat Thalmann N, Thalmann D (1991), A Vision-based Approach to Behavioural Animation, *The Journal of Visualization and Computer Animation*, Vol 1, No 1, pp 18-21.

Reynolds C (1987) Flocks, Herds, and Schools: A Distributed Behavioral Model, *Proc.SIGGRAPH '87, Computer Graphics*, Vol.21, No4, pp.25-34

Reynolds CW (1993) An evolved, Vision-Based Behavioral Model of Coordinated Group Motion, in: (Meyer JA, Roitblat HL, Wilson SW, eds) *From Animals to Animats, Proc. 2nd International Conf. on Simulation of Adaptive Behavior*, MIT Press.

Rodriguez M, Erard PJ, Muller JP (1994) 8: Virtual Environments for Simulating Artificial Autonomy, in: *This Volume.*

Singh G, Serra L (1994) Supporting Collaboration in Virtual Worlds, in: *This Volume.*

Slater M, Usoh M (1994) Body Centred Interaction in Immersive Virtual Environments, in: *This Volume.*

Terzopoulos D, Waters K (1991) Techniques for Realistic Facial Modeling and Animation, in (Magnenat-Thalmann N, Thalmann D, eds) *Proc. Computer Animation '91*, Springer, Tokyo, pp. 59-74.

Wilson SW (1991) The Animat Path to AI, , in: (Meyer JA, Wilson SW, eds) From Animals to Animats, *Proc. 1st International Conf. on Simulation of Adaptive Behavior*, MIT Press.

1

Unpredictability Another Word for Freedom

... and if machines were free ...

Guy Kirsch
University of Fribourg, Fribourg, Switzerland

If interdisciplinarity is to be a useful venture, not just a dangerous adventure, it must be based on disciplinarity and on discipline. Those participating in an interdisciplinary exchange should be and should remain the representatives of their own disciplines. Instead of dabbling in fields which they do not know, they should first of all couch what they know in terms which may be understood by those outside their field of knowledge. Instead of toying with answers in disciplines with which they are not familiar, they should be on the look out for contributions other disciplines might make to the solutions of those problems with which they are only too familiar. The quiet modesty of those who want to know, not the blatant triumphalism of those who know is the prime condition of a fruitful interdisciplinary exchange.

So, if I am about to discuss the idea of *free machines, I* do so as an economist, who has been haunted for the greater part of his intellectual life by the question: How and under which conditions is it possible for free actors to pursue their individual aims and not to get involved in mutually *destructive conflicts?* How and under which conditions do free actors interested in reaching their individual goals engage in a mutually *constructive cooperation?* Which means that as an economist I have mainly been interested in what in German is called "Gesellschaftliche Ordnungstheorie" and which for lack of a better term I shall call *"theory of the social order"*. As to my relation to computer science, it may best be characterized as a relation of interested ignorance. Anything I may know I owe to the patient didactics of my friend Professor *Jurg Kohlas*. And if ever I got something wrong (which is quite a

Artificial Life and and Virtual Reality Edited by Nadia Magnenat Thalmann and Daniel Thalmann

possibility), the fault is mine: My obtuseness was just too great to be overcome by even the most persevered teaching efforts.

1.1. Economists and Computer Scientists Have a Problem in Common

In the recent past, two parallel developments have taken place. *First,* the monocentral hierarchies of the planned economies have collapsed. With a few exceptions the *socialist order* has become a prey to its own deficiencies. The result: Whatever interindividual cooperation had been ensured by the discipline of a hierarchical, i.e. *vertical order* has been engulfed by the destructiveness of interindividual conflicts in a *horizontal disorder.* Slowly and with great difficulties Russia, Poland, Albania, even East Germany, e.g. try to disentangle themselves from the fangs of the present social disarray and to create the conditions of *a polycentral horizontal order.*

Secondly, it seems that more and more the *vertical monocentral architectures of computer systems* run up against difficulties. Instead of solving problems, they tend to create problems for others and for themselves. The vertical order of hierarchically structured computer systems turns out to be inadequate, if and once a certain degree of complexity has been reached. Consequently the new aim is to escape the impending disorder and to design polycentral horizontal architectures of computer systems.

These two developments - the breakdown of the monocentral hierarchy in planned economies and the growing difficulties residing in monocentral vertical computer systems as well as those which derive from their use - are not just parallel in that they happen simultaneously. They are also parallel in that they are congenial as far as their logical content is concerned. To put into a nutshell what I intend to discuss in this paper: *The (impending or actual) collapse of monocentral vertical orders both in planned economies and in computer systems is due to the fact that monocentral hierarchical systems are unable to cope with the novelties they cannot prevent, and that they are unable to generate the novelties they should create. They fall victims to the change they cannot prevent and to the change they cannot induce.*

Now, this seems to be a paradoxical, if not a downright nonsensical thesis. In due time I shall try to show that the thesis makes sense. For the present, the reader is invited to accept it as a mere hint to the plausibility that economists and computer scientists have a problem in common, and that consequently the economists may profit from watching what the computer scientists do, and vice versa.

As I said before, my main interest and my modest domain are economics in general and the theory of the social order in particular. Fortunately for me and hopefully for the computer scientists the economists have been discussing the case "vertical monocentral order vs. horizontal polycentral order" for more than two centuries. Some of the elements of this discussion should be useful when analyzing what is the core of this paper: *unpredictability as another word for freedom,* and *machines as free actors.*

1.2. A Definition of Freedom

The theory of the social order, as it is presently discussed, is a *liberal theory* in that its *methodological starting point is the individual actor* and in that its *normative point of reference is the free individual*. Now, even economists do hardly, if ever agree on what they mean exactly when they are talking about freedom. It does not come as a surprise that computer scientists, who claim to be very crystalline minds, are rather cautious about using the concept of freedom. So, if they are to use the concept of freedom and if a common level of understanding between economists and computer scientists is to be found, we must begin by giving a *definition of freedom* which makes sense to both economists and to computer scientists. Such a definition is one of those bridges which must be crossed, if the findings of one discipline are to be transferred into the other one.

So let me try to formulate such a definition; our later analysis will show whether it is useful or not. We will say that an actor is free, when and to the extent that his future behavior is unpredictable to somebody; this somebody may be the actor himself or somebody else.

The reader may be somewhat reticent about adopting this definition; he may feel that so simple a definition is inappropriate for grasping so noble and grand a concept as freedom. Though this reticence is understandable, it is not reasonable. The ascetic simplicity of this definition is part of its appeal, of its usefulness. A closer look at what this definition means and at what it entails makes this quite evident.

We stated that an actor is free, if his future behavior is unpredictable to himself. (I shall discuss the last part ~f the sentence "and/or to somebody else" in a moment.) Imagine an individual, Peter, who knows for certain that next Saturday night he will go to the movies. He may be unable to face the reproaches of his friend Sheila to whom he has promised a night at the cinema; or: He may have been sentenced by a juvenile court to watch an educational film which is shown next Saturday; or: He may be suffering from a certain neurotic disorder forcing him to go to the movies every Saturday night; or: ... etc. Whatever the reason is, the mere fact that Peter knows in the present what he will be doing in the future allows us to say that Peter, in his own opinion, is not free.

Now, look at Paul who does not know what he will do next Saturday night. He may go to the movies, he may go to bed, attend mass, murder a traffic policeman, read a book, ... etc., you name it, he may do it. In other words: For himself Paul's future behavior is unpredictable. For all practical purposes it is useful to say that Paul, on the contrary to Peter, is free; more precisely: In his own opinion he is free; he considers himself as being a free actor, who is impeded in his actions neither by external forces, nor by moral constraints, nor by neurotic compulsions.

I turn now to the phrase that says: An actor is free who's future behavior is unpredictable to somebody else. If Peter knows for certain that for whatever reasons Paul will go to the movies next Saturday night, Peter does not consider Paul to be a free actor. For all practical purposes it is expedient for Peter not to see a free actor in Paul.

Some further specifications may clarify what is meant by the equation of freedom and unpredictability. First: The definition of freedom based on the notion of unpredictability does not imply that the (un)predictability of an actor's future behavior is necessarily ayes or no affair, it may be a more or less affair. The consequence is that the more (less) unpredictable an actor's behavior is for himself or somebody else, the greater (smaller) is the freedom of this actor.

Secondly, an actor's freedom is defined here in relation to, i.e. as seen by somebody, and this somebody may be the actor himself or some other individual. This implies that in our definition freedom is seen as a relational phenomenon: An actor is free in relation to somebody. Hence in the context of this paper neither do we ask nor answer the ontological question: "Who really is free?" We do not ask this question, because we do not have to find an answer to it. It is up to the moral philosophers, to the theologians to answer the ontological question. As economists and as computer scientists we can just skip such a difficult problem as the ontological question about the presence or absence of man's free will. All we have to care about is the question whether somebody is free in relation to somebody or not.

In other words: We do not define an actor's freedom by referring to what he is able to do, but by referring to what somebody is not expecting him to do. We do not define an actor's freedom by referring to his objective capacity to act, but by referring to somebody's subjective (lack of) knowledge about the actor's future behavior.

The consequence of this is: Even if it could be shown for example by moral philosophers or by neurophysiologists that an actor's behavior is predetermined, i.e. that the agent ontologically is not free, we would say that we consider him to be a free actor, if and when he or somebody else cannot predict his future behavior. The reason why we are allowed to limit our definition on the relational aspect of freedom (and hence ignore the ontological aspect) is, that as economists and as computer scientists we are mainly, if not exclusively interested in the relations individual actors have with themselves or with other actors. We are not interested in their essence, but in the impact of their existence on themselves and on other actors.

It is quite evident that this point is of the utmost importance for the main topic of this paper, namely the freedom of machines. I shall come back to this somewhat later. We will see that any argument saying, that there is an essential difference between men and machines, in that the former are ontologically free and the latter are not, is of no importance whatsoever for our topic. If men and machines are unpredictable, we are entitled, we are even forced to put them on the same level: They are actors whose behavior is - more or less - unpredictable for somebody, and that's all there is to it.

Our definition has yet another implication. An actor may have relations to more than one actor, and his future behavior may be predictable for one actor and unpredictable for another. So Peter may know for certain that he will go to the movies on Saturday night, but Sheila may have no idea what Peter is going to do; or: Sheila may know that she has the means to make Peter go to the movies, whereas for Peter his future behavior is unpredictable. If an actor's future behavior is unpredictable for an actor A and not for an actor B, actor A must consider him to be free, whereas in the opinion of actor B he is not free. Consequently, we may state again, that an actor is not considered free in any absolute sense, but relative to as many actors as he is in relation with. An actor's freedom is not defined relative to him as an actor, but relative to those who are confronted with his actions. This does not exclude that he himself may be one of those who are confronted with his actions.

1.3. The Freedom of Human and Non-Human Actors

The careful reader will have noticed that up to now, with the exception of Peter, Paul and Sheila in the examples, I have carefully avoided to speak of men, persons and individuals. Instead I was using the neutral term "actors". The reason for this is that I do not see any reason why an unpredictable, and hence free actor must necessarily be a *human* being. If and when *non-human* beings, such as animals or machines, act in a way that, for us, is unpredictable, we are not only entitled, but we also do well to consider these beings, as far as we are concerned, as free actors.

Now, there is no question that many machines, ranging from hammers to PCs are predictable, and if ever they are not, we may be sure that they are out of order. Their value for us is strictly instrumental; they do what we tell them to do. They are dependable, because they are predictable. They are sorts of slaves that are reliable, because and insofar as they are not free.

But - and here I accept what computer scientists tell me - there are also machines which are not predictable. Complex computer systems seem to be of that kind. These machines generate an output that is (more or less) unpredictable even for he who knows the hardware and who is informed about the software. And when these machines create unpredictable results, this may be, though it must not necessarily be, the regrettable consequence of some break-down. On the contrary, some of these machines may have been designed and may be operated so as to generate an output which is (more or less) unpredictable. Some other machines may be unpredictable, though the unpredictability of their future behavior is not the end in view of which they were designed. These latter machines may be unpredictable *in principle,* or the shortage of time and/or of resources may *in practice* prevent us from predicting their outcome. I shall not venture on a discussion of the theoretical and of the technical aspects of complex computer systems; this would be definitely far beyond my level of competence. But if my informants are to be trusted, and I trust them, then I must, *as an economist interested in the interaction of free actors, include machines in my discourse on the theory of the social order.*

However before doing so let me caution against a possible and thoroughly dangerous misunderstanding: *Saying that machines may be free does not amount to putting machines and men on the same level.* Those who maintain that, just like men, machines may be free, still have the possibility of claiming that there are fundamental differences in nature and in dignity between men and machines. *Even those who argue that the future output of a given machine is more unpredictable than a certain human actor's future behavior, and who consequently claim that the human actor is less free than the machine, still have the possibility and - as I feel - the obligation of proclaiming that the human actor ranks higher than the ever so complex, unpredictable and free machine.*

Saying that machines are not as free as men (may not be more free than men), because they rank lower in nature and in dignity, would be tantamount to saying that men and machines, because they differ in *one* aspect, may not have *some other* characteristics in common. A social scientist and, as far as I know, a computer scientist should be allowed to do what any physicist does, namely to study phenomena which show up in computers and in human beings.

The consequences of not viewing and treating machines as (possibly) free actors might be just as disastrous as the consequences of another misunderstanding which, with a reversed sign, was quite popular some decades ago: Following the authority of Taylor in the capitalist West and Stakhanov in the communist East, men were, in practice, if not in theory, deprived of their dignity and degraded to the rank of machines, because they could be reduced to the state of quite predictable, i.e. non-free actors.

Granted that the reader has accepted the possibility that machines are unpredictable and hence free, he will most probably also be willing to draw some practical consequences. If he is an economist he will no longer be able to limit his discourse on the social order to the rules governing the interactions between *human* actors; in his analysis he will have to include the regulating of the interactions between *human* actors and *machine* actors. Eventually he will not exclude the interactions between machine actors and other machine actors. It is evident that this expansion of the economist's domain leads to an overlapping with the computer scientist's sphere of analysis. In my opinion this *is not* just another of those exasperating examples of the economists' imperialism; I should rather say that it is just as good an opportunity for interdisciplinary research as any.

As I said before, interdisciplinarity is a two-way-show, it is based on one discipline offering to other disciplines whatever knowledge it may have to give, and on being receptive to whatever knowledge other disciplines have to offer. On the following pages I will mainly concentrate on what the theory of the social order has to say about the conditions and the modes of a fruitful interaction between free actors. Though this knowledge has been gained by studying the relations between *human* actors, there is some hope that at least part of it may be useful when *non-human* actors, i.e. machines are included in the analysis.

1.4. Living Among Unpredictable Actors

The reader will kindly recall the definition of freedom: An actor is free if, when and to the extent that his future behavior is unpredictable for himself or for somebody else. I will concentrate the following argument on the unpredictability of the actor's behavior for *somebody else,* and I shall neglect the question whether the actor's behavior is unpredictable *for himself* or not. As an economist, who is mainly interested in interindividual, in contrast to *intraindividual* relations, *I* feel allowed to do so.

Looking at the unpredictability of an actor's future behavior for others we will notice that the more unpredictable this behavior is, the more others may be *surprised.* In other words: *Somebody is free to the extent that he may surprise others.* The surprises which may be caused by an actor's behavior can be divided into two categories: There may be *positive* and *negative* surprises. The other(s) may feel amazed by the bonanza created for him (them) by the actor's behavior; or: They may be taken aback by the unfortunate consequences which the actor's behavior has for them. In the economists lingo: Free actors create *positive* and *negative external effects;* they create external utilities and external costs, and the unpredictability of these positive and negative externalities, by definition, varies according to the actors' freedom.

Now one might hope that the positive and the negative externalities cancel out, so that on the whole nobody would be positively or negatively affected by an actor's unpredictable behavior. There are no reasons for indulging in this hope; on the contrary, *it is to be expected that the negative surprises will outweigh the positive ones.* The reason for this rather pessimistic thesis is that, if you do not explicitly try to hit a target, you will most probably miss it; occasionally you may and will hit and kill somebody whose existence you did not even notice or about whose welfare you didn't care. In other words: An actor using his freedom to pursue only his objectives will at best be harmless for others, and most probably he will cause negative externalities, although it is not impossible that by chance he may cause some positive externalities. But even if this were so, the positive externalities will most probably not (over)compensate the negative ones.

So, we have to give up the hope that the positive and the negative externalities cancel out, or that the positive externalities even outweigh the negative ones. As we are interested in the actions and interactions of actors in the *social* context, the reader is invited to imagine what it means for the individual to be confronted *with free* actors.

First, he lives in a social environment which is unpredictable; hence it is difficult, if not impossible for him not to be lost, to have any purposeful social life. *Secondly,* he is confronted with the problem of how not to be taken aback by the negative consequences of the other actors' unpredictable behavior, and to profit from the other society members' free behavior. So, the individual is confronted with a twofold problem: *How can he make sure of not falling prey to the freedom of others? And: How is he to make sure of not losing any orientation in a society of unpredictable actors?*

The theory of social order has developed and is still discussing two approaches to these questions: The *monocentral vertical order* and the *polycentral horizontal order,* or which practically amounts to the planned and the market economy.

1.5. The Claim and the Failure of the Monocentral Vertical Order

On the following pages I will avoid concentrating on the institutional arrangements of both the planned and the market economy, but I shall focus on their logical quality. Let me begin by looking at the *monocentral vertical order.* Strictly speaking, it does not *solve* the problem of unpredictability; it makes it disappear by abolishing the actors' unpredictability, i.e. by abolishing their freedom.

A closer look at the theory and the practice of the *monocentral hierarchical* order shows: *It aims at making the subordinates' behavior predictable for their superiors and at making the superiors' behavior predictable for their subordinates.*

The subordinates are supposed to do what they are told to do, no more, no less and nothing else. In a planned economy not only an *underfulfilment,* but also an *overfulfilment of* the plan is seen as a disturbance; if there is to be an overfulfilment of the plan, it has to be planned, and if it is planned, it is compulsory. The superiors are supposed to give orders according to the orders they have been given by their superiors, no more, no less and nothing else.

A subordinates' behavior which is unpredictable *for* his or her superiors is considered and, occasionally, punished as an act *of sabotage.* A superiors' behavior which is unpredictable *for* his or her subordinates is considered and, occasionally, though not so very often, punished as an *arbitrary action.*

In any case we may say that in a monocentral vertical order *any unpredictability is considered to be a pathological aberrance.* The logic of this order is based on the hope that any surprise, and hence any negative surprise can be rendered impossible, and that no actor will be lost in an unpredictable social world.

Unfortunately this hope has been in vain; it has been betrayed by experience and by history. As illustrated by the collapse of the planned economies, the monocentral vertical order, while trying to eschew negative surprises, prevented also the production of positive ones. The deadly sterility, the dull boredom and the lack of innovation were the very characteristics of the monocentrally and vertically ordered societies. There is nothing astonishing about the fact that these societies were rather successful as long as they could rely on standard technical possibilities, as was the case in the first two decades after the war, and that their decline started when these standard technologies no longer would do and when innovation would have been necessary. So, part of these societies' lethal trouble was due to the fact that, having prevented the unpredictable, they also stifled the innovations which might not just have been useful, but which were crucial necessities.

History and experience have taught us yet another lesson. The hierarchical order as it was institutionalized in the planned economies of socialism was not able to prevent all unpredictabilities. Some of these were imported from beyond the national borders; but some others had their origin in the pathologies, in the "sabotage" and the "arbitrariness" at the different levels of the hierarchy. It was not possible to completely crush the individual actors' freedom, i.e. to bring the unpredictability of their behavior to nil. Its rigidity prevented the vertical order from coping with the surprises resulting from this. *In the end, the planned economies have not only been ruined by the innovations they have been unable to generate, but they have also been undermined by the unpredictabilities they have not been able to prevent.*

A least to an external observer, it seems that the negative experience with the monocentral vertical order of planned economies has a strikingly analogous counterpart in data processing. Here too, for quite a long time, the objective has been to build monocentrally and hierarchically structured computer systems. The aim has been to have computers on all ranks of the systems performing no more and no less than the tasks for which they had been designed. Also the aim was to eliminate any "sabotage" and "arbitrariness", in order to avoid unpredictability, lest there should be negative surprises. The aim was to have reliable and predictable computers in order to produce a given positive output.

As with the socialist economies this aim was missed: *Computers showing a certain degree of complexity turned out to be more or less unpredictable; and: trying to build predictable computer systems caused these systems to be more or less unable to react constructively to unpredictability.*

Which brings us to the very diagnosis we have found concerning the socialist planning systems: The innovations being prevented by stalling the unpredictability of the system could not be used as resources and: The unpredictability which one had not been able to eliminate turned out to be the source of disturbances.

There is nothing astonishing in the fact that the diagnosis of the failure of socialist planning and of hierarchical computer systems is the same. Both have tried to gain their ends of avoiding negative surprises by abolishing the freedom of the actors operating in their (social or computer) systems. Insofar as they were successful in the latter, they crippled or even killed any innovation; insofar as they failed, they became the easy prey of what, though it could have been their blessing, was now their doom.

1.6. The Claim and Success of the Polycentral Horizontal Order

Facing this rather bleak picture of failure, it is most fortunate that beside the monocentral vertical order there is a *polycentral horizontal* order. I am going to illustrate the logic of this order by using the market economy as an example. Here too, I shall neglect any institutional aspects and details.

The problem that has to be solved is and remains the same as the problem which should have been solved by the monocentral vertical order: How are actors *not to be hurt by the negative externalities* caused by other actors whose future behavior is unpredictable, i.e. who are free? and: How is it to be achieved, that in a society of mutually unpredictable actors the individual actors are *not lost in a wholly unpredictable social environment?*

The solution which the polycentral horizontal order of the market economy gives is diametrically opposed to the answer given by the monocentral vertical order. The aim of the latter was to put everybody in a predictable society by making the behavior of everybody else predictable; the former claims to create a predictable social environment and to let every individual's behavior be unpredictable for everybody else. The monocentral vertical order aimed at making negative surprises impossible by eliminating any unpredictability. The polycentral horizontal order claims that, though everybody's future behavior will be unpredictable, everybody will have but positive surprises.

Of course this is a rather rough picture of the polycentral horizontal order. Nevertheless it displays clearly enough its logic. This logic has two main elements: *First* every actor is considered to be a center in his own right. The polycentral order is based on the axiom that society does not have *one* center, but that every actor is *a* center. From the standpoint of this theoretical approach, society has as many centers as there are individuals. The order is polycentral, it is not monocentral. *Secondly,* every actor is considered to be equal to any other actor; nobody is to be the instrument of somebody else. The order is horizontal.

It is quite obvious that in the case of the *monocentral vertical* order the approach is diametrically different: Here society has but one center, from which everything is to be analyzed and judged, and towards which everything and everybody is to be oriented; the order is *monocentral.* And: This order being hierarchical, every single actor is a superior in relation to his subordinates and a subordinate in relation to his superiors. The basic idea is the idea of inequality.

In the polycentral horizontal order, every actor's behavior is not just allowed, but also supposed to be unpredictable for the other actors. Which is to say that in a polycentral horizontal order *every actor is not only allowed to be free; he is also supposed to make use of his freedom.* He is not only allowed to be innovative, but he is also supposed to be so.

This brings us back to the twofold problem we mentioned above: Is it possible for individual actors not to be lost in an unpredictable environment, when all single actors are mutually unpredictable? And: How is it possible for individual actors, not to be the victims of the other actors' unpredictable behavior?

The answer to the *first* question is quite simple: In the polycentral horizontal order, as exemplified by the market economy, no individual actor should be able, nor should he be forced, to know any other *individual* actor's behavior, but he should both be able and obliged to know the *aggregate* behavior of whole categories of actors. So a bookseller should neither be able nor be forced to know what book an individual customer will buy, but he should be able and obliged to know what the aggregate demand of a certain title is. Though an individual customer's behavior may, should and will be unpredictable, the aggregate demand will be predictable to a large extent. If and when in a given situation and a given moment the practice of the polycentral horizontal order corresponds to its principle, *the unpredictability of the individual actor's behavior and the predictability of the social environment are compatible.* An analogy may clarify this point: In an hour-glass the sand flowing down forms a nice little heap the form of which is quite predictable. However it is not predictable what route an individual grain of sand will take and what its final position in the heap will be.

While the predictability of the *social* environment is important for an actor, the unpredictability of *individual* members of the society is not, hence he will not care about these; instead he will try to know the evolution of the social environment. In a polycentral horizontal order, market research, though not the investigation of individual economic actors, is a suitable instrument of success.

The answer to the *second* question is just as simple: If the relations among the (more or less) great number of equal actors are based on transferable individual property rights and on a regime of competition, every individual actor has an interest in defending his own freedom, the unpredictability of his own behavior, i.e. to be innovative. To the extent that the market economy corresponds to its own principle, *he who is not innovative, will not survive.* So, if they want to remain centres in their own right, if they want not to be instrumentalized by others, if they want to survive, the individual actors must make every effort to bring forth innovations, to surprise others, to behave unpredictably.

On the other hand, in the polycentral horizontal order of the market economy, every actor should be free and should be forced to react to the innovations generated by others by trying to benefit from them. Everyday experience shows what the theory of the social order explains, namely, that somebody's possibilities of reacting positively to external innovations are the greater, the greater his own adaptability. In other words: *He who is the least predictable to himself has the biggest chance to convert the others' unpredictable behavior into positive surprises for himself: He whose internal freedom is greatest, will suffer least from the freedom of others.*

It is not to be denied - and a critical reader will be right to mention it - that the *practice* of the polycentral horizontal order lives rarely, if ever, up to its *principle. Also* this order has its very own pathology. However it cannot be denied, that it is less affected by its specific pathology than the monocentral vertical order is affected by its own pathology. The reason for this is that, *in the polycentral horizontal order, the consequences of the pathology can and must be dealt with at a micro-level, whereas the monocentral vertical order is inevitably disturbed at its very core by even the slightest pathology.* This explains why in monocentrally ordered hierarchical systems the top officials go to any lengths to know in advance the individual actors' behavior. The "Stasi" in the late German Democratic Republic and the KGB in the ex-USSR are just two examples of this. (By the way, it is quite interesting to see that the polycentral horizontal order, for all its individualistic orientation, does not care about any individual actor, whereas the monocentral vertical order, for all its non individualistic bias, has to care about all individual actors.)

1.7. Conclusion

As it is not up to me to draw from my argument the conclusions that might be useful for computer science, I shall not even try to do so. Instead I will rely on the argument to formulate some open questions with which the economists and the computer scientists are faced in common.

If we are right in saying that human and non-human actors (may) behave in a (more or less) unpredictable way, and hence are (more or less) free, then we face the necessity of regulating the relations between the human and the non-human actors, i.e. to *integrate the human and the non-human actors in one and the same order.* The regulation of the social system and the organization of computer systems tend to amalgamate.

If we are also right in saying that the monocentral vertical order is bound to fail, we will be tempted to opt for a regulation of the inter-actor-relations along the lines of the polycentral horizontal order. As we have seen, this seems to be the optimal way for regulating the relations between free and equal actors: Despite its undeniable shortcomings, the market economy is a remarkably successful economic and social order.

Though as a liberal economist I am in favour of a *polycentral horizontal order, I must warn against extending it to the domain of the relations between human and non-human actors without asking any further questions.* Let me give you the reason for my reserve: The polycentral horizontal order of the market economy as a means for regulating the relations between human actors has been designed simultaneously with the enunciation of the principle: *"Tous les hommes naissent libres et égaux en droits".* As all men were not only supposed to be free, but also to have equal rights, there was no problem to integrate them in an order which puts all actors on the same footing.

However, if we want to design an order which includes human and non-human actors we must decide beforehand, whether to opt for the principle: *"Les acteurs humains et les acteurs non-humains sont libres et égaux en droits",* or whether we would rather say: *"Les acteurs humains et les acteurs non-humains sont libres et inégaux en droits. "* If we opt for the former principle, we may go ahead without any fundamental problems and include all actors in one and the same horizontal polycentral order. On the contrary, if we opt for the latter principle, we are in for trouble; and this is what is happening right now.

On the one hand the freedom of both human and machine actors pleads, as we have seen, in favour of a horizontal polycentral order. On the other hand the differences in dignity and quality, the differences in rights between men and machines plead in favour of a monocentral hierarchical order. Thus we are led into a most *uncomfortable dilemma:* Either we sacrifice at least part of the dignity of men to the advantages which are to be gained by opting for a polycentral horizontal order, or we accept at least part of the shortcomings of a monocentral hierarchical order as a price to be paid in respect of the higher dignity of men as compared to the dignity of machines.

It is at least to be hoped that *we are not willing to abdicate our human dignity and to accept machines as equal partners.* Even if we do not abdicate we have to accept machines as free actors. Most probably the dilemma resulting from this will develop with still greater intensity in the future.

As the dilemma is not too pressing in the present, we do not yet suffer too much from the fact that to this moment there is no satisfactory answer to the question of how to find a way out of the dilemma. This should be no reason to abstain from taking the problem most seriously right now. What the solution will look like is still in the dark. For all that, we may imagine that one possible solution might consist in creating an *anthropocentral hierarchy of polycentral horizontal orders.* How such a complex system of orders could and should be instituted is yet another story.

2

Basic Principles of Topology-based Methods for Simulating Metamorphoses of Natural Objects

Jean Françon, Pascal Lienhardt
Department of Computer Science, Louis Pasteur University / C.N.R.S., Strasbourg, France

2.1. Introduction

For several years, many procedural methods have been developed in order to model natural objects and simulate natural phenomena. For instance, particle systems are defined in order to model "fuzzy" objects and simulating corpuscular phenomena (Reeves, 1983). For generating trees, Aono et al. (1984) use particular branching patterns, Eyrolles et al. (1989) have a combinatorial approach, Prusinkiewicz et al. (1988), Prusinkiewicz and Hanan (1990), Smith (1984) use graftals and L-systems, and de Reffye et al. (1988) have elaborated AMAP in order to achieve a real simulation of plant growth, using botanical knowledge and agronomical measures. Natural leaves, flowers and multicellular structures are studied by de Does et al. (1983), Fracchia et al. (1990), Lück et al. (1986) using L-systems, and by Chen et al. (1992), Lienhardt (1988) and Terraz et al. (1993) using modular maps and their extensions.

We study in this chapter some of these methods (namely, particle systems, AMAP and modular maps) in order to point out their basic principles and some of their particular

Artificial Life and and Virtual Reality Edited by Nadia Magnenat Thalmann and Daniel Thalmann
© 1994 John Wiley and Sons Ltd

characteristics. In order to simulate natural phenomena, i.e. evolution of natural objects, these methods generate sequences of geometric objects $(O_1, ..., O_n)$, O_i being the object at time $t = i$, where t is a discrete time. Moreover, the basic principles of these methods are that of behavioral animation, as studied by Reynolds (1987) and Wilhelms (1990). More precisely, geometric objects are structured into (i.e. composed by) sub-objects; A behavior is associated with each object or sub-object, and O_i is deduced from O_{i-1} by applying their associated behaviors to all its sub-objects, maybe to the object itself. Since an object is structured, control is either local and global. Moreover, behaviors may be parameterized, and thus context-dependent. In what follows, "metamorphosis" denotes such generated sequence of objects. Important aspects of these methods are as follows:

- Handled objects are subdivisions (cellular complexes), i.e. partitions of geometric spaces into cells (vertices, edges, faces, etc.). This partition of an object into cells corresponds to the first level of object structure, on which higher-level types of sub-objects can be defined. Such structures are important for modeling natural objects, which are often structured ones. For instance, a tree is structured into axes: Main axis is the trunk, on which secondary axes (main branches) are inserted, and so on. A natural leaf is structured into lobes, and nervures and limb can be distinguished. Here, studied methods explicitly handle such subdivisions. Subdivisions are classically represented in geometric modeling by a combinatorial model, which represents the topology of the subdivision (mainly, the cells and their boundary relations), and an embedding model, which defines the location of the cells into the usual three-dimensional Euclidean space E^3 (by associating for instance a point with each vertex, a curve with each edge, etc.). Many combinatorial models have been defined during the last years in order to model the topology of subdivisions, for instance by Baumgart (1975), Elter et al. (1993), Guibas et al. (1985), Lienhardt (1989, 1993), Mäntylä (1988), Rossignac et al. (1989), Weiler (1985).
- Basic operations are explicitly defined and used in order to define sub-object behaviors, which are in fact higher-level operations. Such behaviors are parameterized. Topological operations (modifying the topology of a subdivision) are applied for modifying the composition of an object. For instance, growth can be simulated by adding new parts to an object. Other phenomena are simulated by embedding operations, for instance a leaf which bends on itself in autumn.

In the following sections, we will study these aspects of the methods, and try to point out some of their advantages for generating metamorphoses, problems which can be encountered during such processes, and some directions of future works. Methods are studied according to the topological dimension of handled objects, i.e. Section 2.2 (resp. 2.3, 2.4) is devoted to particle systems (resp. AMAP, modular maps and their extensions). Section 2.5 contains some concluding remarks.

2.2. 0-dimensional Objects

Particle systems have been presented by Reeves in 1983 for modeling "fuzzy" objects and simulating corpuscular phenomena, as fire, fireworks, grass, etc. Reynolds has used particle systems in 1987 as a basis for simulating aggregate motion such as that of flocks of birds. Other applications of particle systems are described in literature, and many animation sequences have been realized using this technique.

Basically, a particle system is a set of particles, considered as topologically 0-dimensional objects. In other words, a particle system is a 0-dimensional cellular complex. Each particle is embedded by associating a point of E^3 with it. Moreover, a shape can be also associated with a particle, for instance a sphere, a rectangle, etc. Reynolds uses more elaborated shapes, bird shapes for instance. In other words, the 0-dimensional cellular complex defined by an embedded particle system can be considered as a 0-dimensional "skeleton" of the whole scene (similar techniques are employed by other methods (see Section 2.3). In fact, a particle system is either a set of particles, or a set of lower-level particle systems. So, particles are structured into a hierarchy of systems. We have here a general mechanism for defining structured cellular complexes (more specialized structures are presented in the following sections). In order to simplify, "particle" will denote either a particle or a lower-level particle system. Basic operations defined for handling particle systems consist in:

- Topological operations, i.e. create and remove a particle;
- Embedding operations, i.e. move a particle. Operations exist for handling shapes associated with particles, for instance to modify the size of a shape.

A standard behavior is defined for all particles. A particular behavior is characterized by attributes associated with the particle and with the system itself. These attributes are constant ones, or may vary according to other attributes, e.g. time. Particle attributes are lifetime (a particle is removed according to this value), initial position when it is created, initial speed, etc. The number of particles generated in the system at each step is an attribute of the system. Another one is the "generation shape" which defines the initial location of its particles. In fact, other attributes can be used. Note also that a particle system evolution is controlled by stochastic processes. Many attributes are defined by two values, a mean value and its variance; the value of the corresponding attribute is computed using these two values and a generator of random numbers. Another point is the fact that particle behaviors are defined using a "filiation" principle, i.e. a particle system defines attributes of its generated particles, and thus their behaviors (this mechanism is widely used in many methods).

The standard behavior of particle systems consists in the following sequence of basic operations: Create new particles, define the values of their attributes, remove particles (according to their lifetime for instance), move the remaining particles (according to their current position and speed, for instance). It is clear that the standard behavior is parameterized, by attributes for instance. A very simple example is provided in Figure 2.1.

Assume we intend to simulate a natural phenomenon, consisting in the evolution of a natural object during time. As for classical programming using a general programming language, a user has to analyze the object at each step, and its evolution between successive steps, in order to deduce a "structure" of the model and the corresponding behaviors. Reeves mentions the example of a cloud. A top-level particle system corresponds to the whole cloud, and controls its global motion and appearance. Lower-level systems correspond to areas of the cloud, providing a local control, for instance for modifying the shape of the cloud by moving some parts. A hierarchy of particle systems provide thus either global and local control, for which the structures of the modeled object and associated behaviors are primordial, and complementary. The analysis step is mainly due to the fact that particle systems provide a general technique: No particular application is addressed, as for modular maps and contrary to AMAP (see Section 2.3).

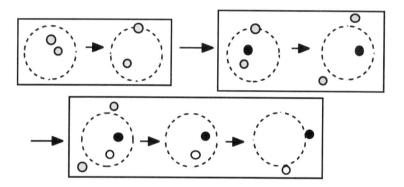

Figure 2.1. Evolution of a particle system during time: each arrow symbolizes the application of an operation modifying the system, and a rectangle symbolizes the application of a behavior. The generation shape of the system is represented by a dashed circle, into which new particles are randomly located. The standard behavior is strictly applied: First, new particles are created, then old particles are removed, and at last, particles are moved (particle lifetime value is 2).

2.3. 1-dimensional Objects

Many methods have been elaborated in order to construct metamorphoses of trees and graphs, mainly for modeling natural trees and simulating their growth (more references are provided in Françon (1991)). Objects are 1-dimensional cellular complexes, consisting in vertices and edges. They can be embedded into E^3 by associating a point with each vertex and a curve with each edge. In fact, for modeling natural trees, many methods associate a shape with each edge, for instance a cylinder, in order to simulate the thickness of a trunk or a branch. Once again, the 1-dimensional cellular complex corresponds to a skeleton of the resulting geometric object.

Most methods are also based on principles of behavioral animation. A very simple metamorphosis example is the construction of a Von Koch curve, in fact of a subdivided 1-dimensional manifold (a simple curve with boundary) which approximates this curve (see Figure 2.2). Two topological operations are defined: Creating an edge, and splitting an edge by a vertex. Two main embedding operations are defined: When a vertex is added during a split operation, the middle point of the segment associated with the splitted edge is associated with the vertex; Such a vertex can then be moved along a direction perpendicular to the original edge, in order to get a continuous motion. A single recursive behavior is associated with all edges, consisting in splitting edges and moving vertices.

Figure 2.2. Recursive construction of a subdivided 1-dimensional manifold. The dashed shape encloses subdivisions resulting from the application at the first step of the recursive behavior, which consists in: First, split an edge, then split the two edges incident to the new vertex, and at last, move this vertex.

Contrary to particle systems, AMAP (Atelier de Modélisation de l'Architecture des Plantes) is a specialized method. Its goal is the definition of a rigorous and faithful model of plants and plant growth, for botanical and agronomical purposes. The method is based on botanical knowledge, and is validated through observations and measures on natural plants. It has been initiated by de Reffye in 1979, by the definition of a mathematical and macroscopic model of plant growth, first applied for the coffee-tree. More details about this approach can be found in the papers of de Reffye et al (1988, 1990).

Modeled objects are embedded combinatorial trees, i.e. 1-dimensional cellular complexes without cycles. A tree is a structured one; This structure corresponds to that of a natural tree (see Figure 2.3), i.e.:

- A vertex corresponds to a node of the tree, i.e. a part of the tree where leaves and buds are inserted; An edge corresponds to an internode, i.e. a part of the tree between two consecutive nodes;
- Vertices and edges are structured into growth units, which correspond to the fact that the growth of a tree consists in two distinct steps. First, a sequence of internodes is produced within a bud (usually in a very short period of time), defining a growth unit; Then, the size of these internodes is increased (usually during a longer period of time).
- Growth units are structured into axes, corresponding to botanical axes: The trunk is the main axis (axis of order 1), on which main branches are inserted (axes of order 2), and so on.

The method principle consists in simulating the activity of buds, which can be:

- Death: Natural death, due to a traumatism or when producing a flower;
- Growth: Either the bud "goes into sleep" (delayed growth), either it produces a growth unit (immediate growth) as shown in Figure 2.4 (the corresponding topological operations are obvious);

- Ramification: This corresponds to the existence of axillary buds, which can produce axes of greater order, reiterations, organs as flowers or palms. A reiteration is a full or partial reproduction of the plant (schematically, this corresponds to a recursive behavior). Reiterations often appear on old trees, or can be consequences of traumatisms (see Figure 2.5, Color Section, showing a pruned tree with traumatic reiterations). Types of ramification are continuous ramification (every node of an axis is the origin of an axis of greater order), rhythmic ramification (some nodes, but not all of them, are origins of axes of greater order) and diffuse ramification (nodes being origins of axes of greater order are located at random). For instance, a fir tree (see Figure 2.6, Color Section) has a rhythmic ramification.

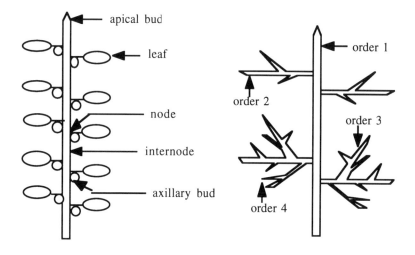

Figure 2.3. Structure of natural trees.

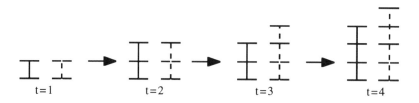

Figure 2.4. Immediate and delayed growth. At each step, the actual size of an axis (number of growth units) is represented at left, and the "normal" size is at right. Steps 1, 2 and 4 correspond to immediate growth, and step 3 to delayed growth.

These events occur according to specific stochastic laws characteristic for each variety and species. Parameters used in a simulation process are plant age, growth speed of an axis, probabilities describing a bud activity (which are functions of the age and order of the bud, for instance), number of internodes per growth unit, etc. Geometric parameters, such as length and diameter of an internode, phyllotaxy (location of axillary buds on an axis), or the branching angles are also calculated according to characteristic specific laws (from a technical point of view, a tree is embedded in a hierarchical way, as shown in Figure 2.7).

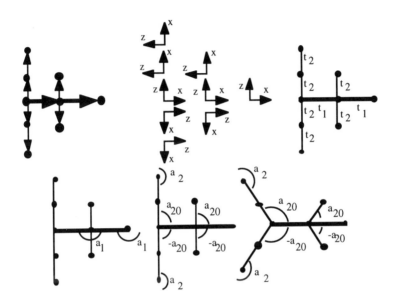

Figure 2.7. Hierarchical embedding of a tree. Top right, an oriented tree (a vertex is the root of the tree). AMAP trees are oriented. This corresponds to a "filiation" relation between cells, related to the fact that a natural tree is oriented, an internode being produced by one (parent) node. Top middle, a reference system is associated with each vertex. Each reference system is computed according to the reference system associated with the previous vertex in the tree (taking the tree orientation into account) and values of length and angles (top right, bottom left and bottom middle). Angles and lengths may vary, according to topological distances computed in the tree (down right), and to other parameters, time for instance. Advantages of such hierarchical embeddings are well-known, and they are not discussed in the chapter.

Other phenomena can be simulated, for instance the fall of branches, or bending of branches according to the theory of material strength, using the geometrical shape of an internode and the elasticity parameter (Young's module) characterizing the wood of the branch. Different growth types can be simulated using these parameters, as shown in Figures 2.8–2.10. For instance, one can obtain the architectural models pointed out by Hallé et al. (1978). The notion of architectural model can be seen as a growth strategy to occupy space. Many plants and trees grow and build their shape in the same kind of way, although the results seem very different from one to an other. There are only 23 architectural models, two of them being illustrated in Figures 2.11 and 2.12.

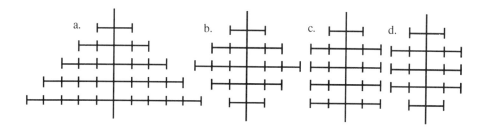

Figure 2.8. Different shapes due to different growth types of secondary axes. (a.) Secondary axis growth is similar to that of the main axis, i.e. when a growth unit is added to the main axis, a growth unit is added to each secondary axis. (b.) The number of growth units of a secondary axis depends on the distance (number of growth units) between its origin and the root of the tree. (c.) All secondary axes have a maximal number of growth units. (d.) Secondary axis behavior is intermediate between those of (b.) and (c.).

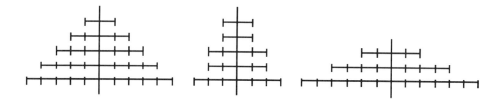

Figure 2.9. Different tree shapes corresponding to different ratios between the growth speed of the main axis and of the secondary axes (from left to right: 1, 2, 1/2).

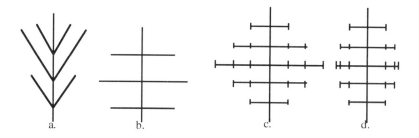

Figure 2.10. (a.) and (b.) Orthotropy (a.) and plagiotropy (b.). The geometric trend of an axis with respect to its bearing axis is also an important parameter. If it is vertical, it is said to be orthotropic (cf. Figure 2.13, Color Section, showing an approximate wild cherry tree with flowers); If it is horizontal, it is said to be plagiotropic (see Fig. 2.6, Color Section). (c.) and (d.) Different shapes, due to different ratios of the geometric length of internodes. Left, all internodes have the same length. Right, the length of an internode of a secondary axis decreases, according to its (topological) distance to the origin of the axis.

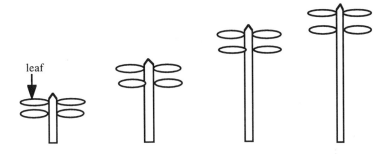

Figure 2.11. Corner model (coconut tree and date palm tree, for instance). There is one axis of order 1, and no ramification.

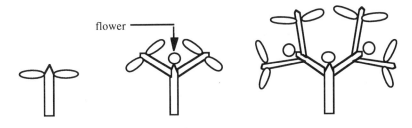

Figure 2.12. Leeuwenberg model (frangipani tree and mistletoe, for instance). Apical buds systematically die after one growth unit, then n axillary buds create n new axes (creating thus a perfect n-ary tree, in graph theory meaning).

Probabilities and parameters are measured on real plants, and simulations validate the model. AMAP method is used for botanical and agronomical purposes, urbanism, image synthesis. Experimentations have also pointed out some botanical phenomena, having for consequences the definition of new concepts and simplifications of the method itself. For instance, a new concept is that of physiological age of a bud and the reference axis notion. A reference axis describes all states of a bud according to its physiological age. The key point is the fact that a single reference axis describes the state of all buds in a plant. So, there is no difference in essence between buds of different axes, but they have different physiological ages. Constructing a tree consists in applying transitions between states of a reference axis, and always from a state to an older one (i.e. the reference axis is oriented according to the physiological age). This corresponds to handling a finite state automaton. The reference axis concept explains many phenomena, as ramification, which corresponds to a transition to an older age, reiteration, which consists in keeping the same state.

Note that some programming aspects are important in order to achieve a true simulation. Several years ago, simulations were realized by constructing different parts of the plant using a sequential order, for technical considerations. So, it was not possible to take several phenomena into account. For instance, the growth of a plant depends on its geometric environment, and the tree itself is a part of the environment of a branch, for instance. It is thus necessary to simulate bud behaviors in a parallel way. This has been achieved by Blaise in 1990 (cf. also Greene's paper, 1989). Figure 2.14 (Color Section) shows a forest.

2.4. 2-dimensional objects

Several methods deal with 2-dimensional cellular complexes (mainly subdivisions of surfaces), for modeling natural leaves, flowers, butterflies..., and simulating their metamorphoses. A simple method used by Eyrolles et al (1989) consists in generating a tree and in adding edges between extremities of the tree, defining thus polygons (see Figure 2.15). The tree corresponds to leaf nervures, which make a tree in first approximation. Simulating a surface metamorphosis is achieved by simulating a tree metamorphosis. A texture is mapped onto the surface, in order to produce the aspect of a natural leaf. The simplicity of the method has some drawbacks. Often, nervures do not end on the boundary of a leaf. It may be difficult to control the shape of the surface when it is not quite planar or regular. But the main problem is related to the fact that it is not possible to control the subdivision of the surface in order to control its color and evolution of color during time. The subdivision defined by color areas of a leaf limb is often quite complicated; Moreover, color areas have complex evolutions (see for instance leaf metamorphoses between spring and autumn). Using the previous method, it is necessary to control texture evolutions during time.

More elaborated methods have been proposed in order to handle more complex subdivisions, for instance the modular map method. At its origin, it was developed for simulating metamorphoses of plant organs (leaves, flowers). It has also been applied for handling other natural surfaces (e.g. butterflies), manufactured surfaces as tissues, and bounding surfaces of natural or manufactured volumic objects (octopus, telephone receiver, etc.). Now, this method and some extensions are also studied in order to experiment combinatorial models defined for representing the topology of subdivisions (namely, combinatorial maps and their extensions) in non interactive applications, that is for programming purposes in geometric modeling. two-dimensional oriented combinatorial maps have been introduced by Edmonds (1960) and studied by many authors, for instance Jacque (1970), Cori (1975) and Tutte (1984), extended by Lienhardt (1989, 1993) for representing n-dimensional subdivided manifolds, and then by Elter et al. (1993) for representing n-dimensional cellular complexes. It is useless to present their definitions in the chapter, but it may be important to give our opinion about the combinatorial models we use, these models being a key part of such procedural methods for constructing metamorphoses of geometric objects. We first present modular maps, and then some extensions of the method which are defined for constructing metamorphoses of any subdivided surfaces and topologically 3-dimensional manifolds, orientable or not, with or without boundaries.

Figure 2.15. A simple method for simulating natural leaf metamorphoses. (a.) A subdivided surface is deduced from a tree by adding edges between extremity vertices. (b.) It can be necessary to control extremity vertices, in order to allow nervures to end inside limb. (c.) For controlling metamorphoses of leaf appearance, it is necessary to define a method for generating texture evolutions.

Modular map method is not specialized as AMAP, but it is not so general as particle systems. Metamorphoses of some subdivisions of planar surfaces with or without boundaries can be constructed. The basic idea here is similar to that of the simple method presented above, i.e. a correspondence exists between a leaf shape and its nervure network. But the limb between two nervures, for instance between two lobes corresponding to main nervures, can be more or less continuous, i.e. the boundaries of the lobes are more or less "glued" together. Sometimes, the shape of leaves, for instance the "degree of gluing" of two adjacent lobes, varies in a plant, according to its age or to the location of the leaf in the plant. In order to simulate this metamorphosis of leaf shapes, it is necessary to control evolutions of this "degree of gluing" between parts of the modeled surface. For this purpose, a modular map is a surface subdivision, structured in the following way (Figure 2.16):

- Some vertices and edges make a tree. Namely, the G-tree, which corresponds to leaf nervures, is composed by G-vertices and G-edges. As AMAP trees, a G-tree is oriented, and a G-vertex is the root of the tree. Moreover, a G-tree is structured into axes, by associating an order with each G-edge. This corresponds to the fact that one can distinguish in a leaf main nervures, secondary ones, etc.;
- Two triangular faces (G-faces) are incident to each G-edge, defining a small limb portion enclosing a part of a nervure; The boundary of a G-face is composed by one G-edge and its incident G-vertices, and by two R-edges and one R-vertex (cells of the subdivision are either G-cells or R-cells);
- R-faces "glue" G-faces; Their boundaries are composed by R-vertices and R-edges. Evolutions of the "degree of gluing" between parts of the modelled surface are achieved by operations on R-faces.

A modular map is embedded by associating a point with each vertex; Embedding of edges and faces is deduced from vertex embedding.

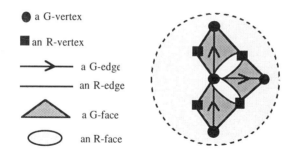

Figure 2.16. Left, graphical representation of G- and R-cells. Right, a modular map composed by 4 G-vertices and 4 R-vertices, 3 G-edges and 12 R-edges, 6 G-faces and 3 R-faces, since the infinite face is an R-face. Note that R-faces can be distinguished in order to model surfaces with boundaries (see Figures 2.17–2.24, Color section).

Figure 2.25. Left, creating an initial modular map. Right, adding a module in an initial modular map (σ is the root of the G-tree).

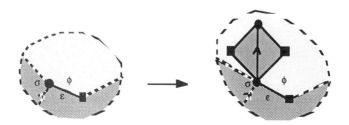

Figure 2.26. Adding a module in a non initial modular map. σ is an extremity G-vertex of the G-tree. The argument of the operation is edge ε, and the module is added within its incident R-face φ.

Four basic topological operations are defined for handling modular maps. They are not complex ones, and produce a wide class of surface subdivisions and metamorphoses. The first operation creates an initial modular map, composed by one G-vertex (root of the G-tree) and one R-face (Figure 2.25). The second operation adds a module in a modular map (a module is mainly composed by two G-faces incident to a G-edge), as shown in Figures 2.25 and 2.26. An example of a subdivision constructed by applying these two operations is presented in Figure 2.27. In fact, these operations produce "skeleton-like" surfaces, and it is necessary to add operations for handling R-faces. The two following operations create and modify R-faces (Figures 2.28 and 2.29). They are mainly used to control and simulate evolutions of the "degree of gluing" of parts of the modeled surface (see creation of octopus tentacles in Fig.2.24, Color Section). Examples of modular maps generated by applying these operations are shown in Figures 2.29 and 2.31).

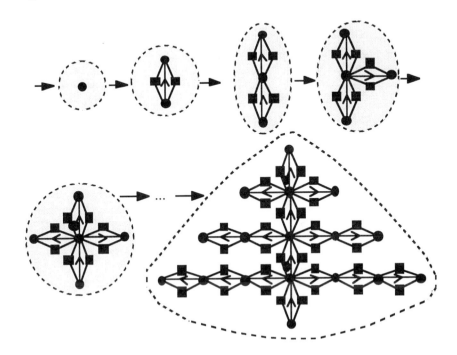

Figure 2.27. A modular map constructed by applying the two operations for creating an initial modular map and adding a module. Assume the external face is distinguished (i.e. its incident edges define a boundary of the object). The resulting object is not a surface stricto sensu, since the neighborhood of each G-vertex is not homeomorphic to a disc. As seen above for AMAP trees, the shape of the G-tree can be characterized by topological lengths of axes and topological distances, for instance between the origin of an axis and the root of the G-tree (see Figure 2.8).

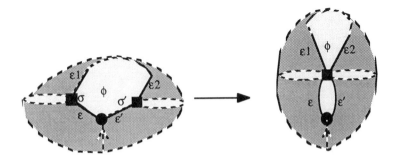

Figure 2.28. Creating an R-face, by identifying two distinct R-vertices σ and σ' (edge ε is the argument of the operation).

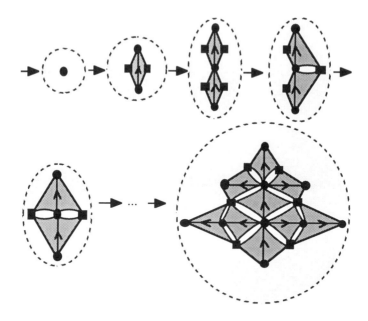

Figure 2.29. Generating a modular map sequence by applying the first three operations. This type of construction is often used in order to simulate growth of leaf lobes whose underlying nervure network is composed by a main axis and secondary axes.

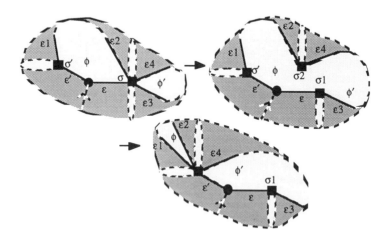

Figure 2.30. Modifying two R-faces. This operation does not create or remove cells, but modifies the boundaries of two faces ϕ and ϕ' (arguments of the operation are edges ε and ε_3). This operation is used in order to modify the internal structure of limb, for simulating metamorphoses of leaf color, and also to precisely control boundaries of surfaces, for instance the "degree of gluing" of adjacent lobes (cf. Figure 2.23).

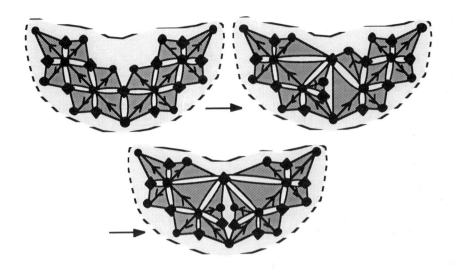

Figure 2.31. Two applications of the operation for modifying R-faces. This operation is often used to simulate a progressive "gluing" of the lobes of a multilobate leaf, and the inverse phenomenon (the operation is its own inverse), as shown in Figure 2.17, where it is used in particular to simulate the metamorphosis of the boundary of leaves of a particular oak (Quercus Ilex).

Behaviors are associated with R-edges, since they are arguments of main topological operations. As for other methods, behaviors are high-level operations defined as sequences of basic operations. They are parameterized, and parameters are similar to those handled by other methods: Time, "birth" time of a cell (and consequently its age), topological distances between cells, behaviors (and consequently states) of other cells, etc. Some of these parameters (and thus behaviors) are context-dependent. They are computed by using adjacency and incidence relations between cells, in a classical way in geometric modeling.

For instance, distances between G-edges in the G-tree allow one to control topology, embedding and color of a modular map. The topology of a G-tree, and thus the topology of a modular map, can be characterized for instance by lengths of axes, which may depend on distances between origins of axes and the root of the G-tree (see Figures 2.7 and 2.27). Color of different areas of a natural leaf is often strongly related to the location of areas in the limb, which can be characterized by topological distances between the area and the origin of the incident nervure or the root of the nervure tree. Similarly, the "degree" of gluing between lobes is also related to distances, showing a metamorphosis of a maple tree, where the "degree of gluing" obviously depends on distances between areas corresponding to main nervures and the root of the nervure tree. Similarly, color becomes darker according to the distance between an area and the root. Other examples illustrate the use of context-dependent parameters, for instance for controlling color of butterflies (Figures 2.19 and 2.20, Color Section), for controlling the shapes of lobes (see Figure 2.22, Color Section, where each petal of the flower has a main axis and secondary axes, and all secondary axes have the same topological length).

Modular map embedding is achieved by mainly embedding the G-tree, in a hierarchical way (see Section 2.3). By varying geometric parameters, metamorphoses of a modular map embedding can be simulated: For instance, a leaf which bends on itself in autumn, or the metamorphosis of a flower into an octopus (Figures 2.21–2.24, Color Section, see creation of the tentacles). Embedding of R-vertices is computed according to the embedding of adjacent G-vertices, using 2 geometric parameters, mainly for precisely controlling the embedding of the boundaries of modular maps (see Figure 2.17, Color Section).

In fact, few behaviors are necessary for constructing complex shapes and metamorphoses shown in Figures 2.17–2.24, Color Section. As discussed in Section 2.2, this is due to the fact that surfaces are structured. For instance, flower petals or leaf lobes have often the same type of behavior, controlled by few parameters (see Figures 2.22–2.24, Color Section). So, some phenomena are easily defined. For instance, some axial deformations (as studied by Lazarus et al. in 1993) are easily controlled by few parameters (natural shapes have often main growth directions, corresponding in modular maps to axes of the G-tree). This produces a very large "amplification database", in Fournier's meaning (1987).

This method has been extended by Terraz et al. (1993, 1994) in order to construct metamorphoses of any subdivision of any surface, orientable or not, with or without boundaries. The topology of these subdivisions is modeled by 2-G-maps, as defined by Lienhardt (1989). A basic structure of subdivisions is defined, on which higher-level structures corresponding to some applications can be defined. The basic structure consists in a tree of faces, structured itself into axes. In fact, behaviors are associated with faces, and a filiation relation is defined on faces (i.e. each face is created by applying to an other face its associated behavior). Faces correspond to nodes of the tree, and filiation relations correspond to arcs of the tree (obviously, the tree is oriented). Orders are associated with faces for defining axes, as shown in Figures 2.32 and 2.33. Simple operations, which are classical ones in geometric modeling, are used in order to handle subdivisions: Creating a face, splitting an edge or a face, identifying two edges. Once again, controlling a surface metamorphosis mainly consists in controlling a tree metamorphosis.

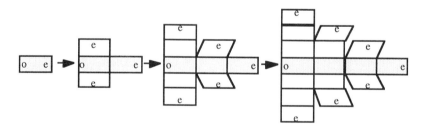

Figure 2.32 Surface metamorphosis. Order of dashed faces is 1, the order of other faces being equal to 2. The corresponding tree of faces is represented in Figure 2.33. 'o' denotes the root of the tree, 'e' denotes the extremity of an axis. This sequence is constructed by adding faces and identifying edges. It is defined by two simple behaviors; One describes the behavior of faces of order one, the other is associated with faces of order 2.

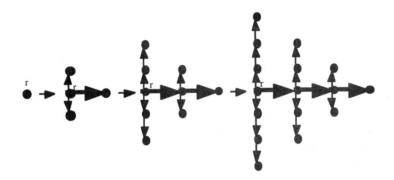

Figure 2.33. Evolution of the tree of faces corresponding to subdivisions of Figure 2.32. Thick arrows symbolize filiation relation between faces of order 1, thin arrows symbolize filiation relation between the other faces. It is clear that the shape of the surface is strongly related to the shape of the tree, as for modular maps. The shape of the tree is controlled as the G-tree of a modular map.

Surface embedding is mainly controlled by a hierarchical embedding of the tree of faces. A planar surface (an ellipse, for instance) is associated with each face, and it is located in the reference system associated with the face. Points are computed on the boundary of the shape, defining an embedding (related to the face) of the incident vertices. Vertices are finally embedded by computing the barycenter of all the corresponding points associated with its incident faces (Figure 2.34).

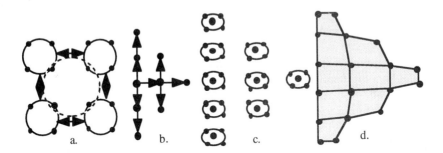

Figure 2.34. Embedding a surface subdivision. (a.) shapes associated with four adjacent faces which share a vertex. Arrows between shapes symbolize adjacency relations between the corresponding faces. The degree of each face is 4, and four points are computed on the boundary of each shape. The embedding of the common vertex is computed as the barycenter of the four corresponding points, enclosed in a dashed circle. (b.), (c.) and (d.) Computing the embedding of a subdivision close to one represented in Figure 2.32. (b.) A tree of faces. (c.) Shapes associated with faces, on which points have been computed. (d.) Final location of vertices, and embedding of the surface subdivision.

Parameters are used in order to control metamorphoses. Since we mainly have to control a tree metamorphosis, many parameters are similar to previously discussed ones. In particular, they can be context-dependent; Consequently, behaviors are also context-dependent. In order to simplify programming, behaviors can be associated with all objects defined in such structured surfaces: Axes, origin or extremities of axes, etc.

Many examples of metamorphoses have been realized using this method: Metamorphoses of "geometric" surfaces (for instance a metamorphosis whose key surfaces are a planar surface, a cylinder, a torus, a Klein bottle, a Moebius strip, an annulus generated by cutting the Moebius strip in its middle, or an annulus and a Moebius strip generated by cutting the Moebius strip at its third part, natural surfaces, as surfaces bounding volumes as fishes (see Figures 2.35–2.36). A higher-level structure of surfaces is defined in order to simulate metamorphoses of fishes, since natural fishes are also structured (head, body, different types of fins, etc.), simplifying thus the definition of such metamorphoses.

This method is also extended in order to construct metamorphoses of subdivisions of topologically three-dimensional objects, for simulating evolutions of natural volumic objects (Terraz, 1994). The basic structure of subdivisions is a tree of volumes, and embedding consists mainly in a hierarchical embedding of the tree, and in associating a volumic shape with each volume.

As for particle systems, we get advantages and drawbacks of a general method: Advantages, since it is possible to construct a wide class of objects and metamorphoses; Drawbacks, since no knowledge is used in the method, contrary to AMAP, in order to help a user. A user has to analyze the object or metamorphosis (s)he intends to construct, for defining a convenient structure and complementary behaviors.

Once again, it is important for our purpose to handle simple combinatorial models for representing the topology of subdivisions, in order to simplify programming of procedural constructions. As for interactive geometric modeling, combinatorial maps and their extensions seem to present both simplicity and rigor required for procedural geometric modeling.

During all these experiments, encountered problems are classical ones in programming (for instance, conflicts may be due to "incoherent" behaviors; Some operations can be applied in a parallel way, other have to be applied in a sequential way). But no particular problem was due to the complexity itself of geometric objects.

2.5. Conclusion

We have studied in this chapter some aspects of procedural methods defined for constructing metamorphoses of geometric objects, i.e. particle systems, AMAP, modular maps and their extensions. All methods explicitly handle structured cellular complexes, using a classical topology-based approach: A geometric object is represented by a combinatorial model which describes its topology, and by an embedding model which describes its location into the usual three-dimensional Euclidean space E^3. Basic topological and embedding operations are defined in order to handle the models. The basic principle of these methods is that of behavioral animation. Behaviors consists in higher-level operations, defined using the previous ones.

These methods have either common and own characteristics. Particle systems is a general method for constructing metamorphoses of 0-dimensional cellular complexes; AMAP is specialized for simulating growth of natural plants, using botanical knowledge and an experimental approach using measures on plants in order to validate the method. Modular map method does not use knowledge of botanics or other experimental sciences for constructing metamorphoses of some subdivided surfaces, but the object structure is strongly related to that of natural leaves and flowers. Extensions of modular maps are more general, and allow one to construct metamorphoses of any subdivided surfaces, orientable or not, with or without boundaries.

Generality or specialization present advantages and drawbacks. For instance, it is possible, using a general method, to construct a wide class of objects and metamorphoses; Conversely, since no knowledge is taken into account in the method, a user has to analyze the natural object or phenomena (s)he intends to simulate, in order to define a well-adapted structure and related behaviors (this aspect is a classical one in programming).

Particle systems and AMAP use a standard behavior applied to all objects, a particular behavior being characterized by parameters. More complex types of behaviors can be used for modular maps and their extensions. In all cases, behaviors are parameterized, and may be context-dependent. For instance, it is possible to compute parameters in modular maps by traversals using adjacency and incidence relations. According to their parameters, methods are either stochastic or deterministic ones. Behaviors of newly created parts of an object are mainly defined using a "filiation" principle: Since each part is created by applying to an other part its associated behavior, this last one will also define the behavior of the first one. It may be important to apply behaviors in a parallel way, in particular when behaviors are context-dependent and they modify the context of an object (for instance when simulating tree growth, where branch growth restricts space around other branches).

We think it could be interesting to compare this type of method with others (with a user point of view for instance), e.g. L-systems, where models, structures, parameters, etc., seem to be more implicitly represented.

One advantage of a topology-based approach is the fact that some operations, as cutting a complex surface for instance, are easily defined using topological operations. Moreover, a procedural approach often simplifies complex constructions, taking advantage of the structure defined on the object (for instance when many similar operations have to be applied to different parts of the modeled object).

As for interactive constructions, but with an increased importance, models and their related basic operations have to present some properties, as simplicity, rigor, etc., in order to allow one to easily define structures and behaviors. In particular, we think that combinatorial models we used for representing 2- and 3-dimensional complexes (namely, maps and their extensions) present good properties, either for interactive and procedural constructions.

About programming metamorphoses, we get all classical problems related to programming, but no particular one due to the complexity of the geometric objects themselves. Nevertheless, it could be interesting to study procedural methods where interactions with a user are allowed during a simulation process. Other directions for future works are:

- Study other formalizations of such methods, i.e. other ways for programming metamorphoses which offer more possibilites than simply constructing objets; For instance, grammars, algebraic specifications, etc., make it possible to study properties of modeled objects by formal computations;
- Apply general methods to particular applications, for instance modular maps and their extensions for botanical or agronomical purposes, since new problems could be pointed out, which do not appear when using such methods for image synthesis and animation. For instance, is it possible that such procedural methods could be of some use for classical applications of geometric modeling, e.g. CAD ?

Acknowledgements

We wish to thank for their help and work: C. Edelin (Institut de Botanique, Montpellier), P. de Reffye, M. Jaeger and F. Blaise (C.I.R.A.D., Montpellier), and all members of the "3D Modelling Group" in Strasbourg.

References

Aono M, Kunii TL (1984) Botanical Tree Image Generation, *IEEE Computer Graphics and Applications* , Vol. 4, No.5, pp.10–34.

Baumgart B (1975) A Polyhedron Representation for Computer Vision, *AFIPS Nat. Conf. Proc.* Vol.44, pp.589–596.

Blaise F (1990) *Simulation de la croissance des plantes par une gestion simultanée des bourgeons actifs, Application aux phénomènes de gêne et d'ombrage*, PhD Thesis, Louis Pasteur University, Strasbourg, France.

Chen X, Lienhardt P (1992) Modelling and Programming Evolutions of Surfaces, *Computer Graphics Forum*, Vol.2, No.5, pp.323–341.

Cori R (1975) Un code pour les graphes planaires et ses applications, *Astérisque* 27.

De Does M, Lindenmayer A (1983) *Algorithms for the Generation and Drawing of Maps Representing Cells Clones*, in Lecture Notes in Computer Science, Vol.153, pp.301–316.

Elter H, Lienhardt P (1993) Different combinatorial models based on the map concept for the representation of different types of cellular complexes, in *Modeling in Computer Graphics*, B. Falcidieno and T.L. Kunii eds., Springer.

Edmonds J (1960) *A combinatorial representation for polyhedral surfaces,* Notices Amer. Soc. 7.

Eyrolles G, Viennot X, Janney N, Arquès D (1989) Combinatorial Analysis of Ramified Patterns and Computer Imagery of Trees, *Computer Graphics,* Vol.23, No.3, pp.31–40.

Fournier A (1987) *The Modeling of Natural Phenomena*, Course # 16, Siggraph'87, Anaheim.

Fracchia D, Prusinkiewicz P, de Boer M (1990) Animation of the Development of Multicellular Structures, *Proc. Computer Animation 1990*, Geneva, Switzerland.

Françon J (1991) Sur la modélisation informatique de l'architecture et du développement des végétaux Colloque, *L'arbre. Biologie et développement*, Naturalia Monspeliensa, C. Edelin ed., Montpellier, France.

Greene N (1989) Voxel Space Automata: Modeling with Stochastic Growth Processes in Voxel Space, *Computer Graphics*, Vol.23, No.3, pp.175–184.

Guibas L, Stolfi G (1985) Primitives for the Manipulation of General Subdivisions and the Computation of Voronoï Diagrams, *Transactions on Graphics*, Vol.2, pp.74–123.

Hallé F, Oldeman R, Tomlinson P (1978) *Tropical Trees and Forests: an Architectural Analysis*, Springer-Verlag.

Jacque A (1970) Constellations et graphes topologiques, *Colloque Math. Soc. Janos Bolyai*, pp.657–672.

Lazarus F, Coquillart S, Jancène P (1993) Interactive Axial Deformations, in *Modeling in Computer Graphics*, B. Falcidieno and T.L. Kunii eds., Springer, pp.241–254.

Lienhardt P (1988) Free-Form Surfaces Modeling by Evolution Simulation, *Proc. Eurographics'88*, Nice, France, pp. 327–341.

Lienhardt P (1989) Subdivisions of Surfaces and Generalized Maps, *Proc. Eurographics' 89*, Hamburg, R.F.A., pp.439–452

Lienhardt P (1993) N-Dimensional Generalized Combinatorial Maps and Cellular Quasi-Manifolds, To appear in the *International Journal of Computational Geometry and Applications*.

Lück H, Lück J (1986) Unconventional leaves (an application of map 0L-systems to biology, in The Book of L, Rozenberg & Salomaa eds., Springer-Verlag.

Mäntylä M (1988) *An Introduction to Solid Modeling*, Computer Science Press, Rockville.

Prusinkiewicz P, A. Lindenmayer A and J. Hanan J (1988) Developmental Models of Herbaceous Plants for Computer Imagery Purposes, *Computer Graphics*, Vol.22, No.4, pp.141–150.

Prusinkiewicz P, Hanan J (1990) Visualization of Botanical Structures and Processes using Parametric L-Systems, in *Scientific Visualization and Graphics Simulation* (Thalmann ed., Wiley & Sons), pp.183–201.

Reeves W (1983) Particle Systems: a Technique for Modeling a Class of Fuzzy Objects, *Transactions on Graphics,* Vol.2, No.2, pp.91–108.

de Reffye P, Edelin C, Françon J, Jaeger M, Puech C (1988) Plant Models Faithful to Botanical Structure and Development, *Computer Graphics*, Vol.22, No.4, pp.141–150.

de Reffye P, Dinouart P, Barthelemy D (1990) Architecture et modélisation de l'orme du Japon, Zelkova Serrata (Thunb.) Makino (Ulmacae): la notion d'axe de référence, Colloque *"L'arbre. Biologie et développement"*, Naturalia Monspeliensa, C. Edelin ed., Montpellier, France.

Reynolds C (1987) Flocks, Herds and Schools: A Distributed Behavioral Model, *Computer Graphics*, Vol.21, No.4, pp.25–34.

Rossignac J, O'Connor M (1989) SGC: A Dimension-Independent Model for Pointsets with Internal Structures and Incomplete Boundaries, in *Geometric Modeling for Product Engineering* M. Wozny, J. Turner and K. Preiss eds., North-Holland.

Smith (1984) A Plants, Fractals and Formal Languages, *Computer Graphics*, Vol.18, No.3, pp.1–10.

Terraz O (1994) *Modélisation et programmation de métamorphoses d'objets tridimensionnels subdivisés*, PhD Thesis, in preparation, Université Louis Pasteur, Strasbourg, France

Terraz O, Lienhardt P (1993) Some aspects of a method for programming metamorphoses of any subdivisions of any surfaces, *Proc. Compugraphics'93*, Alvor, Portugal.

Terraz O, Lienhardt P (1994) *Generation of metamorphoses of any subdivided surfaces, using behavioral animation*, Research report R94–02, Département d'Informatique, Université Louis Pasteur, Strasbourg, France, submitted.

Tutte W (1984) *Graph Theory Encyclopedia of Mathematics and its Applications*, 21, Addison-Wesley.

Weiler K (1985) Edge-Based Data Structures for Solid Modeling in Curved-Surface Environments, *Computer Graphics and Applications*, Vol.5, No.1, pp.21–40.

Wilhelms J (1990) Behavioral Animation using an Interactive Network, *Proc. Computer Animation'90*, Geneva, Switzerland, pp.95–105.

3

Simulating Life of Virtual Plants, Fishes and Butterflies

Hansrudi Noser, Daniel Thalmann
Computer Graphics Lab, Swiss Federal Institute of Technology
CH-1015 Lausanne, Switzerland

3.1. Introduction

In this chapter, we present a general methodology for simulating the life and behavior of creatures and their reaction to their environment. In a larger sense, we can attribute a behavior to each object. Dead objects, like balls, stones, ... move (behave) in their environment according to physical laws. Plants, as all other living creatures, obey also Newton's laws (gravitation, wind, ..), but besides, they grow, reproduce themselves and react to their environment (light, temperature, ...). The behavior of animals is in addition influenced by emotional and instinctive components. Males and females are attracted by each other, or as an other example, a predator is attracted by his victim, which on the other hand is repelled by the predator. For most of the humans and a lot of animals their behavior is strongly determined by their vision, which is a very important channel, by which the environment is perceived. Finally, the highest level of behavior includes intelligence, which is only attributed to humans.

Our approach is based on L-systems, force fields and synthetic vision. With this approach, high level physical and behavioral animation is possible. Vision based actors find their way without collisions in a L-system environment to given destinations. Dynamically created objects, moving in complex 3D vector force fields can interact with each other and branched structures, simulating behavior of herds, flocks, schools or some physical effects.

Production systems and L-grammars, as introduced by Prusinkiewicz and Lindenmayer (1990) are very powerful tools for creating images. From a user-defined axiom and a set of

Artificial Life and and Virtual Reality Edited by Nadia Magnenat Thalmann and Daniel Thalmann
© 1994 John Wiley and Sons Ltd

production rules, the computer creates images with a complexity dependent only on the number of times the productions are applied. The theory of L-systems has been mainly used for the visualization of the development and growth of living organisms like plants, trees and cells. In a previous paper (Noser et al. 1992), we presented the software package LMobject which realizes a timed and parametric L-system with conditional and pseudo stochastic productions for animation purposes. With this software package a user may create realistic or abstract shapes, play with various tree structures and generate a variety of concepts of growth and life development in the resulting animation. To extend the possibilities for more realism in the pictures, we added external forces, which interact with the L-structures and allow a certain physical modeling. External forces can also have an important impact in the evolution of objects.

Prusinkiewicz and Lindenmayer (1990) have proposed two simple cases of external forces. In the first method, the 3D turtle which interprets the symbolic grammar may be aligned horizontal to a vector representing the gravity. Thus, an object (a tree, for example) is able to "feel" the gravity and to react. The second case is specific to plant and tree modeling and allows the simulation of tropism, which is responsible for the bending of branches towards light sources.

In our extended version, tree structures can be deformed in an elastic way and animated by time and place dependent vector force fields. The elasticity of each articulation can be set individually by productions. So, the bending of branches can be made dependent on the branches' thickness, making animation more realistic. The force fields too, can be set and modified with productions. This kind of interaction is based on the principle of tropism as described by Prusinkiewicz and Lindenmayer (1990).

Further, we introduced a third type of force interaction, that affects L-structures. This simulates the displacement of objects in any vector force field dependent on time and position. An object's movement is determined by a class of differential equations Eq.(3.1), which can be set and modified by productions. The mass of the turtle, which represents the object, can be set as well by using a special symbol of the grammar.

$$\ddot{x} = \frac{1}{m} f_x(t, x, y, z, \dot{x}, \dot{y}, \dot{z}, X, Y, Z)$$
$$\ddot{y} = \frac{1}{m} f_y(t, x, y, z, \dot{x}, \dot{y}, \dot{z}, X, Y, Z) \qquad (3.1)$$
$$\ddot{z} = \frac{1}{m} f_z(t, x, y, z, \dot{x}, \dot{y}, \dot{z}, X, Y, Z)$$

To solve the differential equation system, we evolve an initial value problem for Eq.(3.1) using the 4th-order Runge Kutta Method. This vector force field approach is particularly convenient for simulating the motion of objects in fluids (air, water) as described by Wejchert and Haumann (1991).

Behavioral animation was studied in detail by Reynolds (1987). He gives a good overview of different methods and its problematic. Susan Amkraut and Michael Girard showed in the film "Eurhythmy" (Girard and Amkraut 1990) a flock of birds flying around and avoiding collisions between themselves and obstacles in their environment using a force field animation system to realize the simulation. Repulsion forces around each bird and around static objects are responsible for collision avoiding. At the beginning of the animation, the space field and the initial positions, orientations, and velocities of objects are defined and the rest of the simulation is evolved from these initial conditions.

The force field approach in behavioral animation is well suited for modeling an instinct driven, animal behavior for a large number of actors forming schools, herds or flocks. The behavior of intelligent actors, however, needs more sophisticated techniques. To simulate intelligent or human behavior in path searching and obstacle avoidance in a synthetic environment, we have developed a synthetic vision based global navigation module (Renault et al. 1990; Noser et al. 1994). The task of a navigation system is to plan a path to a specific goal and to execute this plan, modifying it as necessary to avoid unexpected obstacles (Crowley 1985). With the use of synthetic vision we simulate the way a real human perceives the environment. Thus, the first step in the simulation of a natural and intelligent behavior is done. Moreover, in a L-system defined environment, where there is no 3D geometric database of the environment because the world exists only after the execution of production rules, synthetic vision gives an elegant and fast way to provide information about the environment to the actor.

In the L-system based animation system, described in (Noser et al. 1992), only a global force field determining the system of differential equations of all objects could be defined in the axiom or in the production rules. Thus, only one movement type could be defined at a given time. Collision detection and object interaction were not possible. In our new approach, each generated object has its own force field acting on other objects or branching structures. This extension allows collision detection and behavioral animation. In addition, each object has its own differential equation, which determines his movement in the global force field given by the contributions of all other objects. So, at the same time several types of movements are possible (falling apple , jumping ball, school of fish, ...).

In this chapter, we also present the implementation of synthetic vision into the L-system based animation software, where the behavior of an actor is at a higher level determined by an automata, which allows an actor to find a path from his current position to a given destination in known or unknown environments by avoiding collisions. Several actors can be generated and personalized in the axiom or in a production rule. More details about our synthetic vision approach may be found in another paper (Noser et al. 1994), including the visual memory representation by an octree and the path searching algorithms (3D), working with heuristics, used to personalize an actor's behavior. In Section 3.2 we present the formal definition of our L-system, explained in (Noser et al. 1992). Section 3.3 and 3.4 describe some theoretical aspects of the new extensions. In Section 3.5 some implementation details are given, as well as the semantic of the symbols 'C' and 'M' of the formal grammar which represent the behavioral features of force field (symbol 'C') and vision based (symbol 'M') animation. As part of turtle interpreted L-systems (or LOGO), these symbols can be considered as high level turtle operation symbols, in contrast to lower level, standard symbols like 'f' (forward) or '+' (rotate), which only advance the turtle or rotate it around an axis by given values. Our new approach allows, for example, an easy animation of flocks of butterflies, of schools of fishes or of path searching actors in a L-system modeled environment. Simple physical simulations, like explosions or bouncing balls are also feasible.

3.2. The L-system

In this section, we introduce the formal description of our L-system; it defines how an object at a certain age is derived by the derivation function D from an initial word (= axiom = sequence of parametric symbols) and the production rules. The symbols of the alphabet are interpreted by means of a 3D turtle, whose current orientation is given by a local orthonormal coordinate system with the axis H(heading), L(left) and U(up). Some symbols control the position and the orientation of the turtle's coordinate system, others represent geometrical primitives, drawn in the turtle's coordinate system, and others perform special operations. For readers not familiar with L-systems we highly recommend the lecture of "The Algorithmic Beauty of Plants" (Prusinkiewicz and Lindenmayer 1990) where different types of L-systems are well introduced. More details about our implementation and extension may be found in (Noser et al. 1992).

We start the formal description of the L-system by giving some elementary definitions.

V: an alphabet

R^+:   the set real positive numbers

N :   the set integer positive numbers

Σ :   a set of formal parameters

$E(\Sigma)$:   the arithmetic expressions in Polish notation

$C(\Sigma)$:   the locical expressions in Polish notation

ω :   an axiom

P : $P = \left\{ p_{a,i} \middle| a \in V, i \in N \right\}$ the set of productions

Π: $p_{a,i} \to [0,1]$ a pseudo-statistical distribution with $\sum_i \pi(p_{a,i}) = 1$

$(a, x_o, \ldots, x_6) \in V \times R^7$ a parametric symbol

The productions of an L-system describe how symbols of a timed and parametric string are replaced if they pass their maximal age during evolution of time.

$P \in V \times R^7 \times C(\Sigma) \times \Pi \times (V \times E(\Sigma)^7)^*$: the production space

$p_{a,i} \in P$: a single production

$p_{a,i}:(a, \alpha, x_1, \ldots, x_6) \xrightarrow{Cond(\alpha, x_1 x_2, x_3, T) \text{ and } \Pi(p_{a,i})} (a_1, f_{10}, \ldots, f_{16}) \ldots (a_n, f_{n0}, \ldots, f_{n6})$

α: maximal age of symbol a

f_{j0} initial age of symbol a_j

x_1, x_2, x_3 3 parameters

x_4, x_5, x_6 values of the evaluated growth functions

$f_{j0} + t$ local age of the symbol

T global time

$f_{j1}, \ldots, f_{j3}$ parameter expressions

$f_{j4}, \ldots, f_{j6}$ growth functions

f_{jk} $f_{jk}(f_{j0}, x_1, x_2, x_3, t, T)$

$p_{a,i}$ a conditional and pseudo-statistical production

In the above definition the symbol a is replaced with a certain probability under a given condition by a parametric string given by the right part of the production. The way, how

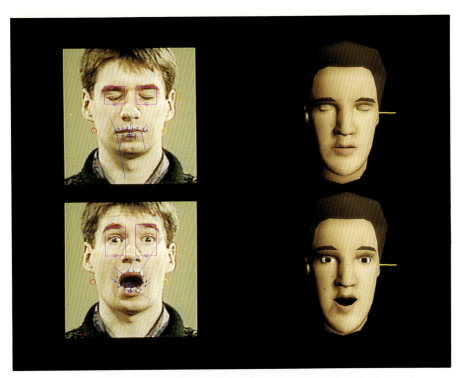

Figure I.2 Communication between a real and a virtual human

Figure I.4 Virtual actress

Figure 2.13 Approximate wild cherry tree with flowers

Figure 2.6 Fir tree with rhythmic ramification

Figure 2.5 Pruned tree with traumatic reiterations

Figure 2.18 Flower petals or leaf lobes have often the same type of behavior, controlled by a few parameters

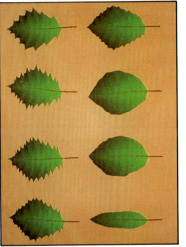

Figure 2.17 Metamorphosis of the boundary of leaves of a particular oak

Figure 2.20 Use of context-dependent parameters, for instance for controlling color of butterflies

Figure 2.14 Forest

Figure 2.19 Use of context-dependent parameters, for instance for controlling color of butterflies

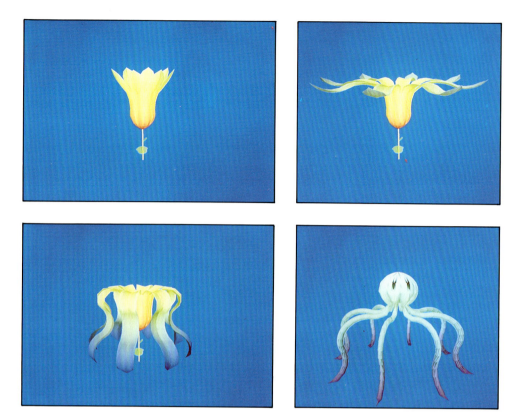

Figure 2.21-2.24 Metamorphosis of a flower into an octopus

Figure 2.35 Fish

Figure 2.36 Fish

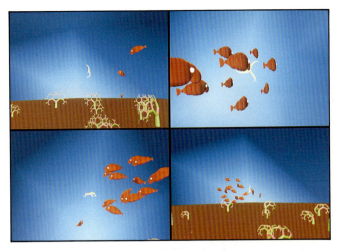

Figure 3.4   School of fish animation sequence

Figure 3.6   Tree-ball interaction

Figure 3.7   A butterfly in a flower field searching its way

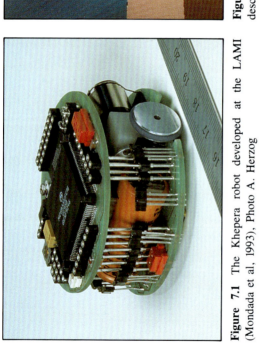

Figure 7.1 The Khepera robot developed at the LAMI (Mondada et al, 1993), Photo A. Herzog

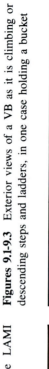

Figures 9.1-9.3 Exterior views of a VB as it is climbing or descending steps and ladders, in one case holding a bucket

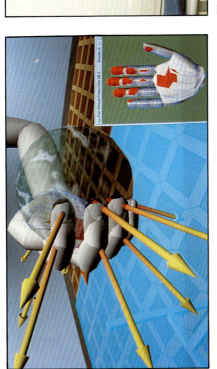

Figure 10.3 Grasping procedure of the virtual hand with a virtual sphere; normal forces and contact areas are shown

Figure 10.4 The control of a grasping procedure in VE performed by means of ARTS glove

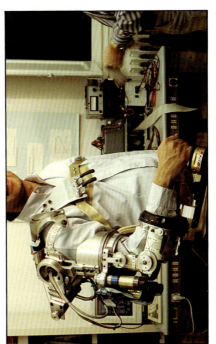

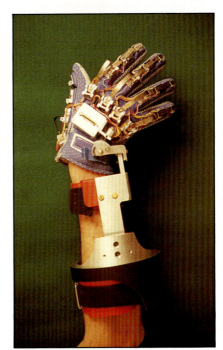

Figure 10.5 ARTS glove

Figure 10.6 Arm exoskeleton system devoted to replicated external forces on the user's hand

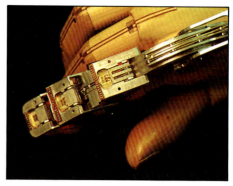

Figure 10.7 Example of the control of virtual object surface exploration task based on force feedback replication to the human arm

Figure 10.8 The prototype of the HFF system

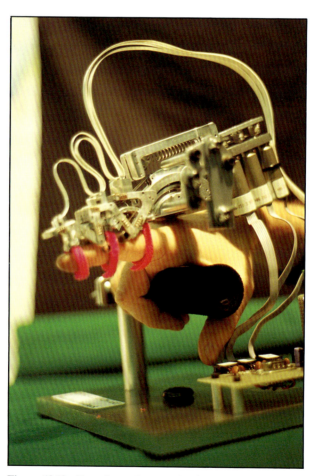

Figure 10.10 Experimental set-up for the characterization of the HFF system

Figure 13.1.a-b Moving a chair and the keyboard in the simulated VR-demonstration of Fraunhofer-IGD. The old shadow of the moving object has to be removed and the new shadow has to be added to the scene. The computation time is about 2 seconds for each task.

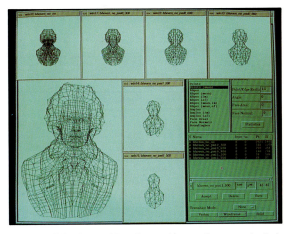

Figure 13.2 Bust of Beethoven (decreasing complexity)

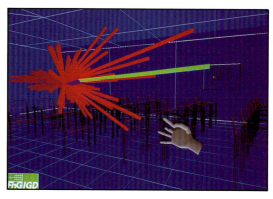

Figure 13.3 Acoustic energy distribution (impulse response)

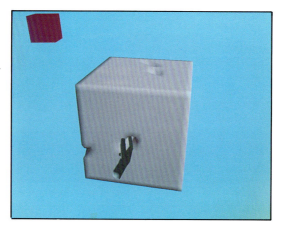

Figure 13.8 Potter (the cube can be modeled in real-time with the index finger)

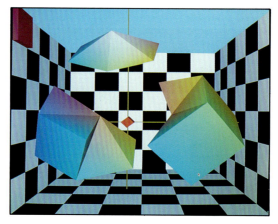

Figure 13.9 Puzzle: assembly task (the pieces can be grabbed and assembled; mutual penetration is checked for exactly)

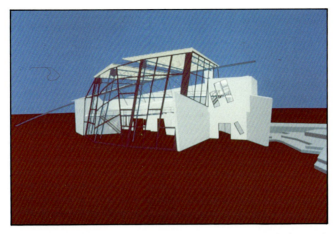

Figure 13.10 Design of a pavilion at the entrance of the park "Englischer Garten" in Munich

Figure 13.11 The virtual model of Darmstadt

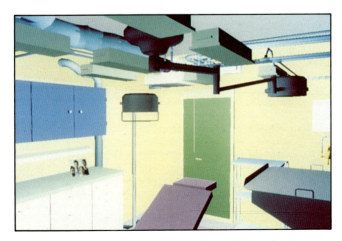

Figure 13.12 Operation room of a hospital area of a ship

Figure 14.4 Dynamic portals

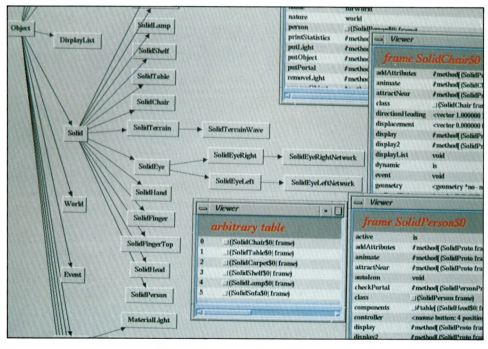

Figure 14.6 A BrickNet visual tool

this replacement is done, is controlled by the derivation function D and its mathematical axioms.

$$D: \left(V \times R^7\right)^* \times R \rightarrow \left(V \times R^7\right)^*$$

Axiom 1: The development of each symbol is independent of each other in time

$$D\big((a_1, x_0, ..., x_6)...(a_n, x_0, ..., x_6), t\big) = D\big((a_1, x_0, ..., x_6), t\big)... D\big((a_n, x_0, ..., x_6), t\big)$$

Axiom 2: The Growth of a symbol before terminal age.

if $x_0 + t < \alpha$ then

$$D\big((a, x_0, ..., x_6), t\big) = (a, x_0 + t, x_1, x_2, x_3, f_4, f_5, f_6)$$

The growth functions are evaluated.

Axiom 3: Application of stochastic production at terminal age

if $(x_0 + t \geq \alpha) \wedge \big(Cond(\alpha, x_1, x_2, x_3, T) = TRUE\big)$ then with a probability $\pi\big(p_{a,i}\big)$

$$D\big((a, x_0, ..., x_6), t\big) = D\big((a_1, f_{10}, ..., f_{13}, x_4, x_5, x_6)...(a_n, f_{n0}, ..., f_{n3}, x_4, x_5, x_6), t - (\alpha - x_0)\big)$$

The initial age and parameter expressions $f_{10}, ..., f_{13}$ are evaluated.

Axiom 4: Selection of random numbers for the productions

$$random\_number = rand\_table\big[(x + y[x]) \bmod z\big]$$

      rand_table: table of size z with uniform random values between 0 and 1

      x   : recursion depth of function D

      $y[x]$: position of the production in the derivation tree of D at the x depth.

To guarantee under certain conditions a continuous growth of the plants the axiom 4 has to be added (Noser et al. 1992) if stochastic productions are used in the plant definition by production rules.

3.3. Behavioral Modeling using Force Fields

In a "force field animation system" the 3D world has to be modeled by force fields. Some objects have to carry repulsion forces, if there should not be any collision with them. Other objects can be attractive to others. Many objects are both attractive at long distances and repulsive at short distances. The shapes and sizes of these objects can vary, too. Space fields like gravity or wind force fields can greatly influence animation sequences or shapes of trees.

The system of differential equations, given in Eq.(3.2), describes the movement of a point object i with mass m_i in a force field. The global force field is given by the sum of all objects' contributions f_{kj}. The individual part g_{ki} of each object determines it's behavior in the global field,

$$\ddot{x}_i = \frac{1}{m_i}\left(g_{xi}(x_i,y_i,z_i,\dot{x}_i,\dot{y}_i,\dot{z}_i,t) + \sum_{j,j\neq i} f_{xj}(x_i,y_i,z_i,x_j,y_j,z_j,\dot{x}_j,\dot{y}_j,\dot{z}_j,r_{ij},t) \right)$$

$$\ddot{y}_i = \frac{1}{m_i}\left(g_{yi}(x_i,y_i,z_i,\dot{x}_i,\dot{y}_i,\dot{z}_i,t) + \sum_{j,j\neq i} f_{yj}(x_i,y_i,z_i,x_j,y_j,z_j,\dot{x}_j,\dot{y}_j,\dot{z}_j,r_{ij},t) \right)$$

$$\ddot{z}_i = \frac{1}{m_i}\left(g_{zi}(x_i,y_i,z_i,\dot{x}_i,\dot{y}_i,\dot{z}_i,t) + \sum_{j,j\neq i} f_{zj}(x_i,y_i,z_i,x_j,y_j,z_j,\dot{x}_j,\dot{y}_j,\dot{z}_j,r_{ij},t) \right) \quad (3.2)$$

where :

i	= index of an object
m_i	= the mass of object i
x_i,y_i,z_i	= position components of object i
$\dot{x}_i,\dot{y}_i,\dot{z}_i$	= velocity components of object i
$\ddot{x}_i,\ddot{y}_i,\ddot{z}_i$	= acceleration components of object i
t	= time
r_{ij}	= distance between object i and object j

The behavior of an object in the global force field is determined by a predefined curve (e.g. spline, fixed) or it's individual part g of Eq.(3.2). The terms of g can depend on the object's actual position and it's speed. Speed dependent terms can be used to model friction properties. The position variables allow it to make the object's behavior position dependent.

Tropism forces act on the articulations of branching structures (Prusinkiewicz and Lindenmayer 1990). The bending of branches is simulated by a rotation of the turtle in direction of the tropism forces. If our dynamically created objects have to interact with branching structures, then their force fields have to be added to the tropism force. The following equations describe this interaction in detail.

$$\vec{M} = \left(\vec{H} \times \vec{F} \right) / e \qquad \text{torque vector (} e = \text{elasticity of articulation)}$$

$$m = |\vec{M}| \qquad \text{torque}$$

$$\vec{A} = \left(\vec{H} \times \vec{F} \right) / \left\| \vec{H} \times \vec{F} \right\| \qquad \text{rotation vector}$$

$$\beta = \sin^{-1}\left(|\vec{A}| \right) \qquad \text{angle between turtle heading } \vec{H} \text{ et } \vec{F} \qquad (3.3)$$

$$\alpha = \beta\left(1 - \frac{1}{1+m} \right) \qquad \text{resulting rotation angle}$$

$$\vec{F} = \vec{f}_{tropisme} + \sum_i \vec{f}_i \qquad \text{global force field}$$

The effective rotation angle is proportional to the torque m, produced by the global force by acting on the turtle's heading vector, but it never exceeds the angle between the turtle heading and the force vector at the turtle's position.

3.4. Vision Based Animation

In our approach to synthetic vision (Noser et al. 1994), a dynamic occupancy octree grid serves as a global 3D visual memory and allows an actor to memorize the environment that he sees and to adapt it to a changing and dynamic environment. His reasoning process allows him to find 3D paths based on his visual memory by avoiding impasses and circuits. The global behavior of the actor is based on the navigation automata, shown in Figure 3.1, representing the automata of an actor, who has to go from his current position to different places, memorized in a list of destinations. He can displace himself in known or unknown environments. After the initialization of his memory and his vision system (off -> mem_set -> vision_set) and the definition of his destinations (end_point_set) the path searching is initialized. Before starting a search, he looks around and memorizes what he sees (look_around). Then, he tries to find a path by reasoning (search_new_path). If he finds one, he follows it (move). If he encounters an obstacle while moving, he stops, turns around, looks for a new path and restarts moving. This process is repeated until he arrives at his destination. There, he takes the next destination from the list and restarts the whole procedure described above.

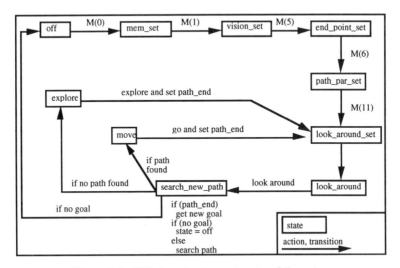

Figure 3.1. Global navigation automata of the actor.

In unknown environments, if he uses a conditional heuristic, he cannot find a path to an invisible destination (behind an obstacle, for example). In this case, he starts to explore his environment according to his heuristic, which will lead him to his destination, if there is any path.

3.5. Implementation of the Behavioral Features

We integrated the physical modeling and behavioral animation features in the LMobject software package (Noser et al. 1992). This L-system is a timed parametric context-free grammar with conditional and pseudo-stochastic productions. All grammar symbols have three parameters and three growth functions. It should be noted, that neither the formal object, nor the graphical object need to be stored completely in memory. Only the formal description of the current state of the derivation function needs to be maintained on a stack, resulting in memory requirements proportional to the recursion depth of the derivation function. Each time the derivation functions encounters a leaf of the derivation tree, it interprets the symbol and executes immediately the corresponding action. This action can be, for example, a turtle operation, a force field declaration, a camera manipulation or the drawing of a graphical primitive in the turtle's coordinate system. The actions are determined by the semantic of the grammar.

The new extension allows us, to dynamically create new point objects with a special symbol **C** of the grammar. Each time the derivation function of the L-system which derives the object from the axiom and the production rules encounters this symbol **C**, it acts on a global interaction table containing the trace of all generated objects. This interaction table has the following structure:

```
typedef struct {
        short    id_depth, id_large;
        float    posVel[6];
        char     *force[3], *eqDiff[3], *type;
        float    mass
} Tinteraction;
Tinteraction InteractionTable[MAX_OBJECTS]
```

The recursive derivation function identifies with its fourth axiom each object in the derivation tree and returns the unique object identification *id_depth* and *id_large*.

If the object is encountered for the first time, it is appended to the global interaction table. The initial position (turtle) and the speed (from the symbol C) are copied into the table posVel and the force (*force) , the differential equation (*eqDiff(3)) and the type (*type) pointers are directed to the corresponding character expressions in the parametric symbol C. This way, the mass of the object can be set as well.

If the object already exists in the interaction table, the derivation function starts an iteration step of the numerical solution of the object's differential equation by regarding all the contributions of the other force fields of the same type in the global interaction table. Then, the turtle is placed at the resulting position. The iteration step is calculated by the method of Runge Kutta of degree four and solves the system of differential equations given in Eq.(3.2). This system describes the Newtonian movement of a point with a mass m in the 3D space under the influence of a 3D vector force field. As the position and speed of each created object are stored in the global interaction table, the relative distances r_{ij} from one object *i* to an other object *j*, can be calculated and thus used in the expressions of the force fields and differential equations. The semantic of the parametric symbol **C**

C (*t*) (*x*) (*y*) (*z*)   (*f1*) (*f2*) (*f3*)

depends on the parameter *x*. If *x* = 1, the expressions *f1*, *f2* and *f3* define the three components of the vector force field of the current object. If *x* = 2, the current object's differential equation is determined in the same way. If *x* = 3, the value of y sets the mass, and the object's movement is started with an initial speed given by the evaluated expressions *f1*, *f2* and *f3*.

Sometimes it is useful, that an object carrying a force field moves along a predefined path. If *x* = 4, the differential equation of the current object is not evaluated, but the object is placed at the position given by (*f1*, *f2*, *f3*). The *fi*'s, for example, can be timed spline defining a 3D path.

The integration of the vision module into the L-system is realized via the special symbol **M** of the grammar. The semantic of **M** depends also on it's parameter *x*. In Figure 3.1, we can see its influence on the state of the actor.

With *x* = 0, the symbol

M (*t*) (0) (*y*) (*z*)   (*f1*) (*f2*) (*f3*)

initializes and scales the visual octree memory of an actor. The values of *f1* and *f2* determine the cube including the whole scene and *f3* sets the resolution of the octree (maximal tree depth).

M (*t*) (1) (*y*) (*z*)   (*f1*) (*f2*) (*f3*)

permits to personalize the actors vision system. With *f1* and *f2* the near and far clipping is set, and *f3* gives the range of interest within which the actor adapts his memory to changes in the environment.

With the symbol

M (*t*) (6) (*y*) (*z*)   (*f1*) (*f2*) (*f3*)

the path searching and exploring procedure can be personalized. The value of *f1* gives the distance, the actor previews along his actual found path, to detect collisions with his environment. By *f2* the size of voxels to be examined during path searching and exploring is set. With *f3,* the user can determine one of the predefined heuristics to use in the path searching or exploring algorithm. It is also possible to set initial positions and look at points, destinations and moving speeds of the actors by using the corresponding parametric symbol **M**.

So, a user can define and personalize one or several actors in the axiom. He can give him several destinations, and then the animation will evolve according to the global navigation automata shown in Figure 3.1. We also implemented the ability to place and orient the camera according to an object's position and velocity so that nice animation from the perspective of an actor with vision or a force field influenced object can be realized.

3.6. Applications

3.6.1. Growing Tree Structure

In this section we illustrate the working principle of the derivation function D by deriving the formal object of a continuously growing simple tree structure at several ages. We consider the alphabet V = {**p, q, +, -, [,]** } with all characters printed in bold. **p** and **q** are timed and parametric symbols with growth functions. To establish the link with the formal description of Section 3.2 we use the following notation.

(**p**, a, x, f(x, t))	the parametric symbol
p	the symbol
a	the parameter x0 which is the actual or initial age of the symbol.
x	the parameter x1
f(x,t)	the growth function f_4
t	the time

The symbols **p** and **q** represent line segments with a length of the actual value of the growth function. The line segment is drawn from the actual position of the turtle in direction of its heading vector H. After having drawn the line segment the turtle is placed at its end without changing its direction. The symbols **+** and **-** of the alphabet V represent rotations of the turtle around its U vector by an angle of +-90 degrees. The brackets [and] correspond to push and pop operations of the turtle state (position and orientation) which are introduced to delimit branches. Thus, the brackets enable the construction of tree structures.

The tree structure is defined by an axiom and one production for the symbol **p**.

Axiom: (**p**, a=0, x=1, f=6xt)
Production: (**p**, α = 1) ------------> (Condition = TRUE, probability = 1)
        (**q**, a=0, x=x, f=6x+t) [+ (**p**, a=0, x = x/2, f=6xt)] [- (**p**, a=0, x=x/2, f=6xt)]

The axiom corresponds to a line segment (symbol **p**) with initial age a=0, a parameter x=1 and a linear growth function f = 6xt = 6t (as x =1). So, the segment will linearly grow until it reaches its maximal age α = 1 given at the left side of the production. The production is applied with a probability of 1.0 without any precondition. Figure 3.2 illustrates some applications of the production

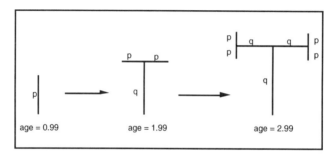

Figure 3.2. Continuous growth of a simple tree.

The line segment p at maximal age of 1 has to be replaced by a segment q of the same length at its initial age of a=0. So, the parameter x of the symbol p (which is replaced) is passed without any change. The growth function fq=6x+t satisfies this continuity condition as f_p(t=1, x=1) = f_q(t=0, x=1) = 6. The term t is responsible for a further linear but smaller growth rate of the segment q. So each branch of the segment continues to grow. The two new branches p should be a factor 2 shorter then the preceding one. Therefore, the parameter x is passed to the new symbols by dividing it by 2 (x = x/2). As they start their growth from zero the same growth function has to be used as for the symbol p in the axiom. Thus, a continuous and consistent further replacement is guaranteed during the following iterations.

In the next paragraph, we provide some details about derivation steps of the formal object. We show how the derivation function D works and when the corresponding axioms of the derivation function D are applied. To avoid some confusion the reader is asked to distinguish between the enumerated mathematical axioms of the derivation function D and the "string" axiom of the tree definition.

Object age t = 0.5:
      D(Axiom, 0.5)= D((**p**, 0, 1, 6xt), 0.5)   =
            (Axiom 2, as a+t = 0.5 < α=1, the growth function is evaluated)
  (**p**, a+t, x, 6xt)   =
  (**p**, 0+0.5, 1, 6*1*0.5)   =
  (**p**, 0.5, 1, 3)

Object age t = 0.9
      D(Axiom, 0.9) = ... = (**p**, 0.9, 1, 5.4)

Object age t = 1.5
      D(Axiom, 1.5) = D((**p**, 0, 1, 6xt), 1.5)   =
      (Axiom 3, as a+1.5 = 0+1.5 = 1.5 > α = 1,
      the parameter x from the preceding symbol p is passed to the symbols of the
      production by evaluating the corresponding expressions)
      D((**q**, 0, x, 6x+t) [+ (**p**, 0, x/2, 6xt)] [- (**p**, 0, x/2, 6xt)],1.5-(α-a)) =
      D((**q**, 0, 1, 6x+t) [+ (**p**, 0, 0.5, 6xt)] [- (**p**, 0, 0.5, 6xt)], 0.5) =
            (Axiom 1)
      D((**q**, 0, 1, tx+t), 0.5) [+D((**p**, 0, 0.5, 6xt), 0.5)][- D((**p**, 0, 0.5, 6xt), 0.5)] =
            (Axiom 2, as a+t = 0+0.5 < α=1,
            the growth functions are evaluated by using the evaluated parameter x)
      (**q**, 0.5, 1, 6.5) [+ (**p**, 0.5, 0.5, 1.5)] [- (**p**, 0.5, 0.5, 1.5)]

3.6.2. School of Fishes

In the following animation fishes with mass m=1 are generated at the same place at a regular rate. Their repulsive force field is given by Eq.(3.4). All these fishes are attracted by a moving object, the bait, with an attractive force field at long distances and a repulsive one at short distances (Eq.(3.5)). The movement of each fish is damped by Eq.(3.6). Figure 3.3 illustrates the bait's force field.

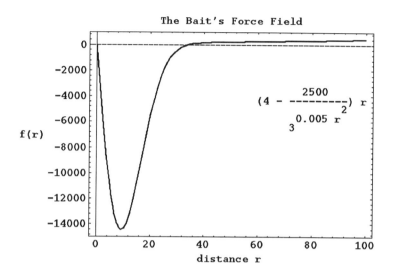

Figure 3.3. The bait's force field.

The fish's force field has about the same form at short distances. At long distances however, it remains zero.

$$\vec{f}_{fish}(r) = -2500 \cdot 3^{-0.005r^2} \cdot r \cdot \vec{n}$$

$$\text{with} \quad \vec{r} = (\vec{X}_{object} - \vec{x}), \quad r = \left\| \vec{X}_{object} - \vec{x} \right\| \quad \text{and} \quad \vec{n} = \frac{\vec{r}}{r}$$

$\vec{X}_{object}$: Position of the object (fish)   (3.4)

$\vec{x}$: position in the the force field

r : distance from the force field center of the object

$$\vec{f}_{bait}(r) = (4 - 2500 \cdot 3^{-0.005r^2}) \cdot r \cdot \vec{n} \tag{3.5}$$

$$\vec{g}_{fish}(\dot{\vec{x}}) = -3\dot{\vec{x}} \tag{3.6}$$

The bait moves along a given 3D path spline. Each new generated fish joins immediately the school, following the bait. The strongly repulsive components of the force fields at short distances of all moving objects, prevent collisions. In Figure 3.4 (see Color Section), we can see some pictures from the whole animation sequence.

Figure 3.5 shows parts of the axiom and the production rules used for the above animation sequence.

Axiom
...... /* some symbols, describing the environment It follows the definition of the bait */
f () () () ()   (0) (0) (0)
    /* the symbol f places the turtle at (0,0,0) and determines the initial bait position*/
C ()   (1) () ()
    $((4-2500*3^{(-0.005r^2)} * (X-x))$
    $((4-2500*3^{(-0.005r^2)} * (Y-y))$
    $((4-2500*3^{(-0.005r^2)} * (Z-z))$
    /* Symbol C with parameter x=1 defines the bait's force field. (X,Y,Z) are the coordinates of the current object (in this case the bait). (x,y,z) is the position of an object, feeling the force field. The variable r is given by r=sqrt((X-x)^2 + (Y-y)^2 + (Z-z)^2), the distance of a fish to the bait. */
C ()   (4) () ()   (spline_1(t)) (spline_2(t)) (spline_3(t))
    /* Symbol C with parameter x=4 places the turtle (= the bait) at the position (spline_1(t), spline_2(t), (spline_3(t)) determined by a predefined timed 3D spline */
z ()   () () ()   () () ()
    /* the symbol z is a germ for the bait. It is an arbitrary geometrical figure, defined by the corresponding production rule, not given here. It is drawn in the turtle coordinate system */
x ()   () () ()   () () ()
    /* The symbol x is a germ for a fish force field declaration */
...... /* some more symbols, describing something arbitrary */
EndAxiom

Production1
x (maximal_age = 1) --------------------->/*symbol x to be replaced by the following symbols*/
    /* it follow the parametric symbols, defining the behavior of a fish */
f ()   () () ()   (50) (50) (50)
    /* the symbol f places the turtle (=fish) at the position (50, 50, 50) and thus determines the initial position of a fish */
C ()   (1) () ()
    $((-2500*3^{(-0.005r^2)} * (X-x))$
    $((-2500*3^{(-0.005r^2)} * (Y-y))$
    $((-2500*3^{(-0.005r^2)} * (Z-z))$
    /* Symbol C with parameter x=1 defines the fish's force field, felt by other objects. */
C ()   (2) () ()   (-3u) (-3v) (-3w)
    /* Symbol C with parameter x=1 defines the individual part of each generated fish of the Eq.(2). The vector (u,v,w) represents the velocity of the current fish. */
C ()   (3) (1) ()   (5) (3) (2)
    /* Symbol C with parameter x=3 starts the evolution of the generated fish with the initial velocity (5, 3, 2) and the mass 1 */
y (1)   () () ()   () () ()
    /* Symbol y represents a germ of a fish with an initial age of 1 */
x ()   () () ()   () () ()
    /* The symbol x is a germ for a fish force field declaration */
EndProduction1

Figure 3.5. Parts of axioms and production rules for the fish animation.

This textual description of the axiom and the production are interpreted and controlled by the derivation function D of the L-system. In this case, at each time interval of 1 (1 = maximal symbol age of a fish germ x) a new fish is generated and immediately starts it's typical behavior. It follows the bait and avoids collisions.

3.6.3. Tree-Ball Interaction

In this example, we show the interaction of a ball and a tree. The ball moves towards a tree. As it carries a repulsive "velocity" force field, the tree and the branches bend under it's influence and try to avoid collision with the ball. The ball's force field is shown in Eq.(3.7)

$$\vec{f}_{ball}\left(r, \dot{\vec{x}}\right) = (18 \cdot 3^{-0.005r^2}) \cdot \dot{\vec{x}} \tag{3.7}$$

Here, the force field is always in the direction of the ball's velocity, even behind the ball, so wind, caused by the movement of the ball is simulated. Figure 3.6 (see Color Section) shows some pictures of the animation sequence.

3.6.4. A Butterfly in a Flower Field

In the animation sequence, illustrated in Figure 3.7 (see Color Section), a butterfly searches his way through a flower field, guided by his vision. It is an example of the use of 3D heuristic search (Noser et al. 1994). The flowers are animated by a wind force field. The butterfly is modeled by some symbols of the grammar just as the flying motor.

The first destination of the butterfly is the reflecting sphere. When it arrives there, it looks around and searches for a path to the second destination at the other end of the flower field. Guided by its vision, it is able to avoid collisions and to find a path, as well as to memorize in its visual memory everything it sees.

3.7. Conclusion

With our current L-system based animation system, simulations in all of the above mentioned domains can be realized and combined in one sequence. As Eq. (3.2) is based on Newton's laws, physical simulations are immediate. Growing and reproduction features are inherent in the L-system. We can realize, for example, animation sequences of a growing tree, producing apples, which contain germs for new trees. These germs develop to new trees, after the apples have fallen to the ground. Thus, a whole forest can develop from a single apple (Noser et al. 1992) Beside the physical modeling, the force field approach allows as well to simulate instinctive or emotional behavior (attractive, repellent forces) of individuals or groups and to interact physically with plants and dead objects. Animation according to the following description are possible:

"A small lake is populated with plants, predators and a fish. The fish spawns. The spawn floats away in a water current. After some time the spawn develops to fish which join to a school following a guide. They avoid the predators. "

The vision based features, allow the actors to avoid collisions and to simulate intelligent behavior. The global navigation automata represents 'intelligent' behavior. It allows an actor to find, for example, the exit of a maze, even if there are impasses and circuits, and to memorize the topology of the seen environment. This learned information he can use in future path searching.

In a future development, we plan to improve the force field animation module. Since most objects' force fields have only short distance ranges, it would save much calculation time if only the force field contributions of nearby objects had to be considered. To solve this problem, we plan to introduce a dynamic space subdivision with octrees, in which the force fields can be placed. Thus, neighboring objects could easily be identified. With such an approach much more complex animation would be feasible at still reasonable calculation times.

The synthetic vision module represents a very universal and powerful tool for future behavioral models. By designing and combining new automata and including more sophisticated actors with walking, speaking and grasping features, high level script based animation can be realized in a extremely dynamic environment with partially autonomous actors.

Acknowledgements

This research was sponsored by the Swiss National Foundation for Scientific Research.

References

Crowley JL, Navigation for an Intelligent Mobile Robot (1985) *IEEE Journal of Robotics and Automation*, Vol. RA 1, No 1, pp31-41

Girard M, Amkraut S (1990) Eurhythmy: Concept and Process, *Journal of Visualization and Computer Animation*, Vol. 1, pp.15-17

Noser H, Renault O, Thalmann D, Magnenat Thalmann D, Vision-Based Navigation for Synthetic Actors, (Submitted for publication, 1994)

Noser H, Thalmann D, Turner R (1992) Animation based on the Interaction of L-systems with Vector Force Fields, *Proc. CGI '92*, Springer, Tokyo

Prusinkiewicz P, Lindenmayer A (1990), *The Algorithmic Beauty of Plants*, Springer-Verlag

Renault O, Magnenat Thalmann N, Thalmann D (1990), A Vision-based Approach to Behavioral Animation, *Journal of Visualization and Computer Animation*, Vol 1, No 1, pp 18-21

Reynolds C (1987), Flocks, Herds, and Schools: A Distributed Behavioral Model, *Proc. SIGGRAPH 1987, Computer Graphics*, Vol.21, No4, pp.25-34

Wejchert J, Haumann D (1991), Animation Aerodynamics, *Proc. SIGGRAPH 1991, Computer Graphics*, Vol.25, No4, pp. 19-22

4

Introduction to Embryonics:

Towards New Self-repairing and Self-reproducing Hardware Based on Biological-like Properties

Daniel Mange, André Stauffer
Logic Systems Laboratory, Computer Engineering Department, Swiss Federal Institute of Technology, Lausanne

4.1. Introduction: Artificial Life as a Bridge from the Natural Sciences to Engineering

Traditionally, the development of engineering (civil, electrical, computer engineering, etc.) and that of the natural sciences (physics, chemistry, biology, etc.) have proceeded along separate tracks. The specialist of the natural sciences is a detective: faced with the mysteries of nature (meteorological phenomena, chemical reactions, the development of living beings), he seeks to analyze existing processes to explain their operation, to model them and to predict their future behavior. The engineer, on the other hand, is a builder: faced with social and economic needs, he tries to create artificial systems (bridges, electrical and electronic devices) based on a set of specifications (a description) and a set of primitives (elementary components such as bricks, beams, wires, motors, transistors).

These two disciplines have drawn closer in these last decades. The specialists of the natural sciences have started to resort massively to the tools created by the engineers. One of the most striking examples of this trend is the systematic use of electronics in the medical

Artificial Life and and Virtual Reality Edited by Nadia Magnenat Thalmann and Daniel Thalmann
© 1994 John Wiley and Sons Ltd

world for such tasks as decoding the human genome, representing graphically chemical molecules of great complexity, tomography, etc.

More recently, engineers have been allured by certain natural processes. Three recent examples illustrate this new direction which, somewhat pompously, has been given the name "*artificial life*":

- *neuromimetic networks* (or artificial neural networks) are based on a rough copy of the way the brain and its associated neural system are supposed to function. These networks have a structure completely different from that of the traditional computer (Von Neumann architecture) and surpass its performance for non-numerical applications such as symbol (handwriting) or shape (drawings, pictures) recognition.

- *Genetic algorithms* are based on the Darwinian mechanism of natural selection. Artificial beings are provided with a genome which fully characterizes them. The cross-breeding (i.e. the fusion of two genomes) and the mutation (i.e. the accidental alteration of the genomes) of these beings produce offspring whose characteristics are subject to a "fitness" factor (natural selection). The effectiveness of these algorithms for certain difficult classical problems of optimization (e.g. the traveling salesman problem) has been established.

- *Embryonics,* which is the subject of this article, is based on the natural mechanism of development of living multicellular beings. Starting from a single mother cell, the zygote, containing the complete description of the organism in the form of a genome, the final organism is achieved through a succession of cell divisions, occurring concurrently with a differentiation of each cell, i.e. a specialization dependent essentially on the physical position of the cell (i.e. on its coordinates) in the given space.

To the best of our knowledge, the word "embryonics" has first been coined by H. de Garis for "embryological electronics" in (de Garis 1993).

4.2. The Foundations of Embryonics

Embryonics, i.e. the quasi-biological development of artificial systems, is based on a *general hypothesis,* which describes the environment in which the development occurs, and on *three properties,* which roughly approximate the biological mechanism of cellular development.

4.2.1. The General Hypothesis: the Environment

The general hypothesis describes the selected environment. In the framework of electronics, it consists of a finite, two-dimensional space of silicon (see Figure 4.1), divided into rows and columns (the third dimension introduced by the physical realization of the system is irrelevant for our purposes). The intersection of a row and a column defines a cell, and all cells have an identical physical structure, i.e. an identical network of connections (wires) and an identical set of operators (logic functions). Each cell includes a random access memory (RAM) whose contents (the *genome*) are also identical in operating conditions (i.e. after the system has been programmed). Some special connections are present on the edges of the space, notably to determine the initial conditions. The transformations, in particular the development of an artificial multicellular organism from a single cell, the mother cell, occur then without supply of material (the network of silicon is present at the start), with a trivial supply of energy (the classical power supply of an electronic system), and with a crucial supply of information.

4.2.2 The Three Properties

The first property is that of *multicellular organization*: the artificial organism is divided into a finite number of cells (see Figure 4.1); each cell realizes a unique function, characterized by a number called the *gene* of the cell.

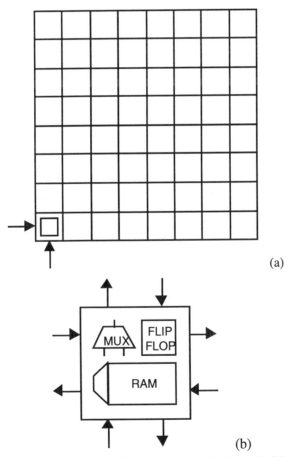

(a)

(b)

Figure 4.1. The environment. (a) The cellular array. (b) One cell of the array.

The same organism can contain multiple cells of the same kind (in the same way as a living being can contain a large number of cells with the same function: nervous cells, skin cells, liver cells, etc.). The maximum number of distinct functions of an organism is then equal to the number of cells of which it is composed, in which case each cell is different from the others. In the example of Figure 4.2, the nine cells, all different, are defined by genes 1 through 9.

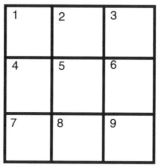

Figure 4.2. A nine-cell organism

The second property is that of *cellular differentiation*. Each cell holds the complete description of the organism, i.e. the genome (see Figure 4.3) and computes its gene by extracting from the genome the function which characterizes it. The gene of a cell depends on its coordinates (X: horizontal coordinate, Y: vertical coordinate), i.e. on its place within the organism.

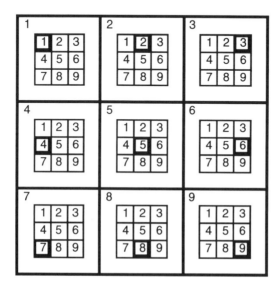

Figure 4.3. A genome in every cell.

The third property is that of *cellular division*. At the beginning (time t0) only one cell, the mother cell, holds the genome of the organism (see Figure 4.4). After a first division (time t1), two adjacent cells (to the north and to the east in the diagram of Figure 4.4) hold a copy of the information of the mother cell. These two cells will then be themselves copied into their own neighbors (time t2), and so on until the plan has been fully implemented. In the proposed example, the farthest cell is duplicated at time t4.

The "comb-like" structure of Figure 4.4 is a particular case of "normal" cellular division, which can generally be represented by a binary tree (Gilbert 1991) (p. 265). It should be noted that while the biological division of a mother cell in two daughter cells occurs to the detriment of the mother cell, which disappears, the artificial system which we propose allows it to remain in place.

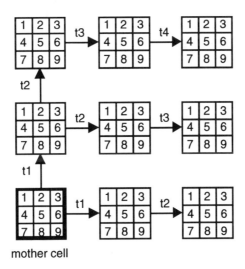

Figure 4.4. Copying the genome from the mother cell into daughter cells.

4.3. The MAJORITY Function Example

In order to illustrate the different steps of our methodology, we have chosen a very simple example: the MAJORITY function of three Boolean variables.

In a first step (Section 4.3.1), we will show that this function, like any other Boolean function, can be represented by a binary decision tree and/or by a binary decision diagram. In a second step (Section 4.3.2), we will suggest that this binary decision tree or diagram can be realized by a new kind of field-programmable gate arrays (FPGAs) satisfying the three basic properties discussed above: multicellular organization, cellular differentiation and cellular division. In the conclusion (Section 4.3.3), we will illustrate the self-repair and self-replication capabilities of this novel architecture.

4.3.1. Binary Decision Tree and Diagram

The MAJORITY function of three Boolean variables MAJ (A,B,C) can be described in the classical truth table of Figure 4.5a; in this table, the input states A,B,C are given in the natural order for the binary number system, from 000 to 111. An important property of this system is made clear in Figure 4.5b: as the sequence is followed, the value of the least significant variable (C) changes at every step, that of the next-to-least significant (B) changes at every second step and of the most significant (A) at every four steps. So by turning Figure 4.5b through a right angle we obtain a rotated truth table which is equivalent to the new representation of Figure 4.5c, the *binary decision tree* (BDT).

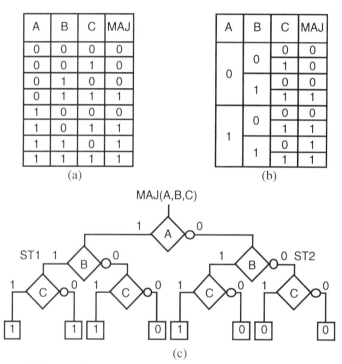

Figure 4.5. Binary decision tree for the MAJORITY function. (a) Original truth table (b) "Light" truth table (c) Canonical binary decision tree

    We define a *complete* (or *canonical*) tree as a binary decision tree for *n* variables having 2^n branches corresponding to the 2^n possible input states: for the tree of Figure 4.5c, $n = 3$ and $2^3 = 8$.

    We see from the tree of Figure 4.5c that two sub-trees (ST1 and ST2) have the following characteristics: all the leaves of these sub-trees have the same value (MAJ = 1 for ST1, MAJ = 0 for ST2). In such a case, it is possible to suppress the corresponding test element and to replace each sub-tree by a single leaf with the unique output value, thus obtaining the new binary decision tree of Figure 4.6, equivalent to that of Figure 5c, but having fewer test elements. Such a tree is a *simplified* tree for the MAJORITY function.

We observe now that the simplified tree in Figure 4.6 has the following characteristics: two sub-trees (ST3 and ST4) are identical. Figure 4.7 gives a new representation, with two branches converging on the same sub-tree ST3 = ST4. Such a tree is called a *binary decision diagram*.

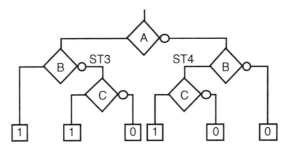

Figure 4.6. Simplifying a binary decision tree.

It is well known that any Boolean or discrete function can be represented by a binary decision tree and/or diagram; these modes of representation and the related methods are described for example in (Akers 1978), (Bryant 1992) and (Mange 1992).

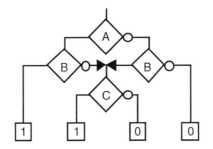

Figure 4.7. Transforming a binary decision tree in a binary decision diagram.

In order to make the final implementation easier, we transform slightly the binary decision diagram of Figure 4.7 and we obtain the *normalized ordered binary decision diagram* (NOBDD) of Figure 4.8a which is characterized by the following constraints:

- each test element (diamond) is located on a rectangular array, at the intersection of a row and a column; each test element can be connected to its nearest neighbors;
- at each level (for each row), the same Boolean variable is tested (A at the upper level, C at the lower level); we obtain therefore a special case of a binary decision diagram, that is an ordered binary decision diagram (OBDD);
- there are no branch crossings.

4.3.2 A New Field-Programmable Gate Array for Multicellular Organization

In order to implement in a piece of hardware any normalized ordered binary decision diagram satisfying the general hypothesis of Section 4.2.1 (2-dimensional regular array of operators and connections) and the first property of Section 4.2.2 (multicellular organization), we have developed a prototype of a new field-programmable gate array based on a fine-grained cell built around a one variable multiplexer and called MUXTREE.

The detailed description of MUXTREE cell is beyond the scope of this chapter and can be found in (Marchal 1994). It will be shown here how this array of multiplexers is programmed in order to calculate the gene of each cell and therefore to deduce the genome of the whole system.

We start from the normalized ordered binary decision diagram of Figure 4.8a and observe that a rectangular array of 3 x 2 = 6 multiplexers (test elements) is necessary to implement the MAJORITY function.

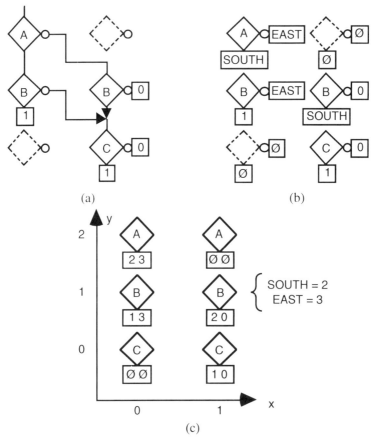

Figure 4.8. A new field-programmable array for multicellular organization. (a) Normalized ordered binary decision diagram (b) Programming the connections of the multiplexer array (c) Coding the genes of the six cells.

In our simple example, programming this array is very easy:

- each output of a test element which is a logic constant (0 or 1) keeps its value in Figure 4.8b (0 or 1);
- each output of a test element heading South is marked "SOUTH" in Figure 4.8b, each output of a test element heading South-East is marked "EAST" in Figure 4.8b;
- each output of an unused test element is marked "Ø" (don't care condition) in Figure 4.8b.

If each "SOUTH" value and each "EAST" value in Figure 8b are coded as, respectively, "2" and "3" in Figure 4.8c, we obtain a two-digit word, i.e. a *gene*, for each test element, i.e. for each cell.

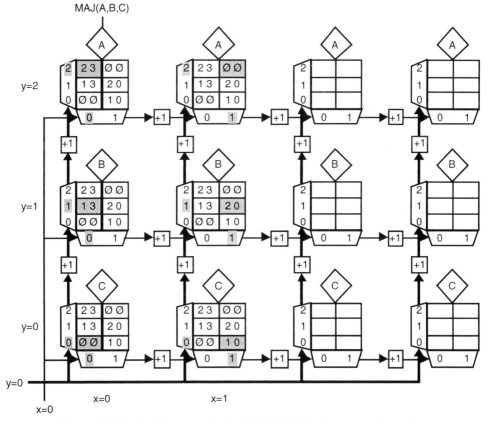

Figure 4.9. Final cellular array for the MAJORITY function: normal operation.

Moreover, if we introduce discrete coordinates (x: horizontal coordinate, y: vertical coordinate), it is possible to address each cell of the array by a word x, y.

The second property of Section 4.2.2 (cellular differentiation) necessitates a copy of the whole genome in each cell's RAM, together with the right coordinates at the right place. A possible implementation is illustrated in Figure 4.9:

- each cell of the MUXTREE array is equipped with a RAM; each RAM contains the whole genome of the MAJORITY function, i.e. the six genes of Figure 4.8c;
- each RAM is addressed by a word x, y, where x is the horizontal coordinate and y the vertical coordinate; the increment of the coordinates x and y is realized by simple adders (marked by "+1" in Figure 4.9); in this particular example, x is a Boolean variable and the adders for this coordinate are modulo 2 adders.

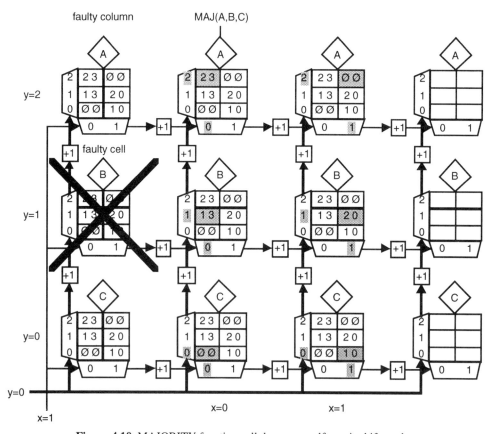

Figure 4.10. MAJORITY function cellular array: self-repair shift mode.

For normal operation, a rectangular array of six MUXTREE cells (with a multiplexer, programmable connections, RAM and coordinate adders) is sufficient. More cells are necessary in case of self-repairing or self-replicating processes.

4.3.3 Self-Repair and Self-Replication Capabilities

Suppose we have a faulty cell in the first column of the MAJORITY array (Figure 4.10) and we have at our disposal one spare column at the right of the array. A built-in self-test (BIST), as described in (Durand 1994), allows us to detect such a fault. It is possible to reprogram the MAJORITY function in the cellular array simply by changing the border conditions. Replacing the border condition x = 0 by x = 1 results in a shift of the whole pattern by one column to the right (thanks to the chain of modulo 2 adders) and thus allows us to obtain a new and correct version of the MAJORITY function.

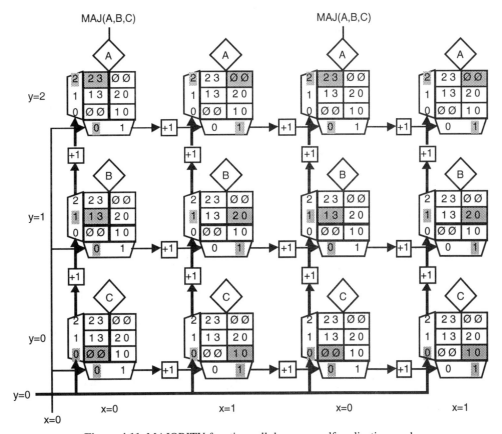

Figure 4.11. MAJORITY function cellular array: self-replication mode.

Using a similar method, it is also possible to duplicate a given function. Suppose we have two spare columns (Figure 4.11). With the original border condition (x = 0 as in Figure 4.9) and assuming a Boolean horizontal coordinate x, the chain of modulo 2 adders ("+1" in Figure 4.11) will produce the following values for the horizontal coordinate x, read from left to right: 0,1,0,1. Combined with the vertical coordinate y which is unchanged, the pattern of the horizontal coordinate x produces two copies of the original array of Figure 4.9 and, therefore, two copies of the same MAJORITY function.

4.4. Conclusion

At the moment, we are not able to guess all the consequences and repercussions of such a project. However, we know that it is feasible; we have built and tested two hardware prototypes showing:

- the implementation of a logic system in a regular cellular array using MUXTREE cells;
- the realization of a possible division/specialization process through the use of a genome RAM in each cell, and a system of horizontal and vertical coordinates;
- the shift method of the self-repair and self-replication processes.

The most important point is the following: we feel that this methodology could lead us to very complex integrated circuits, beyond the present possibilities of technology, with biological properties such as self-repair and self-replication. Also, we hope that this bridge between computer engineering and molecular biology could perhaps bring something new to biology itself: particularly concerning the very significant part of DNA (90%) which has not yet been decoded and which may support control functions, instead of the well-known data functions (production of proteins in accordance with the decoding of the DNA language).

References

Akers SB (1978) Binary Decision Diagrams, *IEEE Transactions on Computers*, Vol. C-27, No 6, June 1978, pp. 509-516.

Bryant RE (1992) Symbolic Boolean Manipulation with Ordered Binary-Decision Diagrams, *ACM Computing Surveys*, Vol. 24, No 3, September 1992, pp. 293-318.

de Garis H (1993) Evolvable Hardware, *Proc. Artificial Neural Nets and Genetic Algorithms*, Innsbruck, April 1993, pp. 441-449.

Durand S, Piguet C (1994) FPGA with Self-repair Capabilities. To be presented at the *1994 ACM International Workshop on Field-Programmable Gate Arrays*, Berkeley, February 13-15, 1994.

Gilbert SF (1991) *Developmental Biology*, Third Edition, Sinauer Associates, Sunderland (Mass.).

Mange D (1992) *Microprogrammed Systems: an Introduction to Firmware Theory*, Chapman & Hall, London.

Marchal P, Stauffer A (1994) Binary Decision Diagram Oriented FPGAs. To be presented at the *1994 ACM International Workshop on Field-Programmable Gate Arrays*, Berkeley, February 13-15 .

5

Artificial Consciousness?

Igor Aleksander
Department of Electrical and Electronic Engineering, Imperial College London

5.1. Introduction

There has been a recent renewal of interest in the question of whether an explanation of consciousness can (Dennett 1991) or cannot (Penrose 1989) be captured by some formal theory. The aim of this paper is to present a theory of consciousness centered on the concept of a neural state machine. The theory is based on the conditions that may be necessary to synthesize consciousness in constructed artefact. This is given the name "artificial consciousness" so as to create grounds for a discussion of the difference between the synthetic product and that which is normally thought to be possessed by human beings.

During the last 40 years, under the heading of "artificial intelligence", there has been an effort to program computers so as to make them perform functions which, if done by humans, would be said to require intelligence. This has been done by programming the machine with the ability to follow logical rules developed by a programmer. It is not uncommon to point to the poverty of this approach as logical rules do not capture a sense of intentional subjectivity (Searle 1992) or a sense of "being" (Winograd and Flores 1986). This argument is sometimes extended to suggest that *no* computing artefact is relevant to discussions about consciousness (Penrose 1989). In this article it is argued that as a result of novel neural approaches to computation where *learning* is the prime process for acquiring a function, subjectivity and discussions about consciousness are not outside the scope of either formal theory or the implementation of an artificial consciousness on a neural computing device.

Artificial Life and and Virtual Reality Edited by Nadia Magnenat Thalmann and Daniel Thalmann
© 1994 John Wiley and Sons Ltd

5.2. Theory

The theoretical framework used in this work has one fundamental postulate from which follow seven corollaries. This kind of framework has been inspired by the work of George Kelly (1955) who used it in his theory of personal constructs.

The Fundamental Postulate: Consciousness and Neural Activity.

> *The personal sensations that lead to the consciousness of an organism are due to the firing patterns of some neurons, such neurons being part of a larger number which form the state variables of a neural state machine, the firing patterns having been learned through a transfer between sensory input neurons and the state neurons.*

The words of this postulate are intended to have specific meanings which need to be stressed so that the corollaries which follow should make sense.

Personal sensation: Much of the controversy surrounding consciousness comes from the problem of infinite regress. Here it is implied that neural activity leads directly to personal sensation so dismissing the problem of infinite regress.

Firing patterns: Neurological terminology has been adopted to refer to the output activity of a group of neural elements. In an artificial system 'firing patterns' could refer to any measurement of the output quantity of the elements which constitute that system.

Neurons: This adoption of this neurological term is used to indicate that the theory is that of a cellular system where "neuron" is the name given to a basic cell.

Neural state machine: A state machine is the most general model of a finite computing process - it calls on the concept of an inner state which is a function of input sequences. Neural versions assume that neurons generate the variable values which, when taken together, form a state. (Corollary 1 formalizes this notion and the generality of neural state machines has been argued elsewhere (Aleksander and Morton, 1993)).

Learned: Neurons are assumed to be plastic and it is this plasticity which allows them to learn meaningful, representational, firing patterns.

Iconic Transfer: This key property relates to the source of information which controls the learning of the neurons. It will be seen that distal, sensory information is postulated to impose output patterns on neurons so that may be learned learned and recalled in the absence of input. It is this transfer that creates inner perception in the conscious organism.

Sensory Neurons: These are transducer neurons that transform energy from environmental input into the distal, sensory signals which are control iconic transfer.

Corollary 1: The brain is a state machine

The brain of a conscious organism is a state machine whose state variables are the outputs of neurons. This implies that a definition of consciousness be developed in terms of the elements of state machine theory.

Corollary 1 is a statement of the intent in the fundamental postulate that the theory of artificial consciousness be based on the generality of state machine theory. State machines can model any system with inputs outputs, internal states and input-dependent links between such states. The states and their links form a state structure. Such machines can be probabilistic where links between states are defined as probabilities, they can have a finite or an infinite number of states. The fact that any conscious organism must have something called a brain with an attendant state structure is evidently true and not controversial. The key question is whether enough can be said about the nature of the state structure of organisms that are said to be conscious which distinguishes consciousness itself. This becomes the task for the corollaries which follow - to define the characteristics of state structure that are necessary for and specific to organisms that are said to be conscious. Here the material of corollary 1 is stated in a formal way.

Formalization 1

In any state machine, five items need to be defined:

i) The total *input* to the neural state machine is a vector **i** of input variables $i_1, i_2 ...$

$$\mathbf{i} = [i_1, i_2 ...]$$

The i_1, i_2 .. variables are the outputs of sensory neurons.

In living brains the number of such variables, being the number of neurons involved in the early layers of all sensory activity, is very large but finite. There is also some debate about whether it is important for these variables to be considered as binary (firing or not) or real (firing intensity per unit time). While it will be seen that this decision does not alter the course of the theory, it is assumed here that these variables are binary. This is done without loss of generality but with the gain that, using the methods of automata theory, it becomes possible to develop non-linear models.

Also, **I** is defined to be the set of all possible input vectors.

ii) The total **output** of the neural state machine is a vector **z** of output variables $z_1, z_2 ...$

$$\mathbf{z} = [z_1, z_2 ...]$$

The z_1, z_2 .. variables are the outputs of 'actuator' neurons.

Again the variables $z_1, z_2...$ are considered to be binary, and, in living brains, would be seen as the output parts of the brain which are responsible for muscular action .

Also, **Z** is said to be the set of all possible output vectors.

iii) The ***inner state*** of the neural state machine is defined as a vector **q** of variables q_1, q_2 ..

$$\mathbf{q} = [\, q_1, q_2 \ldots]$$

The q_1, q_2 .. variables are the outputs of 'inner' neurons.

Again, variables q_1, q_2 ... are binary, and, in brains, would be the states of neurons neither involved in input sensing nor output generation.

Also, **Q** is said to be the set of all possible input vectors.

iv) The ***state dynamics*** of the neural state machine are determined by the equation

$$\mathbf{q'} = \text{ß}(\mathbf{q,i})$$

where **q'** is the "next" state, **q** is the current state and ß a function, which in the case of a finite number of binary variables may be expressed as the mapping,

$$\text{ß}: \quad \mathbf{Q} \times \mathbf{I} \rightarrow \mathbf{Q}.$$

where x is the Cartesian product. (In the general case this mapping is considered to be probabilistic in the sense that every pair (**q,i**) of **Q** x **I** maps into every element of **Q** with some probability.)

v) The ***output function*** of the neural state machine is determined by the equation

$$\mathbf{z} = \omega\,(\mathbf{q})$$

where ω is a many-to-many mapping which in the general case is probabilistic.

$$\omega: \quad \mathbf{Q} \rightarrow \mathbf{Z}.$$

In addition to the above group of five properties which are required in the definition of any state machine, the definition of a *neural* state machine contains the following property which relates to the generalization of the neurons.

vi) The state dynamics and output functions of the neural state machine ***generalize*** in the
     sense that:

if q' (in **q'**) $=$ ß(q,i) where q is in **q** and i is in **i**,
then there are several q_1, q_2 ... all in **q**, and i_1, i_2 .. all in **i**
such that q' = ß(q,i) .
q_1, q_2 .. are said to be similar to q
i_1, i_2 .. are said to be similar to i..

Similarly, q_1, q_2 ... can lead to a single output z .

The following three corollaries are stated together because their justifications are interleaved.

Corollary 2: Inner Neuron Partitioning

The inner neurons of a conscious organism are partitioned into at least three sets:
Perceptual Inner Neurons : responsible for perception and perceptual memory;
Auxiliary Inner Neurons : responsible for inner 'labelling' perceptual events.
Functional. Inner Neurons : responsible for 'life-support' functions - not involved in consciousness.

Corollary 3: Conscious and Unconscious States

Consciousness in a conscious organism resides directly in the perceptual inner neurons in two fundamental modes:
Perceptual : which is active during perception - when sensory neurons are active;
Mental : which is active even when sensory neurons are inactive.
The activity of the inner perceptual neurons ranges over the same states in for both these modes.

The same perceptual neurons can enter semi-conscious or unconscious states that are not related to perception.

Corollary 4: Perceptual Learning and Memory

Perception is a process of the input sensory neurons causing selected perceptual inner neurons to fire and others not. This firing pattern on inner neurons is the inner representation of the percept - that which is felt by the conscious organism. Learning is a process of adapting not only to the firing of the input neurons, but also to the firing patterns of the other perceptual inner neurons. Generalization in the neurons (i.e. responding to patterns similar to the learnt ones) leads to representations of world states being self-sustained in the inner neurons and capable of being triggered by inputs similar to those originally learned ones.

Comment on corollaries 2, 3, 4

i   All three corollaries stem from the statement in the fundamental postulate that a conscious organism is conscious through *owning* the sensation-causing firing patterns of its inner neurons.

ii. All three corollaries meet the requirement that an organism could not be said to be conscious unless sensations due to sensory input may be sustained in the absence of such sensory input, albeit in reduced detail. (The organism is conscious even with its eyes closed and other senses shut off).

iii   Allowing for unconscious function in a brain-like organism, corollary 2 indicates that perceptual states occur in a subset of inner neurons. That is, not all inner neurons store perceptual memories - some may be encode concepts such as duration, ordinality or even 'mood', while others just keep the organism "alive".

iv   Corollary 3 indicates that the fundamental postulate leaves open the possibility that not all the states of the perceptual inner neurons have direct sensory correlates. This allows the model to account for effects such as sleep or anaesthesia.

v   Corollary 4   suggests that the formalization   of the fundamental postulate should account for the creation of perception-related states by reference to the learning properties of the neuron. This includes a formalization of the process of retrieval of inner perceptual states.

Formalization of corollary 2

The inner state variables $\mathbf{q}$ are partitioned into three subvectors $\mathbf{q}^p$ (perceptual), $\mathbf{q}^a$ (auxiliary) and $\mathbf{p}^f$ (functional). That is:

$$\mathbf{q} = \mathbf{q}^p \vee \mathbf{q}^a \vee \mathbf{p}^f, \quad \mathbf{q}^p \,\&\, \mathbf{q}^a \,\&\, \mathbf{p}^f = \emptyset$$

($\vee$ is conjunction, & is disjunction, and $\emptyset$ the empty set).

Formalization of corollary 3

A perceptual input i_w has a state correlate q_w in $\mathbf{q}^p$, so that

$$q_w = \beta(i_w, q_w), \text{ the perceptual mode.}$$

Also if i_w is replaced by a neutral input $\emptyset$

$$q_w = \beta(\emptyset, q_w), \text{ the mental mode.}$$

The set of all input related states q_w is $\mathbf{q}^w$ which is a subset of $\mathbf{q}^p$, the remainder of $\mathbf{q}^p$ contains states not related to perception, unconscious and semi-conscious states.

Formalization of corollary 4

Learning is the process of first associating an input i_w and an arbitrary state $q_\emptyset$ to form the element of the forward network function ß,

$$q_w = \beta(i_w, q_\emptyset).$$

The key factor is that there is μ, a fixed sampling mapping which transfers some of i_w into q_w, causing q_w to be defined by i_w:

$$q_w = \mu(i_w).$$

To create an attractor for i_w, ß is further defined by:

$$q_w = \beta(i_w, q_w).$$

(This is the "iconic" training methodology fully described in Aleksander and Morton, 1993).
The generalization of the neurons as formalized in corollary 1, ensures that the requirement of corollary 3:

$$q_w = \beta(\emptyset, q_w), \text{ the mental mode,}$$

is satisfied.

Corollary 5: Prediction

> *Relationships between world states are mirrored in the state structure of the conscious organism enabling the organism to predict events.*

Prediction is one of the key functions of consciousness. An organism that cannot predict would have a seriously hampered consciousness. It can be shown formally that prediction follows from a deeper look at the learning mechanism of corollary 4.

Formalization of corollary 5

Say that i_x follows i_w as a result of world state changes. Say that the organism is in state q_w in response to i_w. If the input changes to i_x and iconic learning is taking place, the following element of ß will be added:

$$q_x = \beta(i_x, q_w), \quad \text{followed by}$$

$$q_x = \beta(i_x, q_x), \quad \text{where } q_x = \mu(i_x).$$

In the mental mode, the following two transitions become equally probable:

$$q_x = \beta(\emptyset, q_w), \quad q_w = \beta(\emptyset, q_w).$$

This means that, in time, state q_w will lead to q_x in the mental mode, completing the prediction.

Corollary 6: The Self

> *As a result of iconic learning and feedback between output and the senses, the internal state structure of a conscious organism carries a representation of its own output and the effect that such an output can have on world states. This includes a representation of what can and cannot be achieved by the organism itself.*

A salient characteristic of self-awareness is the ability to distinguish between changes in world states that are caused by the organism's own actions and those that occur in a way that is not controlled by the organism. Here it is argued that this ability follows from the prediction corollary and implies that the organism stores the knowledge.

Formalization of Corollary 6

The objective of this formalization is to involve the output of the organism as part of the input. Let $z_\emptyset$ be a special "no output" condition and let all other output actions perceivable the input be:

$$z_1, z_2 \dots z_j$$

Any input i_w therefore contains at least two components:

$$i_w = \{j_w, z_j\}$$

(note that if the output is $z_\emptyset$ then $i_w = j_w$.)
It follows from the iconic learning function $q_w = \mu(i_w)$ that

$$q_w = \{k_w, s_j\}, \qquad \text{where } \{k_w, s_j\} = \mu \{j_w, z_j\}.$$

Hence iconic learning leads to parts of states such as s_j which are internal representations of the organisms own actions.
    Now suppose that the world is in some state i_a and that this has been learned with $z_\emptyset$, producing therefore a direct iconic representation $q_a = \mu(i_a)$, suppose that action z_1 changes the world state to i_1 where it remains even if the action ceases (i.e. the output reverts to $z_\emptyset$) . The system will learn the following linked internal representations.

$$q_a \rightarrow \{k_a, s_1\} \rightarrow \{k_1, s_1\} \rightarrow \{k_1, s_1\} \dots \rightarrow q_1$$

Hence iconic learning leads to representations of the way in which the organism's own actions achieve changes in the world state.

Corollary 7: Representation of Meaning

> *When sensory events occur simultaneously or in close time proximity in different sensory modalities, iconic learning and generalization of the neural state machine ensures that one can be recalled from the other.*

It is said that a conscious organism knows the meaning of input (e.g. words or events) is through the association of the one with the other. The word "knows" translates in this theory to the association of a complete iconic internal representations that are retrieved from partial inputs. Association of this kind is a basic property of a neural state machine and can be formally stated. However, this is also the area in which much of the controversy of whether a machine can or cannot "know" the meaning of words and phrases arises (Searle 1980).

5.3. Language

Language is obviously a vital part of human consciousness. Its full treatment is left for a publication that is currently in preparation (Aleksander 1994). Here it can be said that first the neural state machine through being a state machine has the computational power for representing language. However, the principle on which language gets into the state structure is through instruction by another organism that already has the skill. It can be shown that state machines can learn and generalize from positive examples and "near misses" demonstrating that the problem of "poverty of stimulus" does not apply. Where the theory of artificial consciousness departs from conventional approaches to natural language processing is in its use of iconic representations. In this sense language has been devoted to a trigger between world events and conscious iconic states learned through the iconic transfer mechanism discussed in this paper.

5.4. Conclusions

A preliminary case has been made for a formal, computational theory of artificial consciousness. Despite the fanciful sound of this assertion, it is felt that the concept perhaps makes more sense that "artificial intelligence". In the quest for better human machine interfaces, it may be important for the machine to be conscious in a subjective sense than simply have the computational power to solve problems which if solved by humans would be said to require intelligence.

This chapter also leaves a challenge: can human consciousness be shown to have properties not implied by the theory presented here?

References

Aleksander I (1994) *The case for artificial consciousness* (in preparation).
Aleksander I, Morton HB (1993) *Neurons and symbols: the stuff that mind is made of*, Chapman and Hall, London.
Dennett, DC (1991) *Consciousness explained*, Allan Lane/Penguin, London.
Kelly G (1955) The theory of personal constructs, Noton.
Penrose R (1989) *The emperor's new mind*, Vintage, London.
Searle J.R. (1980) Minds Brains and Programs, *The Behavi. and Brain Sci.* Vol.3, pp.417-457.
Searle JR (1992) *The rediscovery of the mind*, MIT Press, Boston.
Winograd T, Flores, F (1986) *Understanding computers and cognition*, Abelex, New Jersey.

6

Managing Entities
For an Autonomous Behavior

Michèle Courant, Béat Hirsbrunner, Kilian Stoffel
Institut d'Informatique, Université de Fribourg, Fribourg, Switzerland

6.1. Introduction

6.1.1. From the Hypothesis of Control to the Hypothesis of Autonomy

The concept of distributed systems introduced by parallel MIMD architectures and the wide spreading networks, marks a turning point for the methodology of informatics.

While the last forty years have been dominated by the Von Neumann model and the associated imperative-functional algorithmic tradition, a radical change affects all levels of software, in particular the level of application development environments, the level of operating systems and even the level of communication mechanisms.

This fundamental change is due to a shift of the approached problem. From the classical *assembling* problem, which was until now the foundation of the whole computer science methodology, we turn over to an *integration* problem. This shift is itself rooted in a renewal of hypotheses about the manipulated entities: from a *compositionality* hypothesis, we pass over to an *autonomy* hypothesis of the system components. This means nothing less than the abandoning of the grounding principle of all classical algorithmic, i.e. the "divide and conquer" of top-down analysis, for a synthetic approach that has yet to be defined.

Artificial Life and and Virtual Reality Edited by Nadia Magnenat Thalmann and Daniel Thalmann
© 1994 John Wiley and Sons Ltd

6.1.2. Motivations for an Hypothesis of Autonomy

In the context of parallel MIMD architectures, or more generally of distributed systems, the component autonomy hypothesis is based upon two arguments. First, the distributed systems confronts us with a change of scale which requires a large adaptability:

- *External adaptability* is required because of the increased risk of failure. The systems must be able to lose components or accept new ones without being excessively perturbed;
- *Internal adaptability,* i.e. self-organization, is required because distributed systems should recover from possible defectiveness of components and should permanently be capable of adapting to changing requirements.

Secondly, the change of scale of the available resources also affects the *complexity* of the target applications. This complexity increases in such a way that the expression or the prevision of all possible cases becomes prohibitive. This leads to the progressive abandonment of imperative languages and to the increasing success of declarative languages, mainly with logic and constraint programming. We see an evolution revealing clearly that we desire not only to use the computing resources of the machines, but also to exploit their potential of *creativity*.

Finally, the increasing complexity of the target applications, coupled with their critical status, due to their direct impact on our ecological, economic and political[1] environment, demands a greater accessibility of the systems in order to improve the transparency of their decisions (Hendrix and Walter 1987). One promising but certainly not exclusive way of reaching this objective is that the decision-making mechanisms of the systems match the decision-making mechanisms of the users. Starting from this point, it is legitimate to aim at distributed systems, whose decision-making units interact with each other according to a human-like social organization, this means some order induced by autonomous agents.

Hence adaptability, openness and self-organization: qualities which lead us, perhaps not to living, but at least to natural dynamic systems. Accessibility, which asks us to respect the models of cognition and of social organization, and therefore to aim at autonomous behaviors.

6.1.3. Plan

This chapter takes up the question of managing entities from the perspective of autonomy. In Section 6.2, we try to explain how the concept of autonomy is methodologically significant for the domain of software development. Sections 6.3 and 6.4 then illustrate the use of this concept by two examples: one at the application level, the other at the operating system level. In the conclusion, we discuss the hypothesis formulated for the management of autonomous entities and the question of the status of these entities with respect to human agents.

---

[1] Let us think for example, systems controlling energy producing centers or providing assistance to financial decisions...

6.2. What is Autonomy ?

Autonomy is a notion crystallizing a scientific challenge which goes far beyond computer science and concerns the whole of natural and human sciences. Trying to define autonomy is then very ambitious: doing so would be no less than formulating a unified theory of natural and artificial, physical, biological and cognitive systems !

Starting from the work of Varela (1980) we modestly try to grasp the concept of autonomy. We first give a minimalist definition of autonomy, opposed to allonomy, and then a maximalist definition in terms of self-organization and autopoiesis. Finally, we identify some operational aspects of autonomy for computer science (Courant and Le Peutrec 1994).

6.2.1. A Minimalist Approach to Autonomy: Autonomy Versus Allonomy

Autonomy means literally "own law" and designates the capacity of a system to define itself.

In this sense, autonomy is opposed to allonomy, which means "other law" and designates the characteristic of a system to be defined from the outside. The notion of allonomy refers to systems with inputs and outputs, whose dynamics may be defined in terms of a function f of E in E, where E is the environment of the system. An allonomous system is therefore governed by a control schema: as it is shown in Figure 6.1a, the fluxes which connect it to its environment are informational fluxes in the Shannon sense.

An autonomous system on the other hand, at least for interacting systems rooted in some physical substratum with which we are concerned[1], has the capacity to determine its own inputs and outputs: therefore it has a non reducible "freedom" vis-à-vis its designer or any observer. While they are open behavior systems, rather than speaking of inputs/outputs, whose predefined nature is too emphasized, we prefer to speak of *interactions* in the case of autonomous systems. The interaction flux is no more an informational flux, although an informational interpretation of this flux by an observer remains possible. In this case, this observer reduces the system to an allonomous correspondent, for example by only considering a limited period of observation or of prediction and/or by exploiting its perceptive filters: this is what is illustrated in Figure 6.1b.

This prime distinction between allonomous system and autonomous system shows clearly that the concepts of allonomy and autonomy refer to the relationships between a system and another. Consequently, they are not concepts directly expressible in a *first order schema*, i.e. a schema based upon intrinsic properties of its elements, such as Chomsky's hierarchy.

Actually, autonomy does not circumscribe any computable or non computable system class. It only defines the non-controllability of a system by a referential system, such as an environment, a designer or a simple observer. However, some correlations may be

---

[1] We do not consider here the special cases of autonomous systems, such as the whole universe, whose actions are internal by definition, and whose dynamics is totally reflexive.

established between the non-controllability and the nature of a system. It is often admitted for example, that *every* physical (natural or artificial) system is necessarily non-controllable: a simple quartz oscillator realizing a clock, as well as the most complex living organism, until the tiniest particles, becomes then autonomous. Nevertheless, we notice that this assumption is only acceptable because the more general current physic theories brought out a fundamental no-knowledge of matter.

The concept of autonomy fits into a *second order schema* integrating an infinite recursive observation relation, whose closure may be captured in a *limited perceptability* principle. The non-controllability of a system feeds on the no-knowledge inherent in the *exteriority* hypothesis of a system, and vice versa. On the contrary, the control schema characterizing allonomy expresses a kind of *interiority* of a system. Allonomy and autonomy then represent two dual approaches of a same "reality": the first one, related to interiority, is a cognitive approach, while the second one, related to exteriority, is a perceptive (and active) approach. This perceptive approach results in a behavioral non determinism of autonomous systems, i.e. their behavioral *unpredictability* (Kirsch 1994).

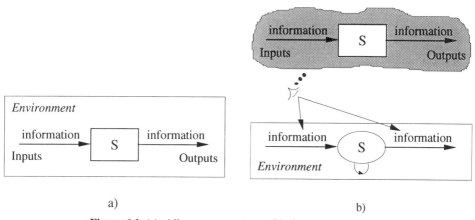

a)   b)

Figure 6.1. (a) Allonomous system   (b) Autonomous system

6.2.2. A maximalist approach to autonomy : Self-organization and autopoiesis

A minimalist definition of autonomy, strictly grounded on a simple basis of "own law" and non-controllability, hardly escapes from some more requirements.

In fact, in cybernetics as well as in cognitive psychology, autonomy has always been strongly connected with self-organization. Hence, computer scientists sometimes prefer to take as a basic definition of autonomy *"the capacity of a system to maintain its viability in various and changing environments"*. In fact, this is merging autonomy with autopoiesis (i.e. literally "capacity of self-producing"), which is only considered as one of its particular cases by Varela (1980). But, in the physical domain, autopoiesis is precisely one of the best candidates for defining life!

Therefore, autonomy is somewhere between two extremes: on one hand, the whole set of physical systems, on the other, only the set of autopoietic (or living) systems. And this gap is highly significant. It reveals that fundamental scientific questions are still open. World-wide debates focus in particular on the following ones:

- Do non autopoietic (i.e. living) physical systems exist?
- Do non physical autopoietic systems exist?
- Is there an equivalence between autopoietic, living and physical systems?

6.2.3. Conclusion: Operationality of Autonomy

In the software and hardware development domain, the minimalist approach of autonomy has several operational consequences.

First, it suggests to design entities fitted with own laws, including in particular local decision-making capacities.

Secondly, it advocates to recognize the necessary autonomous status of implemented systems, by integrating from the beginning their non totally controllable character in the models. We can notice that, despite a "losing" appearance, this recommendation will bring up an increase of power (because accepting unforeseen situations brings up the opportunity to deal better with them!).

Thirdly, it encourages one to use declarative approaches, and then to aim at specifications in terms of laws (behavior laws, interaction laws, evolution laws, emergence laws, formation laws, etc.).

Fourth, it enlightens the hiatus underlying autonomy, that is desiring its only advantages (creativity of the systems, economy of expression,...) and refusing the even possibility of undesirable behaviors. Hence, it encourages one to look for tools and methods allowing both to provide systems with a certain (perception, decision and action) freedom and to set some barriers in order to prevent some catastrophic situations.

Starting from self-organization, or even autopoiesis, the maximalist approach of autonomy stresses the potential advantages of designing autonomous systems.

No consensus exists about measuring either the "autonomy degree" or the "autopoiesis degree" of a system. However self-organization, and autopoiesis in particular, shows quite well that autonomy is not an absolute concept. Actually, autonomy remains compatible with some kind of "control" because the structural coupling between the system and its environment (Varela 1980; Courant and Le Peutrec 1994) provides us with numerous possibilities of *influencing* the system. And the more a system is autopoietic, and therefore resilient to environment perturbations, the more it opens itself again to our influence. Though this influence is only a kind of indirect control, without any guaranteed effects, it is very powerful, and maybe the best key for a long term reliability.

Consequently, autopoiesis reveals its most interesting facets when it becomes powerful enough to generate a *continuum* in the perception-action loop binding man and machine. Hence, it requires that the machine cognition will be based on more and more human-like sensorial and emotional notions.

6.3. Application Software and Autonomous Agents

6.3.1. Introduction

As an illustration of the use of the concept of autonomy, we now present an interaction model for autonomous agents, whose implementation is integrated into a programming language based on the paradigm of a society of agents.

The goal of the model is to describe a reactive envelope for agents situated in an environment. A priori, the interaction language derived must allow the encapsulation of different types of agent kernels, such as sequential machines, Kohonen neural networks implementing associative memories with self-organizing dynamics, as well as declarative or procedural kernels. It is then destined to interface programming languages to agent kernels with a large range of applications. The only constraint imposed is that the agents must be situated and must evolve in an environment with a suitable distance definition.

The model is as basic as possible in order to hold up further refinements or successive abstractions, yielding to higher level interaction primitives. It is entirely constructed on the hypothesis of an attraction/repulsion dynamics and inspired by a naïve physics based on the notions of charge and force fields.

6.3.2. Interaction Model and Interaction Description Language

The interaction model assumes that the agent's envelope, which is the agent's interface with the environment, is formed of a set of charges. A charge is an instance of a charge type, whose value is to conform to the type specification and inherit its dynamics. A charge type is defined by:

1. Its **domain of intensity**, composed of a sign, normally bivalent, and a domain of absolute intensities. We choose for example domains such as $[0, +\infty[$ for a continuous model, and $\{0, +\infty\}$ for a model with quanta.

2. Its **interaction protocol**, which specifies the attraction/repulsion laws governing the type instances. For a bivalent sign we can have typically rules such as:

   (R1)   Identical signs attract, opposite signs repel.
   (R2)   Identical signs repel, opposite signs attract.

3. Its **propagation function**, which specifies how a charge is propagated, that is attenuated or intensified, in the environment.

4. Its **force function**, which specifies what is the force induced on a charge situated at a point P1, by a charge of the same type situated at a point P2.

5. Its **composition function**, which specifies as a vector sum, what is the total force exerted on a charge by all the charges of the same type carried by the other agents.

6. Its **manipulators**, which specifies the interface of an agent with its charge, i.e. how the agent can act upon it. The existence of one or several manipulators associated with a charge type implies that the dynamics of an agent system may be expressed by the internal dynamics of the charges. On the other hand, the absence of a manipulator associated with a charge type indicates fixed charges and agent systems whose dynamics is obtained only by moving of agents according to the forces exerted on them.

Defined in this way, the model allows a large number of possible interaction modes between agents. The interaction protocol allows first to induce, either classifying phenomena (see rule (R1)), or coupling phenomena (see rule R2)).

The propagation function then allows a multitude of variants. For example, it may be parameterized by the distance only, in case of a charge propagating uniformly in all spatial directions, or is it may be modulated by a position parameter. We can also have the cases of charges whose influence decrease and increase respectively with the distance. The first case allows for example the simulation of interaction mechanisms by sonic waves or of communication mechanisms by diffusing chemical factors such as the pheromones. The second can be adequate to produce aggregation phenomena governed by laws such as *"the further an individual is from its nest, the greater it desires to return to it."*

Figures 6.2a and 6.2b show the possibilities offered by propagation functions with sign changes. The first case, combining a sign change with a directional parameter, allows us to obtain behaviors governed by the attraction/repulsion laws induced by magnetic fields. The second case allows the modeling of complex interaction laws generating alternate concentric influence zones.

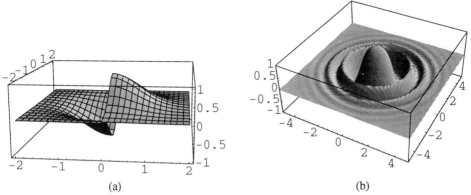

(a)   (b)

Figure 6.3.2 (a) Directional propagation with sign change (b) Directional propagation with periodic change of sign.

The model intends that an agent can gather within its envelope several charges of different types. Thus, the dynamics of a system of agents interacting according to the model obeys to the concurrent action of the charges. Due to this, situations of conflict or non-determinism can appear within the agents. According to the principle of the autonomy of agents, it is then the agent kernel which is responsible to resolve the conflicts or to manage the non-determinism, within the limits of the constraints inherent to the charge types.

The model is currently being implemented in the form of an interaction language. The syntax of this language and its implementation in the concurrent logic programming language Strand on the Intel iPSC/2 MIMD architecture are described in detail in (Ludwig 1994). This implementation notably uses sensors associated with the charge types permitting agents to perceive what forces act on them.

6.3.3. Illustrations

Despite -or perhaps because of- its very primitive attraction/repulsion dynamics, the model forms a very general purpose programming tool. The applications for which it has been used up to now concern problem solving, with the reformulating of "classics" such as sorting, coloring, and puzzles problems. These "classics" support in turn more specific applications, notably within the framework of distributed artificial intelligence. Thus, the model tackles domains as diverse as the automatic processing of natural language, the simulation of prey-predator behaviors or of mobile robots, or the sharing of tasks and resources in a society of problem solving agents. Figure 6.3 shows how, in robotics, the famous canyon problem may be solved by a dynamic adjustment of charges.

However the model is not limited to a goal oriented use. It can also be used for modelling dynamic systems in general, in other words for experimentation concerning artificial life (Langton et al. 1992).

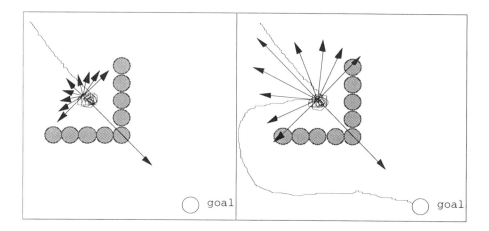

Figure 6.3. Use of concurrent charges in robotics. The robot is attracted by the goal and flees the obstacles. By temporarily loosening its attraction to the goal, the robot can escape from the canyon.

6.3.4. Conclusion

The interaction model presented integrates two aspects of autonomy. First, it gives to the agents the capacity of taking local decisions, which allows them to balance or influence the system by adjustment of their charges or moving in the environment. Second, this results in a self-organizing dynamics of the system.

Although based on a naïve physics, the model is surprisingly powerful, due to the variety of interpretations to which it can be used, either to capture certain adaptive aspects of cognition, or to formulate in reactive terms obstacles avoidance problems in robotics, or to give a concise distributed formulation of problems such as puzzles, etc.

Nonetheless, it opens onto many possible extensions, in particular of giving the charges their own laws of evolution, or of constructing more complex interaction mechanisms using the charges types. For example, a whole range of biosensors can be envisaged.

Note that the formalism derived from the model is a declarative formalism in that it exclusively describes laws, and not directly algorithms. On this point, it can be compared to the other declarative formalism presented in (Noser 1994) which are L-systems, and be precisely considered as a dual formalism: one is dedicated to the description of internal formation (i.e. substantial) laws, as well as the other focuses on interaction (i.e. relational) laws.

Various models, similar to the presented one, have been defined in different contexts. Among others, we find potential fields and symmetric force fields especially dedicated to obstacle avoidance problems, but also numerous models of dynamic systems inspired from physics and chemistry (Langton et al. 1992). However, none of these models have yet led to a general purpose programming language.

6.4. Operating systems and Autonomous Entities

6.4.1. Introduction

The new context of massively parallel MIMD architectures on the one hand, and of increasing complexity applications on the other hand, also deeply affects the operating system software.

In addition, the control software of a parallel computer should provide the users with an interface that allows simplified programming. Part of such an interface has to be an allocation system (Ludwig 1993), that assumes the role of sharing a parallel program across the computer. We describe here how one such system has been built, with the idea of an arbitrary large parallel computer in mind.

6.4.2. Structure of the Allocation System

An essential idea of the system presented here is that each node of the parallel computer decides autonomously how it should behave. The interaction between the nodes is restricted to the information exchange between neighboring nodes. The neighborhood relation can be defined through the communication net of the computer. It can also be defined by special properties common to certain nodes (for example I/O nodes). Or it can be a purely logical neighborhood relation.

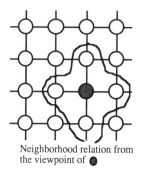

Neighborhood relation from
the viewpoint of ●

Figure 6.4. Structure of the allocation system.

Figure 6.4 shows the neighborhood relation in a 2D net based on the communication system. The bold nodes are the neighbors of the darker node. The information exchange passes by the bold lines. The allocation system of the dark node therefore receives information from the nodes present in its neighborhood relation. An ideal state is calculated on the basis of this information. Using its local strategy the node then tries to reach its ideal state. An identical allocation system is present on every node of the computer. Each node has its own definition of neighborhood and has also in principle its own allocation strategy. One example of such an allocation strategy is described in the next section.

6.4.3. Definition of the Allocation Strategy

A node must decide, based on the information that it receives from its neighbors, from which nodes it should accept tasks and to which node it should give tasks. This part of the system is defined using a fuzzy logic controller in order to simplify the specification of the allocation strategy by the user (Stoffel et al. 1993). The behavior of each node can be defined using simple fuzzy rules, such as:

- **If** overloaded **And** number of tasks rising **Then** migrate many tasks;
- **If** overloaded **And** number of tasks falling **Then** migrate few tasks.

It is easy to imagine other such rules which allow each node of the computer to decide autonomously how it has to behave in a particular situation.

Such a rule system has two main advantages in comparison with the conventional binary system. On one hand, the behavior of the system is better balanced, due to each rule being neither false or true. This continuous passage from Yes to No makes the system much more stable. On the other hand, rules can be written in a form such that every programmer has already used them intuitively in his common life.

Massively parallel computers are no longer used exclusively as number crunchers, but also for a much broader range of applications. It is therefore necessary to adapt the allocator to other program types with very different requirements. In the next section, we show how this can be automated.

6.4.4. Adaptation Mechanism

The fuzzy expressions used in the previous section such as "overloaded", "many tasks" can be defined in many different ways within a fuzzy system. These values can be altered with different applications. The node allocation system is embedded in a neural net in order to automate these alterations and to allow each node to adapt individually to its particular situation with the whole system. Using these neural nets, the parameters of the fuzzy system can be "learned", i.e. adapted (Jang 1990). For this allocation system, a back-propagation network was used.

To find the parameters for a given program, first an initial set of parameters is chosen and the program is executed with this set of parameters. The state of each node is periodically recorded. Once the program terminates, these stored values are used as training data for the back-propagation network. Once the neural net has found a new set of parameters, the program is re-executed with this parameters. This continues until a near optimal state is reached. Using this method, each node can find its own near ideal set of parameters.

This method is suitable for programs that are often executed, and therefore require an ideal set of parameters. Opposed to this, are programs that are only executed a few times. In this case one does not wait until the program is ended, but calculates during the program execution a new set of parameters. This method allows us to calculate a locally optimal set of parameters. However, these parameters may not be optimal for the program execution considered globally.

6.4.5. An Example

In this example a node behavior that should behave like a sinus function is simulated. Two curves are given in Figure 4.5a. The full curve shows the desired sinus function and the dashed curve the behavior of a non-adaptive node. The curve of an adaptive node is not given here because before $\approx \pi/4$ it is practically identical with the dashed one, and after $\approx \pi/4$ with the black one. The former is due to the fact, that the adaptive nodes are started with the same initial values as the non-adaptive nodes. The latter is due to the fact that the parameters are adapted too often and causes the system to over react; if the learning phase of the system is extended, these errors can be eliminated.

The errors of the adaptive an non-adaptive nodes are shown in figure 6.5b. If one considers the different forms of behavior of the adaptive vis-à-vis the non-adaptive nodes, one sees that the non-adaptive always leads to the same error. The adaptive nodes on the other hand, after a short initial oscillation, from 0 to $\approx\pi/4$, approach the desired sinus function very closely. After this initial oscillation, the nodes enter into a phase where the same error appears periodically. This error is however much smaller than the error of the non-adaptive nodes.

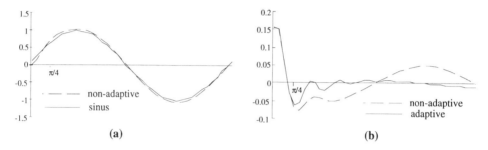

Figure 6.5 (a) Desired sinus function (b) Error function

6.4.6. Conclusion

The allocation system described in the previous section shows how an unconventional concept such as autonomy could become an important part of future operating systems on parallel super computers. The results achieved are comparable with those of conventional systems. In many domains they are even better. An essential advantage is their arbitrary scalability. The allocation is therefore already prepared for larger scale parallel computers.

6.5. Conclusion

Through two examples relative to the application software and the operating system software of massively parallel MIMD architectures, we have illustrated the operationality of autonomy and the advantages of managing complex systems by self-organization laws.

This approach based on autonomy abandons the objective of absolute control and of "local" optimality for relying on general laws, such as laws of homeostasis, to lead the systems to "globally" optimal behaviors. Thus, it prevents sudden and catastrophic crunching of competence and performance of systems, due to their inevitable limitations and the unforeseen states that they produce. Finally, even if it seems paradoxical, giving up the perfect controllability of the systems leads to much more secure, much more predictable behaviors. In this way, we obtain the behavioral accessibility and transparency, whose importance gradually increases with the complexity of systems.

These considerations raise a number of ethical and scientific questions, on which we have already touched through the notion of autonomy.

We have developed highly adaptive systems, capable of self-regulation, of self-regeneration, i.e. quasi autopoietic. What is in fact the difference between these systems and the natural autopoietic systems, except their material substratum? By technological means, did we not create inadvertently a new form of "life"?

In a wide perspective, human activity is strongly interwoven with artificial autopoietic systems. Meanwhile, our interactions with these systems were relatively confined within a very high level, and hence remain hidden behind the "silence" of cognitive exchanges. However, when more "sensorial" and "emotional" connections will be established, will it still be possible for us to believe that the screen is a glass shield separating two distinct parallel worlds, and relegate these autopoietic systems to *virtuality?* Would we still be able to deny that the artificial autonomous (and eventually "living") entities that we created and ourselves, share one *unique reality?*

References

Courant M, Le Peutrec S (1994) Living Systems Dynamics: a New Approach for Knowledge Representation, *International System Dynamics Conference*, Stirling (UK), July 11-15.

Hendrix GG, Walter BA (1987) The Intelligent Assistant, *Byte*, December, pp 251-258.

Jang R (1990) *ANFIS: Adaptive-Network-Based Fuzzy Inference System*, Department of Electrical Engineering and Computer Science, University of California, Berkeley.

Kirsch G (1994) Unpredictability - Another Word For Freedom... And If Machines Were Free?, In: *this volume*.

Langton GG, Taylor C, Doyne Farmer J, Rasmussen S (Editors) (1992) *Artificial Life II*, Proceedings of the workshop on Artificial Life held in February 1990 in Santa, New Mexico; Addison-Wesley.

Ludwig M (1994) *Conception et réalisation d'un langage de description d'interactions pour des systèmes d'agents autonomes*, Thèse de doctorat l'Université de Fribourg (à paraître).

Ludwig T (1993) *Lastverwaltungsverfahren für Mehrprocessorsysteme mit verteiltem Speicher*, Doktorarbeit, Technische Universität München, München.

Noser H, Thalmann D (1994) Simulating the Life of Virtual Plants, Fishes and Butterflies, In: *this volume*.

Stoffel K, Law I, Hirsbrunner B (1993) Fuzzy Logic Controlled Dynamic Allocation System, *13th International Joint Conference on Artificial Intelligence*, Chambéry, France, August.

Varela FJ (1980) *Principles of Biological Autonomy*, Elsevier North Holland.

7

A Constructivist Approach for Autonomous Agents

Philippe Gaussier* **, Stéphane Zrehen*
*Laboratoire de Microinformatique, EPFL-DI, CH-1015 Lausanne
**ENSEA ETIS , Allée des Chênes Pourpres, F-95014 Cergy-Pontoise

7.1. Introduction

In recent years, a new approach to Artificial Intelligence (AI) has developed: the Animat Approach (AA) (Meyer and Wilson 1990; Stewart 1991). Its aim is to study artificial intelligence with a bottom-up vision. Cognition must be understood as an emerging phenomenon in systems interacting with their outside world. This means cognition must be embodied. Basic behaviors should be obtained before higher level capabilities emerge. Thus such abilities as manipulating abstract symbols or speaking a language should emerge from lower levels, and not be given a priori.

In theory, this approach should avoid the "symbol grounding" trap, as all knowledge, and a fortiori symbol meaning if symbols exist, is built through experience. Its natural field of study is to replicate basic behaviors of simple animals like ants or rats: navigation, object and scene recognition and object stacking. The problems met in this branch of research are actually the same as in Virtual Reality (VR): How are objects represented inside an agent? What is needed to ensure autonomy of agents? How should objects be represented to ensure identification? What kinds of interactions are allowed between agents? What are the needed basic capabilities for solving given tasks?

VR is fraught with the same difficulties as classical AI: when a large number of parameters must be taken into account, mathematical modeling becomes almost impossible as all the possible interactions between the "agents" and their "external world" cannot be analyzed in advance. The use of symbolic processing is no longer possible because

Artificial Life and and Virtual Reality Edited by Nadia Magnenat Thalmann and Daniel Thalmann
© 1994 John Wiley and Sons Ltd

definition of the needed symbols is not available. Most of the time, in either AI or VR, what is perceived is ambiguous, which leads the tree-search programs to well-known dead-ends.

Our general goal is to design control architectures for autonomous robots capable of adapting to an unknown world. This leads us to draw our inspiration from biological systems. We try to bring together different results from neuro-biology, ethology and psychology to build neural-like control architectures which allow the emergence of interesting observed behaviors such as localization, navigation, obstacle avoidance or scene recognition.

Thus, we exclude all a priori symbolic representation of the world. On the contrary, the main functioning basis of our systems is adaptation: "knowledge" is built and transformed while interacting in the world. Our main claim is that acting in the world is necessary to the interpretation of perceived signals, i.e., to the emergence of a "cognition." In this chapter, we will show through several examples how:

• Performing an action modifies the subsequent perceptions, thus reducing the complexity of the recognizable scenes.
• Action helps remove the ambiguities from perceived signals.
• Choosing an action avoids exploring all the interpretation possibilities.
• Action simplifies "reasoning programs". We will show how it is possible to retrieve a given position without any global knowledge about how to navigate.
• Action simplifies learning: dynamic aspects of the action-perception loop can be taken into account. The learnable patterns are then easily identified.

We will present several neural networks implemented on mobile Khepera robots (see Figure 7.1, Color Section) which solve given tasks by acting on the environment. The first one is a neural network which allows obstacle avoidance. The second one is stacking of scattered objects by a group of robots with a behavior gimmicking that of ants. Both of these neural networks have no learning capacity: their synaptic weights and hence the observed behavior is fixed. These types of networks correspond to a "behaviorist" vision in psychology, and are therefore limited in their capacities as showed by new trends in psychology.

In the following part of this chapter, we will propose neural networks that allow internal representations of the world, thereby escaping the behaviorist paradigm. However, those representations are not, as in classical AI, programmed in advance: they build themselves upon perceived signals, and history plays a determinant role in the final representation. Learning is driven by internal motivations and by error signals such as pain due to a wrong decision (see Figure 7.2). We will emphasize the importance of perception to action and action to perception loops.

We will propose three applications for these networks: scene recognition with a moving robot eye, target retrieval with the help of vision identification of landmarks in the environment. At the end, we show how the use of a Topological Neural Map, the Probabilistic Topological Map (PTM), can improve the networks performances.

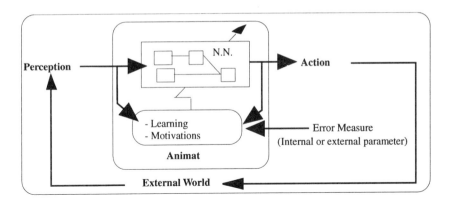

Figure 7.2. General Neural Architecture for an Autonomous Agent. Perceptions lead to an action through the neural network. The action in turn modifies perceptions, and learning is driven both by the error signals (either internal or external) and by internal motivations such as hunger, pain, tiredness...

About these latter networks, we should stress the role of chance, which makes a Neural Darwinism possible (Changeux 1985; Edelman 1987): chance helps each neural module to generate diversity and to select choices which have proved successful in the interactions with the environment, through cooperation-competition mechanism.

7.2.   Hard-Wired Neural Networks for Animats

In this section, we present how to build autonomous robots in a constructivist view. We use a bottom-up approach like in Brooks's subsumption (Brooks 1986). We will first describe an application of obstacle avoidance which is controlled by a very simple Neural Network (N. N.). Then we will add neural groups to allow our robot to recognize object and to pick them up in order to solve a collective task in an emerging fashion.

7.2.1. Basic Neuron Model and Braitenberg Vehicles

Mc Culloch and Pitts first proposed a computational model of biological neurons in the form depicted on Figure 7.3a: a neuron is connected to other neurons by synaptic links of various strengths (Rosenblatt 1954). The neuron activity is equal to the output of a non-linear function applied to the weighted sum of all its inputs. Learning consists in modifying synaptic weights, and it has been shown that such units can perform logical operations and approximate numerical functions (Hertz et al. 1991).

In his famous booklet "Vehicles", the neuroanatomist Valentino Braitenberg (Braitenberg 1984) proposed a series of simple vehicles with sensors and effectors whose extremely simple neural control architectures gives rise to interesting behaviors. In all these vehicles,

motors are assimilated to formal neurons as described above, whose inputs are the output of
the sensors. By choosing the appropriate connection graph between the sensors and the
effectors, it is possible to avoid obstacles, to run after them or to make circles around them.
For instance, the connection graph depicted on Figure 7.3b corresponds to an obstacle
avoiding robot when the sensors have a response that is a decreasing function of the
distance to objects. The velocity of each motor is equal to the weighted sum of the response
of the sensors. Right-left connections are inhibitory, while connections on the same side are
excitatory. Thus an obstacle on the left gives a larger response on the left sensor than on the
right. The left motor response is greater than that of the right, and the robot turns on the
right.

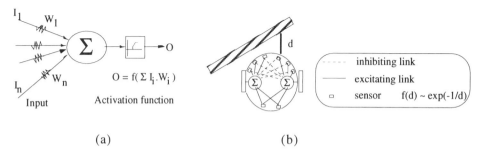

| (a) | (b) |

Figure 7.3. (a) The MacCulloch and Pitts formal neuron (b) An obstacle avoiding Braitenberg
vehicle.

7.2.2. Collective Sorting of Objects by Ant-like Robots

In this part we show how action can modify perception and allow a simple emergent
behavior. The experience depicted here is inspired from ethological studies. Deneubourg
proposed a replication of ants' behavior about food collecting and sorting (Deneubourg et
al. 1991). The basic behavior of every ant is probabilistic: when it meets a concentration of
food, it grabs it with a given probability, and if it already carries food, it drops it with
another given probability. If the probability of removing an object from a heap decreases
with the heap's size, and that of depositing it increases with that size, then heaps are built
progressively, by the repeated action of several ants on their environment. This is performed
without any map of the environment and without any knowledge about the location of the
heaps or of the other ants. There is no central control of the whole process. It illustrates how
to take into account interaction with the environment to simplify the programming task.

   This behavior was implemented on the Khepera robot. Khepera has eight infrared sensors
that saturate at a distance of about 2 cm: four on the front, one on each side and two behind.
An object can thus be identified by the saturation of one or two sensors on the front. When
more sensors are saturated, the sensory signal should be seen as an obstacle and provoke a
Braitenberg avoidance behavior. Khepera is equipped with a hook on its backside which
allows to grab objects through a half-turn rotation (see Figure 7.4a-g).

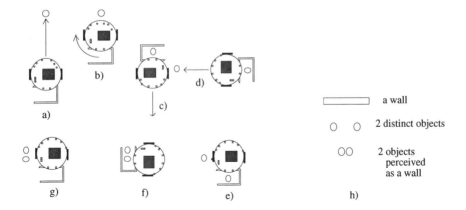

Figure 7.4. Robot actions and perceptions. (a) to (g) How a robot grabs an object with its hook and deposits it when it meets an isolated object. (h) How a simple robot action can modify perception: two objects pushed one against the other are perceived as a wall.

The behavior is programmed as follows: when an object is met and Khepera is not carrying an object, then it grabs it. On the other hand, when it does carry an object and meets another one, then it leaves it there by a rotation in the other direction. In between Khepera moves randomly.

In this implementation, where several Kheperas are placed on the playground simultaneously (see Figure 7.5a), it is not possible to control the probabilities as in simulations; they are imposed by the physics of the problem: when a heap is met under a certain angle, then it can be mistaken for an obstacle and the carried object is not deposited. Those conditions lead the heaps to take a somewhat linear form, which in turn divides the space into "closed" zones in which certain robots specialize (see Figure 7.5b). The robots can be in competition or can cooperate according to the spatial situation. However, the position of the heaps cannot be known in advance. The kind of equilibrium reached by this interaction is essentially dynamic: the size of the heaps is never fixed as there is always a chance that a robot seeing the heap from the right angle takes away an object. However, there is a statistical equilibrium (see Figure 7.5c).

The individual behavior described above can be implemented by the neural network depicted on Figure 7.6: IR sensor values are an input to the obstacle avoidance mechanism and to the object recognition group. This last group is necessary in order to make the difference between an obstacle and an object. Its synaptic links to the sensors are as follows: positive from two contiguous sensors and negative from the next on each side. Thus, more than two saturated contiguous sensors is not recognized as a seizable object. This group is a Winner-Takes-All (WTA): the most active neuron remains the only one active. This property is the result of a competition mechanism between neurons.

One interesting behavior occurs when one Khepera takes one of its mates for an object (see Figure 7.7): it leaves the object it carries, and the second Khepera grabs it. This cooperation of two robots can be seen as a form of elementary communication which emerges through interactions with the environment.

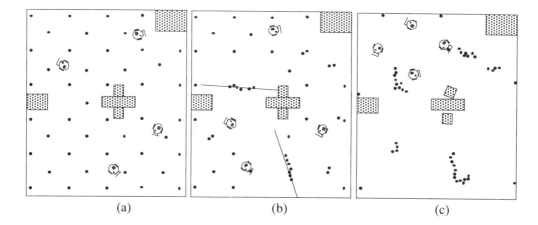

Figure 7.5. A collecting task for four robots. (a) The initial situation. (b) During process: linear stacks are being built. This corresponds to a competition between robots for given zones. (c) The situation after 30 min.

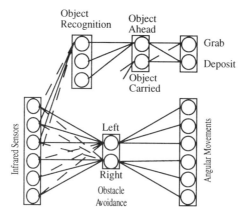

Figure 7.6. A neural network for object collecting behavior. Object recognition, obstacle avoidance and angular movements are performed by WTA groups.

We have thus designed a neural network that allows robots to solve a clustering task but that does not describe precisely the task. By only analyzing the network architecture, it is impossible to understand why the robot makes clusters of more than two objects. Clustering is really an emerging capability of the robot program. It is due to the interactions of the robots with its environment. The same goes for the cooperation or the competition between the robots.

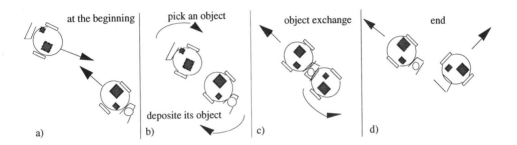

Figure 7.7. How a recognition mistake allows two robots to exchange an object.

7.3.   Neural Networks that Learn

The neural networks described above do not adapt: the behavior they provoke is fixed. In this section, we introduce learning in our constructivist view. We first present an application of active vision performed by a moving eye which focuses on different parts of the image. Then we propose an application of vision results to target retrieval.

7.3.1. Active Vision with a Moving Eye

Vision is a central issue for realizing machines that can interact with their environment or survive in a hostile world. Animals have developed sensors and neural architectures adapted to their specific problems depending on the reaction time needed, the size and the complexity of the objects to recognize. Optical illusions can provide a key to our understanding of human visual perception (see Figure 7.8). We try to associate psychological evidences that agree our choice to our N. N. simulations, as well as neurobiological results that justify the N. N. structure. Our approach is inspired by the "Gestalt theory". We consider that a relevant request is due to an intensity variation and we consider that sensory features are perceptually ambiguous (Köhler and Wallach 1944; Treisman 1988).

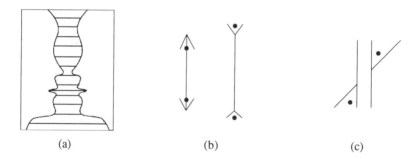

(a)   (b)   (c)

Figure 7.8. Optical illusions. (a)What is it? A single candlestick or two people facing each other ? (b) (c) examples of optical illusions explained by boundary diffusion (Muller Lyer's and Poggendorff's illusions).

The simulation software Prometheus (Gaussier 1993), emulates a robot with a single eye. It is able to move its eye to explore a scene. It has foveal and peripheral vision. We implement an active vision approach and we will show it reduces the analysis complexity. Prometheus somehow imitates human behavior in front of an "unknown" object.

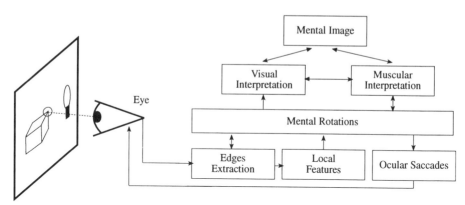

Figure 7.9. General architecture of the "Prometheus" robot.

Prometheus's "brain" has several cortical areas associated to the primary visual areas, to the visual recognition, to the motor control of the ocular saccades and to the association of visual information and motor information (see Figure 7.9). First, a primary visual area is involved in the edge extraction and in the edge enhancement due to the feedback of the interpretation (Grossberg and Mingolla 1985). A diffusion mechanism applied to the contour image provides local maxima which correspond to characteristic points (which gives account of the optical illusions on Figure 7.8b and 7.8.c). A visual interpretation is performed through a mechanism that simulates the mental rotations. Next, a motor map is used to control the eye movements or the focus of the attention in association with the visual recognition. Both visual and motor data are joined in a kind of "frontal area". They define a *sub-symbolic* mental representation of the studied object. The robot uses the same scan path during learning and during the utilization phase (Norton and Stark 1971).

We distinguish two connected levels of processing (see Figure 7.10). The first one performs low level processing and extracts characteristic points (Watt and Morgan 1983) which are associated with retina capabilities and primary visual areas. A very simple implementation will produce two groups of feature maps. These maps will be used in the next part to control the ocular saccades and to perform the analysis. The second one processes a state space transformation of the input picture, tries to recognize the objects to learn and it proposes a reconstruction to confirm recognition. Learning is performed immediately. A first part of this N. N. tries to locate an interesting feature in the picture, whereas the second one tries to recognize what it is. Those two pathways correspond to parietal and temporal regions of the cortex (Burnod 1989). The first one is associated to a massively parallel computation and the second one to a sequential and temporal analysis.

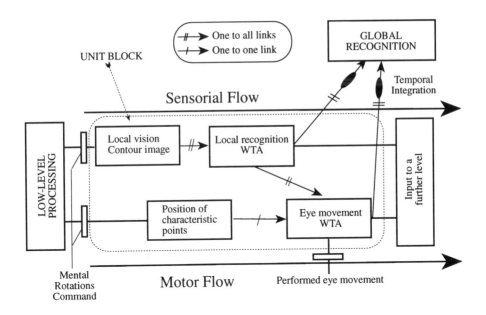

Figure 7.10. General scheme of Prometheus' neural network.. The low-level part extracts primitives from the perceived image. The neural network that allows the local recognition and the subsequent eye movement constitutes a "unit block". Two flows of information are present: one sensorial and one motor. The global recognition group is not part of this processing chain: it belongs to another area in Prometheus' brain. "One to all" links means that a neuron in the group pointed by the arrow is linked to all neurons in its input group. "One to one link" means each neuron is connected to a single neuron in its input group.

During training, the robot extracts the characteristic points of one object and it performs an invariant transformation from each of these points. We suppose learning of primary visual areas is completed or stabilized (no more plasticity in the primary visual cortex). The learning phase studied here is similar to the sensory-motor phase during which the human baby learns for instance to associate vision and touch (Piaget 1936). If the previous learning phase wasn't finished, it would be difficult to master in a single step the learning of different levels of increasing complexity without a supervisor and a back-propagation type algorithm.

During the interpretation (see Figure 7.11), the robot focuses its eye on a characteristic point, performs an invariant transformation (i.e. a polar logarithmic transformation) and then a mental rotation to match the present target with the learned representation. This is made possible by the use of an internal representation which we do not describe here. To complete its interpretation or to remove any ambiguity, the robot focuses on the other characteristic points used during learning. Objects thus can be recognized in a real scene even if they are partially occluded or rotated or if there is noise. A switching mechanism emulating mental rotations is used (see Figure 7.10) in this application and in the target retrieval task presented in the next paragraph. For details, see (Gaussier 1993). At last, a mechanism of time integration is introduced to simulate a short time memory. Thanks to it, Prometheus will be able to interpret a particular area according to the previous interpretation. All these processes are performed by neural nets. In a feed-forward point of view, the whole system is made of less than ten layers to remain biologically plausible. Obviously, several maps can be used in parallel and do not increase the global computation time.

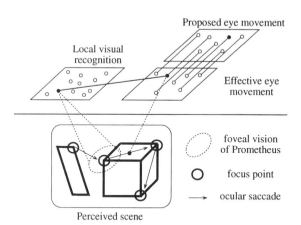

Figure 7.11. Functioning of Prometheus. Three neural groups are involved (see Figure 7.10). Prometheus focuses its eye on one of the cube's vertices. The ocular saccade it will perform is due to the combined activation of one neuron in the local recognition group and a neuron in the proposed eye movement group. The performed saccade thus corresponds to the one learned when exploring this cube's vertex for the first time.

With this architecture, an "a priori" meaning of the focus points needs not be given. Moreover the image topology related information is not lost. The most interesting aspect is that we can take into account the dynamics of the recognition process. We explicit the cooperation between sensory and motor information. Thus our approach tries to propose a solution to the symbol grounding problem in the field of autonomous agents and active perception machines. The important feature about our system is that it exhibits the useful behavior of learning and recognition. The power of this approach lies in the ability of the network to find its own solution to a particular problem and this is done without explicit programming.

7.3.2. Landmark-based Location Retrieval

How to retrieve a target location from a point where the target is not visible? AI solutions usually require an x-y map and a way to locate oneself and the target. Then geometrical operations would give the direction of movement. We do not wish to use such a method, because we do not know how to explain the ability to use an absolute map. In an autonomous agent vision, coordinates are essentially self-centered. However, the main problem remains: for any point in the environment a direction that reduces the physical distance to the target should be found. We will show that learning a few positions around the target and the direction that leads from these positions to the target is sufficient.

Looking to biology, we learn that insects use relative positions to fixed landmarks in the environment for localization. Indeed, it has been observed that bees circle around their nest before leaving it. A famous experiment (Tinbergen 1969) consists in placing a few stones in a geometrical fashion at the entrance of the bee's nest. When the bee is away, this arrangement is displaced by a few meters. On its way home, the bee is misled and heads to the new position of the stones.

Our goal is thus to devise a neural network that uses landmarks for localization and target retrieval, in the manner of bees. (Zipser 1985) proposed a computational model for rats' hippocampal place fields, where the response of given cells are a function of the distance to a given location relative to landmarks. Such cells can be used for localization as any x-y position can be identified by the vector of angles between that position and the landmarks (see Figure 7.11a). Our neural network will consist mainly in a group of place fields for localization and a motor group coding the directions of movement.

In the previous paragraph, we showed how to combine visual and motor data to recognize a scene. Here, we will use as input to the localization group both the motor and visual information about the scene. We suppose there is a reflex link that allows the robot to move in the direction of what it observes. This information is extracted from the same flow that commands eye movements. It corresponds to the second pre-processing box shown on Figure 7.18. Visual data are used to identify the landmarks, and motor data correspond to their angular position relative to the next landmark. This information is collected from any point when exploring the scene, through a given eye scan path (see Figure 7.12b). It is recombined in a neural group shown on Figure 7.13, which plays the role of an input to the place-fields group. Each line corresponds to a landmark and each column to an angular variation according to a discretization chosen in advance.

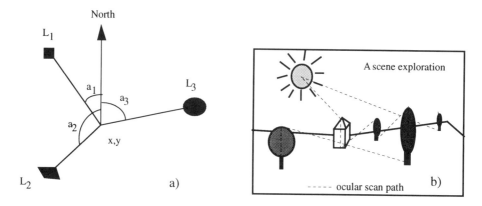

Figure 7.12. Place field localization using landmarks. (a) Each position is recorded as the vector made of the angles between the actual position and the landmarks. It is possible to use an absolute direction such as the north. (b)The straight line represents the eye ocular scan path. That motor information is used to find the object size and the angle between two objects.

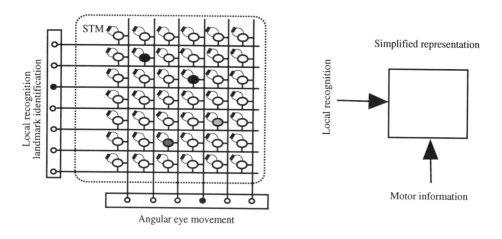

Figure 7.13. Input to the place field group. It is a neural group which recombines local visual information with the angular information corresponding to the movement from one landmark to the other. One neuron in this group is activated only if both its input neurons are active (logical AND operation). A Short Term Memory allows the neurons corresponding to previously observed landmarks to remain active for the global scene recognition.

We claim that it is necessary to learn only a few place fields. However, in order to allow target retrieval, they should respond maximally to locations disposed evenly around the target (see Figure 7.14a). Moreover, the direction from those key locations to the target should be known. Therefore, we propose the following protocol that resembles bees' behavior: once the target has been found, the robot starts circling around it and learns the position corresponding to several place fields, i.e. it records at different points the visual angles between landmarks (see Figure 7.14a). During this local exploration, it also records the direction that leads from these key positions to the target, i.e. it learns the association between given neurons in the localization groups and other neurons in the motor group.

Then, when away from the target (see Figure 7.14b), the robot performs at each time step the movement associated to the place field closest from its position (according to the angular distance measure). Thus at each time step, the distance to the target is reduced.

The choice of the most active place field is performed by a competition mechanism: this group of neurons is a WTA. If it always results in the choice of the most active exclusively, then the trajectories are rather hectic as shown on Figure 7.14b . On the other hand, if one takes a probabilistic mechanism doubled with an integrator, it is possible to smooth the trajectories: over one integration period (several time steps) the movement performed is the vector sum of the movements associated to the most active place fields. This is particularly efficient on the boundaries of the place fields' preference subspaces.

During the exploration around the target, positive associations between recognition neurons and a given direction are learned: the corresponding synaptic weights are set to a positive value. During target retrieval from another point in the environment, forbidden zones (obstacles) may be met. In that case, inhibition between some new positions and particular directions should be inhibited. This is why the recognition group should contain more neurons than the ones learned during exploration. But inhibition must be limited to a small portion of the environment, in order not to prevent movements far away from the obstacle. A threshold function must therefore be applied to the inhibiting links.

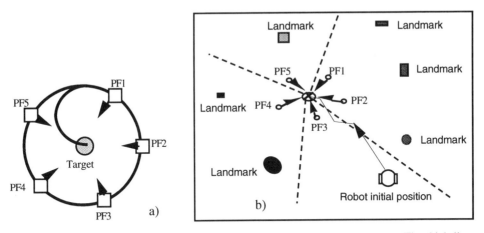

Figure 7.14. Target retrieval behavior. (a) Local exploration around the target. The thick line represents the trajectory of the robot once it has found the target. The robot records at certain points PFi (represented by squares) their relative position to the landmarks and the direction to the target. (b) From any point, the robot makes one step in the direction associated to the closest place field PFi. The dotted lines represent the boundaries of the preference spaces of the place fields.

We simulated this complete architecture on a computer. The results are shown on Figure 7.16 where 100 trajectories starting from all over the environment are represented.

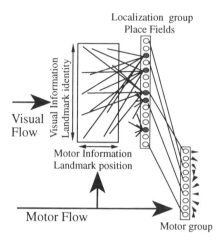

Figure 7.15. The basic neural network for localization and target retrieval. The input to the recognition place-field group is a combination of the visual and motor information extracted from the ocular scan path (Figure 7.13). Gray cells designate the place fields that have learned something.

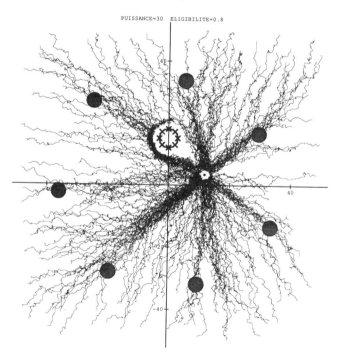

Figure 7.16. Trajectories using a probabilistic competition mechanism. Landmarks are represented by large gray dots. The activation zone of the inhibiting recognition neurons is represented by thick circles. The straight lines represent the Voronoi boundaries of the recognition neurons, and their intersection is the location of the target.

7.4. Topological Neural Maps

In the previous paragraphs, WTA groups have been used as a support for internal memory. Their use requires that all the links from the WTA to a further group must be learned independently for each neuron. As a consequence, complete learning may require a long time. Moreover, the generalization capacities are limited to the sub-space in which a given neuron wins.

It is possible to improve the functioning of a WTA by adding a topology preservation property: the neurons should be arranged in an array and two similar input patterns should be coded on neighboring neurons. Such an enhancement of a WTA is called a Topological Neural Map (TNM). Its main advantage is that all links to a further group need not be learned: The choice of a winner N on the TNM leads to an activation of its neighbors, which decreases with their distance to N. Thus if a neuron close to N happens to be the winner at a further stage, the link from N to the further group is enough and elicits the same neuron in the further group. It is therefore not necessary to learn a new link (see Figure 7.17).

We have devised a TNM for large-dimensional binary input that self-organizes locally in one step (Gaussier and Zrehen 1994a). This means that an activity bubble is produced on the single presentation of an input. This map has been applied successfully to the control of a mobile robot whose task is to learn how to avoid obstacles (Gaussier and Zrehen 1994b).

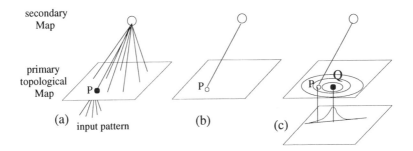

Figure 7.17. Usage of a Neural Topological Map. (a) Each neuron in the secondary map receives afferences from all cells in the primary topological map. (b) Input I is presented and P is the winner in the primary map. Only the weight between P and the maximally responding cell in the secondary map is modified by reinforcement learning. (c) Input J is presented and Q is the winner in the primary map. The activity in the secondary map cell decreases with the distance between P and Q.

7.5. Conclusion

In this chapter, we have tried to present a synthetic approach to control mechanisms for a mobile robot. The interest to use a real mobile robot is to simplify the simulation phase and to avoid problems linked to toy universes. Moreover, it helps to take advantage of the possible emergent behavior of our robot due to its interaction with the world in unforeseen situations.

Nevertheless, the most important part of the control systems we have shown consists in simulating neurons and "brains". All those mechanisms may be implemented without modifications to autonomous agents in a virtual world. This could indeed be very helpful when the task is to experiment on large robots in extraterrestrial worlds for instance.

We have presented different kinds of intelligent systems. First we have seen that simple robots can interact with their environment and cooperate to perform a task in an emergent fashion. On another level, we have studied a vision architecture to control a robot eye. We have shown that simple neural mechanisms can explain complex recognition tasks. We also proposed a way to use this visual system to control a mobile robot. We have explained how to combine motor and recognition information to build an efficient information to a navigation neural network. In all those applications, the N. N. had the same structure. An important aspect of these networks is their systematization: the neural network that allows target retrieval is simply grafted on the unit block that allows visual scene recognition (see Figure 7.18). In any case, the systems have two data streams: one associated to a sensorial and another to a motor information. The intelligent behavior is due to the learning of links between these two pathways: the association of a sensorial recognition to a motor action for instance.

In this vision, the information stored on individual neurons (for WTA) or groups of neurons (in TNMs) can be interpreted only in relation with the groups to which they are linked. In other words, perceptual categories are identified by the actions associated to them. No a priori meaning must be given to categories: it emerges through the agent's experience.

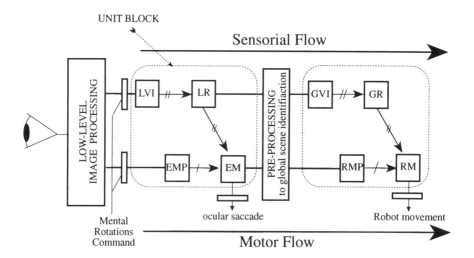

Figure 7.18. The complete neural network for target retrieval. It is made of two unit blocks (see Figure 7.10). LVI: local vision input. LR: local recognition. EMP: Eye Movement Proposal. EM: Eye Movement. GVI: Global Vision Input. GR: Global Recognition. RMP: Robot Movement Proposal. RM: Robot Movement.

Acknowledgements

This research is supported by the Swiss National Fund's PNR 23 program. We wish to thank Prof J.-D. Nicoud for his support of this research as head of the LAMI, and F. Mondada, E. Franzi and A. Guignard for designing the robot, and T. Cornu, J. Godjevac, P. Ienne and S. Rouche for their precious comments on the manuscript, and the French Ministry of Foreign Affairs who allowed Ph. Gaussier to perform his civil service in the LAMI.

References

Braitenberg V (1984) *Vehicles: Experiments in synthetic psychology*, MIT Press, Cambridge.

Brooks RA (1986) A robust layered control system for a mobile robot. *IEEE Journal of Robotics and Automation* RA-2, pp.14-23.

Burnod Y (1989) An adaptive neural network : The cerebral cortex, Masson, Paris.

G.A. Carpenter and S. Grossberg (1987) Invariant Pattern recognition and recall by an attentive self organizing ART architecture in a nonstationary world, *Proceedings of Neural Network*, vol 2, pp.737-745

Changeux JP (1985) *Neuronal Man : The Biology of Mind*, Oxford University Press, Oxford.

Deneubourg JL et al. (1991) The Dynamics of Collective Sorting: Robot-Like Ants and Ant-Like Robots, *From Animals to Animats, Proceedings of Simulation of Adaptive Behavior*, MIT Press, Cambridge.

Edelman G (1987) *Neural Darwinism : The Theory of Neuronal Group Selection*, Basic Books, New-York.

Gaussier P (1993) *Simulation d'un système visuel comprenant plusieurs aires corticales*, Doctoral Thesis. Paris XI - Orsay.

*Gaussier P, Cocquerez JP (1991), Neural Networks For Complex Scene Recognition: Simulation Of A Visual System With Several Cortical Areas, *in Proceedings of IJCNN*, Baltimore, Vol. 3, pp. 233-259.

Gaussier P, Zrehen S (1994a) The Probabilistic Topological Map (PTM): a self organizing and fast learning neural map that preserves topology, Submitted to *Neural Networks*

Gaussier P, Zrehen S (1994b) A Topological Map for On-Line Learning: Emergence of Obstacle Avoidance in a Mobile Robot, *submitted to SAB 1994.*

Grossberg S, Mingolla E (1985) Neural Dynamics of Form Perception: Boundary Completion, Illusory Figure, and Neon Color Spreading, *Psychological Review*, Vol.38, No2, pp.141-171.

Hertz J, Krogh A, Palmer RG (1991) *Introduction to the theory of neural computation*, Addison Wesley Redwood City

Köhler, Wallach (1944) Figural After-Effects: An Investigation of Visual Processes, *Proceedings of the American Philosophical Society*, 88, pp.269.

Meyer JA., Wilson S (1990) From Animals to Animats, *Proceedings of Simulation of Adaptive Behavior*, MIT Press, Cambridge.

*Mondada F, Franzi E, Ienne P (1993) Mobile Robot miniaturization: A tool for investigation in control algorithms, *Proceedings of Third International Symposium on Experimental Robotics*, Kyoto, in press.

Norton D, Stark L (1971) Eye Movements and Visual Perception, *Scientific American* 224(6), pp.34-43.

Piaget J (1936) *La naissance de l'intelligence chez l'enfant*, Delachaux et Niestlé Editions, Genève.

Rosenblatt F, (1954) *Principles of Neurodynamics*, Spartan Books, Washington D.C.

Stewart, J (1991) Life=Cognition: The epistemological and ontological significance of Artificial Life, *Proccedings of SAB 91 Paris,* Bourgine P. and Varela F. eds, MIT Press, pp 475-483

Tinbergen N (1969), *The Study of Instinct,* Clarendar Press Publishers, Oxford.

Treisman A (1988), Features and Objects: The Fourteenth Bartlett Memorial Lecture, *The Quarterly Journal of Experimental Psychology*, 40A (2), pp.201-237.

Watt RJ, Morgan MJ (1983), The Recognition and Representation of Edge Blur: Evidence for Spatial Primitives in Human Vision, *Vision Results*, 23(12), pp.1465-1477.

Zipser D (1985) A Computational Model of Hippocampal Place Fields. *Behavioral Neuroscience* 99, 5, pp.1006-1018.

---

* not referenced in this chapter

8

Virtual Environments for Simulating Artificial Autonomy

Miguel Rodriguez, Pierre-Jean Erard, Jean-Pierre Muller
Institut d'Informatique et d'Intelligence Artificielle, Université de Neuchâtel

8.1. Introduction

Cognitive Sciences have traditionally studied the nature of knowledge and its functions. Nowadays, the scientific community working on Artificial Intelligence (AI) collaborate actively either simulating biological systems or modeling and building artificial systems (animats). In this context, understanding and realizing artificial autonomy becomes a central question.

On the other hand, research on Virtual Reality has recently produced new means of simulation, providing more flexible environments for experimentation.

This chapter

a) introduces a particular model of autonomy through an architecture which is decomposed in three levels of abstraction: physical, behavioral and cognitive (Sections 8.2 and 8.3).

b) discusses two opposite approaches to the nature of the cognitive knowledge: the objectivist one and the subjectivist one (Section 8.4).

c) presents the possibilities introduced by virtual environments: either in world modeling or in the sensory-motor apparatus modeling (Section 8.5).

d) brings up some epistemological questions about simulating an artificial agent in a virtual environment (Section 8.6).

Artificial Life and and Virtual Reality Edited by Nadia Magnenat Thalmann and Daniel Thalmann
© 1994 John Wiley and Sons Ltd

8.2. The Concept of Autonomy

Who, nowadays, does not understand the term *autonomy*? Yet, it has variable meanings according to the context: the autonomy of a car (mobility range), the region autonomy (political independence), biological autonomy (life), etc.

In general, a system (social individual, biological organism, artifact, the Common Market, ...) is autonomous only if it is able to give to himself its proper laws, its conduct, opposite to the hetero-nomous systems which are driven by the outside. This general approach has grown as an ambitious and extremely interesting challenge for several disciplines of cognitive science.

Amongst the outstanding approaches, the concept of *autopoiesis* (Maturana and Varela 1980) tends to extract the fundamental characteristics of life. So, it covers certainly the concept of autonomy. Despite of the richness of this model, it is hard to interpret and to use in computer science, because it develops notions like identity or emergence which are quite abstract for computer applications.

What follows is an attempt to characterize autonomy in an artificial context. We try to extract certain dimensions of autonomy, modeling and building an agent. Let us be precise that we use the term *agent* in the rude but general meaning of "artificial system having capacities of perception and action"; in particular, a mobile robot.

Artificial autonomy
What properties needs an agent *to be* autonomous?

Answering this question through two different points of view - the observer and the designer - gives a new light.

8.2.1. The External Point of View

The appreciation of the agent's autonomy is made by a particular observer: it depends of his past, his abstracted knowledge and intentions, ... the point of view is, in this case, external to the agent.

As observers, we also take such an external point of view when we try to analyze the agent's capacities.

The evaluation criteria
In order to facilitate our judgment, we introduce two evaluation criteria:

    a) to preserve (alone) its physical and energetical integrity [survival].
    b) to satisfy (alone) the tasks given by the society [social role].

The first criterion is substantial for the agent. The second one is a utility criterion for the designer. These criteria do not pretend to characterize exhaustively the notion of autonomy; they limit to be a practical tool to judge the degree of autonomy of an agent.

From an external point of view, we consider that the agent which is able to exhibit behaviors satisfying the evaluation criteria is an autonomous agent.

8.2.2. The Internal Point of View

From the other side, the phenomenon of autonomy relies on the internal agent's structure and organization. The architecture and the internal dynamics determine the agent, independently of any observer.

As connectors, we adopt such an internal point of view in the modeling process.

AI successively considered autonomy as a 'reasoning capacity' (in the cognitive paradigm) then as 'action capacity' (in the behavioral paradigm). Nowadays, a new thread emerges from these two paradigms.

Reasoning

Reasoning (and representation) is a central topic in the cognitive paradigm. Problem solving - and planing, in particular - can be roughly presented as a search process in a solution space. Invariably, the search space size grows exponentially with the size of the problem. Thus, cognitivist programs use specific heuristics and control mechanisms to manage this combinatorial explosion.

Furthermore, these reasoning programs are mostly inspired from the common sense understanding of human thinking.

Activity

Action is the intrinsic nature of any agent; it is immersed in an environment and can't avoid interacting with it.

The behavioral paradigm, through a part of the AI community (Braitenberg 1984; Brooks 1986; Anderson and Donath 1990), took action in real environments (*Activity* from here on) as a central topic, inspiring from the life sciences and applying to mobile robotics. These works enhanced the value of *situated action*[1] as a good solution to the activity problem. They treat actions as stimulus-response loops, spatially and temporally localized: only immediate environment at the present instant is considered. In real environments, that approach ensures reactivity in front of unpredictable events.

These works lead into sensory-motor systems, producing *situated agents* which are inspired from the animal world (insects in particular).

Activity and reasoning

Practical results from the two paradigms appear opposite in the schema of Figure 8.1:
- situated agents are able to deal with real environments but has no capacity (or only have a little) of reasoning. By this fact, their behavior is limited to simple reactions and they are essentially driven by the environment.
- planning programs have high reasoning capacities (in the symbolic level) but they are generally applied to simulation domains, due to their incapacity to satisfy timely response constraints.

---

[1] "*Actions taken in the context of particular, concrete circumstances*" (Suchman 1987).

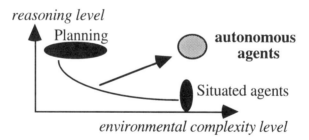

Figure 8.1. Reasoning, Activity and autonomy.

The first systems are *situated* (reactive behaviors), the second ones are *goal oriented* (finalized behaviors). Our approach lay on the strong conviction that situatedness and goal-orientedness, apparently opposing, form, from an internal point of view, a propitious base for artificial autonomy. Our architecture integrates both dimensions.

Some authors are yet trying to reduce the gap between reasoning and Activity: (Firby 1987) and (Schoppers 1987), amongst others, work on reactive planning, (Malcolm et al. 1989) advocates to place a classical planning system on situated agents (see (Maes 1990a) for some examples). As far as we know, the growth on one dimension results in a loss on the other dimension.

From an internal point of view, we consider that an agent likely to be autonomous should be able to orientate its situated Activity.

8.2.3. Discussion

We just presented artificial autonomy from two points of view: evaluation criteria for external judgment and the internal capacity of the agent to efficiently integrate activity and reasoning.

The architecture presented hereafter summarizes the second point of view. Nevertheless, the evaluation criteria remain the only mean to appreciate the agent's autonomy.

8.3. An Autonomous Agent Architecture

8.3.1. Three Levels of Abstraction

The architecture is conceptually decomposed in three levels of abstraction: physical (0), behavioral (1) and cognitive (2).

Level 0 holds the physical agent, composed by sensors and effectors. It establishes the dialogue with the environment (perception-action).

Level 1 holds the behavioral processes. It introduces the activity and converts the physical agent in a situated one. Each behavior is linked to a set of features extracted from the sensors (the stimuli) and computes, depending on the particular stimuli configuration, the action to generate. The behavior is then a sensory-motor loop linking perception to action (internally) and action to perception (externally) through the environment.

Finally, level 2 contains the knowledge and several cognitive processes which structure the knowledge and manage the behaviors of level 1. This level introduces the capacity of reasoning and converts the situated agent in a cognitive one, likely to satisfy the evaluation criteria.

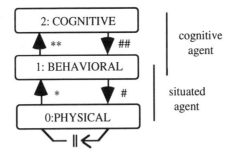

Figure 8.2. The general architecture.

Each abstraction level provides information to its upper level: channel * passes on the sensors state and link ** the behaviors state (state of stimulation). Similarly, each level controls its lower level: link ## permits to select the behavioral attitude and link # permits that the selected behavior directly controls the effectors.

8.3.2. Properties

This architecture demonstrates some interesting properties:

- **Synthetic approach**: the physical capacities are the limited base of behaviors which are the limited base of the cognitive capacities. These strong dependencies introduce important constraints that must be considered in the modeling process.
- **Conceptual modularity**: Activity and reasoning are distinctly separated through the levels of abstraction. This choice facilitates the reflection about the particular needs of each level and their interactions.
- **Hybrid architecture**: It integrates, in a simple and natural way, the reactive and cognitive approaches suggested by (Malcolm et al. 1989).
- **Generality**: Each level remain opened. The architecture is independent of any choice of robot, set of behaviors and cognitive model. We uniquely specify the interface between levels and the nature of behaviors (situated, realized by sensory-motor loops).

- **Study support for the 'action selection' problem**[2] (Maes 1990b, Tyrrel 1993). The control is clearly specified and the cognitive level do not impose any particular cognitive model.

This architecture has been implemented in our institute. It was used for navigation tasks in the corridors of the laboratory. The distributed nature of the architecture is treated in (Müller 1993). Levels of abstraction are developed and illustrated in (Rodriguez 1994).

Related to the new possibilities offered by virtual environment applications, we now develop one originality of our approach: the subjectivist nature of knowledge considered at the cognitive level.

8.4. Knowledge: Objectivist versus Subjectivist Representation

Knowledge-based systems build in the cognitivist paradigm essentially contain *a priori* knowledge given by the designer. It describes objects, facts, properties of objects, items of know-how (rules) or meta-knowledge. It corresponds to the designer's point of view about a particular domain and often reflects the limits of human expertise. This representational approach is said *objectivist*: input information is pre-categorized according to the designer interpretation. As an example, one input of the system could be: "I observe a frog"! Now, observing a frog results from complex mechanisms which are internal to the agent.

Opposite to the objectivist approach, some authors (Mataric 1990; Drescher 1991; Booth and Stewart 1993) take an internal (empirical) approach said non-objectivist or *subjectivist*. In this case, inputs are not pre-categorized: this process is achieved by the agent itself. Furthermore, the internal categories don't correspond to physical objects laying in the world: they are close to the signals given by the sensors. This methodological choice usually exploit learning capacities for the acquisition of knowledge, by the agent itself.

Supposing that different levels of cognition exist, the objectivist representations would correspond to a 'high level cognition' while subjectivist representations would correspond to a 'low level cognition'.

The subjectivist approach naturally meets our synthetic architectural approach: it is a synthetic representational approach, through the successive levels of abstraction. Ideally, it should lead to an internal notion of object. It is the new attitude which characterizes our approach to the knowledge of the autonomous agent.

In this frame, the knowledge managed by the cognitive processes:

- is empty at the beginning and acquired synchronically by the agent.
- refers to the world-agent interaction, observed (stimuli), interpreted (sensory-motor history) and structured (cognitive maps) by the agent itself.

---

[2] *"how to choose, at each moment in time, the most appropriate out of a repertoire of possible actions"* (Tyrrel 1993).

- serves as a prediction tool in order to facilitate an adequate management of the behavioral capacities.
- is sensory-motor in nature, because it restrictively lays on the information extracted at the behavioral level of the architecture.

This approach meets the same concerns as others which contemplate the agent as an embedded system and model autonomy from an internal point of view (Schwartz 1992, Bourgine and Vullierme 1993). Our purpose is to pursue this reflection and to make it concrete in the experimental framework constituted by mobile robotics.

8.5. Virtual Environment

Building up a virtual environment is useful because it gives to an agent an artificial environment that tests his behavior, varying arbitrarily the parameters of this environment. In simulation that means that the information coming from the real world by others is replaced by others which are generated by a computer program in such a way that the consequences upon the results of the process are not essentially modified. For example, the well known discreet event simulation generates sequences of events, which are distributed in the time by the same law, as they were in the real world. Obtained results are therefore statistically equivalent to those we had obtained through real measurements. In a virtual environment, the senses of an agent are simulated by virtual senses and *stimuli* stemming produced by them which must produce the same behavior and responses in the agent, as if they would come from a real world.

8.5.1. Limits of Direct Experimentation

For example, the experimentation in mobile robotics as it is usually carried out in laboratories nowadays is limited by the configuration constraints of the laboratory, the motion (effectors) and sensorial (sensors) capabilities of the robot. Building up a virtual environment is a way to overcome these constraints, not only the ones related with the design of the world where the robot is embedded and increasing the robot's functionalities but especially of the sensors which can be modeled taking in account perturbing factors influencing their behavior in a real world. Building a virtual environment consists of implementing in a computer the components forming the natural environment of the robot and thus to give the ability to extend the field of investigation. It simulates a particular or critical situation which could not occur except in a laboratory.

8.5.2. Architectural Frame

In the general architectural frame of the autonomous agent (Section 8.3.1), it comes down to replacing the physical layer (level 0) by a virtual layer, maintaining, unchanged, the protocols (pointed out by * and #) which links it to the behavioral layer (level 1). Maintaining these protocols has the effect that the *sensory-motor* dynamic remains unmodified. Hence in the *stimulus-response* process the events that originate the stimuli are assumed to be independent of the agent, and appear randomly.

Nevertheless whenever an agent is merged in a real world, he can move and act within it (for example by moving objects). This leads to modification of some structures and therefore the influence of the world upon the agent. This fact has to be kept in the representation of a virtual environment where the agent by acting and moving within it, can also change the image it receives from it. This shows the interlinking role of the sensor which is the perceptual organ of the robot. Though even if a virtual robot belongs to the world where it is acting, the perception of that world can only be carried through the sensors. Sensors are therefore the articulation between the virtual world and the behavioral, cognitive autonomous agent.

8.5.3. Components of the Virtual Environment

A virtual environment is made up of three parts, the world which is the physical environment (floor, walls, obstacles) of the robot, the robot itself, which as part of this world that follows the same mechanical laws (i.e. collision problem) and virtual sensors which simulate the senses of it.

The last part is more complex than the two others. In a real world a sensor emits a signal and measures the response the world gives to it. For a virtual sensor, this answer must be determined regarding the objects of the world and their properties. The design of a virtual sensor has to take in account not only the ability of responding to the sensor signals of the objects of the virtual world (like color, texture, reflection properties, mechanical resistance), but also the sensors where several algorithms are needed in order to determine the responses to the emitted signals, such as the ray tracing algorithm by sensors which use an echo (i.e. sonars) or collision and proximity detection algorithms for those which are sensible to a mechanical (i.e. bumpers) or electromechanical contact.

8.5.4. Discussion

Virtual robotics offer a fascinating investigation area insofar as it joins together robotics and virtual reality research domains. Replacing a real environment by a virtual one bring an extension of the experiment range and more flexibility, which were not possible in the real world. It opens an important field of investigation, especially in the realization of the designed abstractions, virtual robot, virtual world which must change consequently to the robot's actions and the virtual sensors, the goal of them is to build the received signals taking into account the abstract configuration of the virtual world.

8.6. Epistemological Constraints on Virtual Sensors

When simulating agents in a virtual environment, it is possible to use both an objectivist or subjectivist cognitive model:

- to compute the virtual reality images, the computer needs precise models of the objects, lightning, etc. For this reason, the objects and their identity are available and easily accessible to the simulated agent if asked for.
- the same models can compute the projection of these objects on simulated sensors (virtual retina or others), simulating the actual stimulations on the agent sensory apparatus.

Which one to use is not just a matter of taste but an important question which eventually depends on what we want to do with our simulated agents. There are roughly two possibilities:

- if we want just an agent to behave from an external point of view as realistically as possible, moving through a cluttered flat, taking objects here and there, the best answer seems to exploit the information which is just there with simulated sensors producing high-level information like "there is a green cup filled with cherries just there". However and as an example, we have seen robot arms moving in a more human-like way with simple associative networks than complicated inverse kinematics equations.
- if we want to experiment with models of what is really going on from an internal point of view, having sensors delivering object-level information is missing the point. Constructivist models as advocated by Piaget (Piaget 1967) clearly show the incremental construction of the objective world by coordination of subjective sensory-motor schemes. However, to simply reproduce the retina images could be going too far because we also know from recent neurophysiology results that we already access highly structured stimuli built through phylogenesis (Tabary 1994).

As a conclusion, to simulate an artificial agent in a virtual world, one has to be very cautious on the point of view one wants to take. The external point of view focuses on the realism of the observed behavior. The internal point of view on the realism of the architecture produces the observed behavior. However, in either cases, the most obvious solution is not necessarily the best and it is possible that the two points of view will eventually meet because the behavior is the only phenomenon simultaneously recognizable as identical by an observer and by the agent itself through introspection (Merleau-Ponty 1942).

References

Anderson TL, Donath M (1990) Animal behavior as a paradigm for developing robot autonomy, in *(Maes 1990a)*.

Booth M, Stewart J (1993) Un modèle de l'émergence de la communication, *Premières Journées Francophones IAD & SMA*, Toulouse, Avril.

Bourgine P, Vullierme JL (1993) Les Machines pensantes ont-elles un Ego?, *1er Congrès de l'association française des sciences et technologies de l'information et des systèmes*, Versailles, juin.

Braitenberg V (1984) *Vehicles: Experiments in Synthetic Psychology*, MIT Press, Bradford Books.

Brooks, RA (1986) A Robust Layered Control System For A Mobile Robot, *IEEE Journal of Robotic and Automation*, Vol. RA-2, no. 1, March 1986.

Drescher GL, (1991) Made-Up Minds, *A Constructivist Approach to Artificial Intelligence*, The MIT Press, Cambridge, Massachussets, London, England.

Firby RJ (1987) An Investigation into Reactive Planning in Complex Domains, *The Sixth National Conference on AI*, R. Engelmore (ed.), Morgan Kaufman Publishers, August.

Maes P (ed) (1990a) *Designing Autonomous Agents, Theory and Practice from Biology to Engineering and Back*, MIT Press.

Maes P (1990b) How to Do the Right Thing, *Connection Science Journal*, Special Issue on Hybrid Systems, pp. 291-323, Spring.

Malcolm C, Smithers T, Hallam J (1989) An Emerging Paradigm in Robot Architecture, Intelligent Autonomous Systems, *Proc. Intern. Conf.*, Amsterdam, December.

Mataric MJ (1990) Navigating with a rat brain: A neurobiological-inspider model for robot spatial representation, in *Proc. of the First International Conference on Simulation of Adaptive Behavior* (Meyer J, Wilson JS, editors), MIT Press, Bradford Books.

Maturana H, Varela F, (1980) *Autopoiesis and Cognition: The Realization of the Living*, Dordrecht: Reidel.

Merleau-Ponty M (1942) La structure du comportement, Presses Universitaires de France.

Müller JP, Rodriguez M (1993) A Distributed System Architecture, Application to Mobile Robotics, *IEEE, International Conference on Systems, Man and Cybernetics*, Le Touquet, October.

Piaget J (1967) *La construction du réel chez l'enfant*, Delachaux et Niestlé, Neuchâtel.

Rodriguez M, (1994) Modélisation d'un agent autonome: architecture comportementale et représentation sensori-motrice, in *Actes du Premier Colloque Jeunes Chercheurs en Sciences Cognitives*, ARC et IN COGNITO, Isère, Mars.

Schoppers M (1987) Universal Plans for Reactive Robots in Unpredictable Environments, in *Proc. of the Tenth International Joint Conference on AI*, 852-859, Menlo Park.

Schwarz E (1992) Un modèle générique de l'émergence et de l'évolution des systèmes naturels, *Deuxième Ecole de Systémique*, AFCET, Mont Ste. Odile, Octobre.

Suchman L (1987) *Plans and situated actions*, Cambridge University Press, Cambridge.

Tabary, (1994) *Autonomie biologique et ...* , Thèse de la Sorbonne, Paris.

Tyrrel T (1993) *Computational Mechanisms for Action Selection*, PhD Thesis, University of Edinburgh.

9

Body Centered Interaction in Immersive Virtual Environments

Mel Slater, Martin Usoh
Department of Computer Science and London Parallel Applications Centre,
Queen Mary and Westfield College, University of London, UK

"Well then, what about the actual getting of wisdom? Is the body in the way or not...? I mean, for example, is there any truth for men in their sight and hearing? Or as poets are forever dinning into our ears, do we hear nothing and see nothing exactly?" (Socrates, Phaedo, 65A.)[1]

9.1. Introduction

The technology to immerse people in computer generated worlds was proposed by Sutherland in 1965, and realized in 1968 with a head-mounted display that could present a user with a stereoscopic three-dimensional view slaved to a sensing device tracking the user's head movements (Sutherland 1965; 1968). The views presented at that time were simple wire frame models. The advance of computer graphics knowledge and technology, itself tied to the enormous increase in processing power and decrease in cost, together with the development of relatively efficient and unobtrusive sensing devices, has led to the emergence of participatory immersive virtual environments, commonly referred to as "Virtual

---

[1] Socrates: Great Dialogues of Plato, translated by W.H.D Rouse, A Mentor Classic, 1956.

Artificial Life and and Virtual Reality Edited by Nadia Magnenat Thalmann and Daniel Thalmann
© 1994 John Wiley and Sons Ltd

Reality" (VR) (Fisher 1982; Fisher et. al. 1986; Teitel 1990; see also SIGGRAPH Panel Proceedings 1989; 1990).

Ellis defines virtualization as "the process by which a human viewer interprets a patterned sensory impression to be an extended object in an environment other than that in which it physically exists" (Ellis 1991). In this definition the idea is taken from geometric optics, where the concept of a "virtual image" is precisely defined, and is well understood. In the context of virtual reality the "patterned sensory impressions" are generated to the human senses through visual, auditory, tactile and kinesthetic displays, though systems that effectively present information in all such sensory modalities do not exist at present. Ellis further distinguishes between a virtual space, image and environment. An example of the first is a flat surface on which an image is rendered. Perspective depth cues, texture gradients, occlusion, and other similar aspects of the image lead to an observer perceiving three-dimensional objects. The second, a virtual image, is the perception of an object in depth, leading to accommodation, convergence, and possibly stereopsis - for example, as might be generated by a pair of binocularly separated pictures fused to provide a stereoscopic image. The third, a virtual environment, incorporates the observer as part of the environment, so that head motions result in motion parallax from the observer's viewpoint, and a number of physiological and vestibular responses associated with focusing and object tracking are stimulated.

The human participant is "immersed" in the virtual environment (VE) in two ways. First, through the VE system displaying the sensory data depicting his or her surroundings. Part of the immediate surroundings consist of a representation of the participant's body and the environment is displayed from the unique position and orientation defined by the place of the participant's viewpoint within the environment. (We mean "display" and "viewpoint" with respect to all sensory modalities). Body tracking devices, such as electromagnetic sensors enable movements of the person's whole body and limbs to become part of the dynamic changes to objects in the VE under his or her immediate control (see Kalawsky, 1993). This is the second aspect of immersion: that proprioceptive signals about the disposition and dynamic behaviour of the human body and its parts become overlaid with consistent sensory data about the representation of the human body, the "Virtual Body" (VB). Putting this another way: proprioception results in the formation of an unconscious mental model of the person's body and its dynamics. This mental model must match the displayed sensory information concerning the VB. The VB is then under immediate control of the person's motor actions, and since the VB is itself part of the displayed VE, the person is immersed in the VE. We call such environments "Immersive Virtual Environments" (IVEs).

The term "immersion" is a description of a technology, which can be achieved to varying degrees. A necessary condition is Ellis' notion of a VE, maintained in at least one sensory modality (typically the visual). For example, a head-mounted display with wide field of view, and at least head tracking would be essential. The degree of immersion is increased by adding additional, and consistent modalities, greater degree of body tracking, richer body representations, decreased lag between body movements and resulting changes in sensory data, and so on.

Immersion may lead to a sense of presence. This is an emergent psychological property of an immersive system, and refers to the participant's sense of "being there" in the world created by the VE system. Note that immersion is a necessary rather than a sufficient condition for presence - immersion describes a kind of technology, and presence describes an associated state of consciousness.

In addition to the necessity of an immersive technology, the interaction techniques in a Virtual Reality may also play a crucial role in the determination of presence. For example, if through the limitations of body tracking, people must carry out everyday activities in an unnatural or artificial way, for example, moving through the world by pointing, this may lever them out of the illusion provided by the VE, thus reducing the sense of presence. In this chapter we introduce a paradigm for interaction in IVEs called "Body Centered Interaction" (BCI). The fundamental idea is that interaction techniques that maximize the match between proprioceptive and sensory data will maximize presence, within the constraints imposed by the display and tracking systems. A corollary is that whole body gestures are those which correspond to the semantics of the interaction.

In the next section we examine the role of the body in everyday reality, and the VB in virtual reality. We consider presence more closely in Section 9.3. The BCI paradigm is examined in detail in Section 9.4, together with a number of examples, including walking, scaling and communication. In Section 9.5 we discuss the use of the VB in communication between human participants. Conclusions are presented in Section 9.6.

9.2. The Body

9.2.1. The Physical Body in Everyday Reality

Possession of a body is so obvious that its major functions can be overlooked (Synnott 1993). It fulfils several crucial functions. It is:

- The physical embodiment of self;
- The medium of interaction: through the use of our bodies we interact with and are able to change the world;
- The anchor of the self in the sensory world: our sensory organs receive data about external reality which our mind/brain system interprets as perceptions of the world;
- A medium of communication: it allows us to communicate with other humans through the use of sound and gestures. By changing the world we construct powerful media of communications.
- It is the social representation of self in several respects: we recognize the existence of others through their bodies, we decorate our bodies in various ways to indicate aspects of our social status, and so on.

The body is our connection with reality, it is the means through which we participate in everyday reality. Our sensory organs take in data about external reality which leads to perception, cognition and eventually to behavior which converts this information into meaningful action through which we change external reality.

It is a relatively recent view that it is through the body and sensory perception that we come to understand reality. For example the ancients held the belief that the body is what prevents us from knowing reality:

Socrates:
> "And I suppose it [the soul] reasons best when none of these senses disturbs it, hearing or sight, or pain, or pleasure indeed, but when it is completely by itself and says good-bye to the body, and so far as possible has no dealings with it, when it reaches out and grasps that which really is." [2]

It is a fundamental part of modern scientific, and perhaps common sense thought, that sense perceptions are the ultimate foundation of our knowledge about ourselves and the world.

9.2.2. Proprioception

Proprioception is defined by Oliver Sacks as "... that continuous but unconscious sensory flow from the movable parts of our body (muscles, tendons, joints), by which their position and tone and motion is continually monitored and adjusted, but in a way which is hidden from us because it is automatic and unconscious" (Sacks 1985). Proprioception allows us to form a mental model that describes the dynamic spatial and relational disposition of our body and its parts. We know where our big left toe is, without looking, by relying on this body model. We can touch our nose with our right forefinger, with closed eyes, similarly by relying on this unconscious mental model formed from the proprioceptive data flow.

Sacks quoted the philosopher Wittgenstein in pointing out the fundamental nature of the proprioceptive sense, considered by many as a kind of hidden "sixth sense":

Wittgenstein:
> "The aspect of things that are most important for us are hidden because of their simplicity and familiarity. (One is unable to notice something because it is always before one's eyes). The real foundations of his enquiry do not strike a man at all".

Proprioception is best appreciated when lost: Sacks describes the case of a woman who lost this sense, and was unable to move her body under conscious control. It was only through visual feedback, by looking in a mirror, that she was eventually able to move with conscious volition.

---

[2] Plato,The Phaedo, op. cit.

9.2.3. Virtual Bodies

Virtual Reality offers a challenge to the everyday relationship between mind and body. This relationship is so fundamental that we normally do not think about it. Only in times of injury and crisis does the relationship come to the fore. However, entering into a Virtual Reality can be a shock: based on sensory data the mind may be fooled into the illusion of being in an alternative world - the results of head tracking strongly confirm this, since a turn of the head to the right swings the world to the left as in everyday reality. Motion parallax and stereopsis provide further evidence. And yet - look for what you would expect to see - your own body, and it may be missing, perhaps replaced by a disembodied polygonized "hand".

The proprioceptive stream is informing us, as always during the conscious state, that the body is still there as usual. The sensory data contradicts this, there is no body. The virtual body concept is an attempt to reduce the contradiction between sensory data and proprioception by constructing a body representation slaved to the available tracking devices.

The programs and experiments outlined in this chapter were implemented on a DIVISION ProVision200 system. The ProVision system includes a DIVISION 3D mouse, and a Virtual Research Flight Helmet as the head mounted display. Polhemus sensors are used for position tracking of the head and the mouse. Scene rendering is performed using an Intel i860 microprocessor (one per eye) to create an RGB RS-170 video signal which is fed to an internal NTSC video encoder and then to the displays of the Flight Helmet. These displays (for the left and right eye) are colour LCDs with a 360 × 240 resolution and the HMD provides a horizontal field of view of about 75 degrees. The frame update rate achieved during the experiments was about 10-15 frames per second.

With the VB we have used throughout, participants see a representation of their right hand, and their thumb and first finger activation of the 3D buttons on the DIVISION 3D mouse, are reflected in movements of their corresponding virtual finger and thumb. The hand is attached to an arm, that can be bent and twisted in response to similar movements of the real arm and wrist. The arm is connected to an entire but simple body representation, complete with legs and left arm. Forward movement is accompanied by walking motions of the virtual legs. When participants turn their real head around by more than 60 degrees, then the virtual body is reoriented accordingly. So for example, if they turn their real body around and then looked down at their virtual feet, their orientation lines up with their real body. However, turning only the head around by more than 60 degrees and looking down (an infrequent occurrence), results in the real body being out of alignment with the virtual body.

9.3. Presence

9.3.1. The Absence of Presence

An IVE may lead to a sense of presence for a participant taking part in such an experience. Presence is the psychological sense of "being there" in the environment based on the technologically founded immersive base. However, any given immersive system does not necessarily always lead presence for all people: the factors that determine presence, given immersion, is an important area of study (Barfield 1993; Held and Durlach 1992; Heeter 1992; Loomis 1992a; Sheridan 1992; Slater and Usoh 1994a; 1994c; Zeltzer 1992).

Like proprioception, presence is so fundamental to our everyday existence that it is difficult to define. Imagining the loss of presence is more difficult than imagining the loss of proprioception. The concept of presence "no where" is logically unsound, since presence implies a "somewhere". Equating loss of presence with loss of consciousness does not lead to any further understanding. However, it does make sense to consider the negation of a sense of presence as the loss of locality, such that "no presence" is equated with no locality, the sense of where self is as being always in flux. Interestingly, Sacks describes the case of a man without the capability for present day memory. It was essentially impossible to have a conversation with him, since the context would be lost after a few moments, when he forgot who he was talking to, and what the conversation was about. This is a kind of neurological loss of presence. Imagine a VR system that continuously and randomly changed the environment, so that the human participant could form no stable sense of locality, and no relationship with any object: everything being continually in flux. Such an environment would not be presence inducing.

9.3.2. Presence and the Body

It can be argued that there is an inherent logical connection between the degree of presence and the VB. If the match between proprioception and sensory data about the corresponding dynamics of the body is high, then the person immersed in the VE is likely to identify with their VB. If sensory data confirms that this VB functions effectively within the larger (computer generated) environment, then there must be presence within that environment. The VB has become identified with "self", the VB is immersed within a particular environment, therefore self must be in that environment.

There is empirical evidence from a number of case-control studies providing evidence for this idea. The first pilot study divided 17 subjects into two groups, experimental and control. The experimental group had a VB as described in Section 9.2, and the control group had a very impoverished VB consisting only of a 3D arrow pointer that responded correctly to (right) had movements and orientations. All subjects carried out the same tasks, which involved moving from a corridor into a number of rooms, and each room exercised a different aspect of the experiment. For example, in one room objects spontaneously flew towards the face of the subjects, and in another, they were perched on a plank over the edge of a precipice.

In this experiment presence was measured in two ways. The first was by a particular question in a questionnaire administered after the experience (To what extent did you experience a sense of being "really there" inside the virtual environment?). This was measured on a six point scale, from 1 = "Not at all really there" to 6 = "totally there".

The second method was to observe the reactions of the subjects to "danger" - in particular did they exhibit the looming effect when objects flew towards their faces (i.e. did they "duck"), and second, did they react in an observable manner, including verbal exclamations, when over the virtual precipice. The results suggested a positive association between the VB and the observed reaction to "danger". If a reaction to danger indicates presence, then possession of a VB did positively influence presence. These results are extensively reported in (Slater and Usoh, 1992; 1993a). A first analysis did not find a positive relationship between VB and reported sense of presence as indicated by the responses to the questionnaire.

The situation was more complex than this, however. We were puzzled by the fact that these 17 people had all had very similar experiences, and yet their reactions were so different to one another, including their responses to the presence question. The human participant in a VE does not simply absorb the VE generated sensory data, but processes this through the mental models and representation systems typically employed by the person in everyday reality. Since people have different models of the world and corresponding preferences in (unconsciously) processing sensory data, and since the VE typically offers very biased sensory data (i.e. very much biased towards the visual), this might explain the variation in people's responses.

We carried out a post-hoc analysis of the questionnaire data, including an analysis of essays written by the subjects 24 hours after the end of the experiment. This was based on a neuro-linguistic programming (NLP) model of subjective experience, which states that all such experience is encoded in terms of three main representation systems, Visual, Auditory and Kinesthetic (VAK) (Dilts et. al. 1979). The Visual system includes external images and remembered and constructed internal images. The Auditory system includes external sounds, and internal remembered and constructed sounds. It also includes internal dialogue, that is the person talking to him or herself on the inside. The Kinesthetic system includes kinesthetic and tactile sensations and also emotional responses (which are decomposed into specific patterns of internal tactile and kinesthetic sensations). The model claims that people have a tendency to be dominant in one or other of these systems, and that such dominance may be reflected in language patterns: specifically, in the (visual, auditory, kinesthetic) predicates and references they tend to use. For example, when a person says "I see what you mean", this is taken not just as an arbitrary and accidental choice of expression, but as an indication of their internal processing - they may be literally making an internal picture of the situation under discussion. They could equally well have said "I hear what you're saying" or "I have a feeling for what you say", but instead chose the visual predicate.

NLP also distinguishes between egocentric and exocentric perceptual positions. The perceptual position is the standpoint from which the person experiences and remembers events. A person might remember an event from an associated (egocentric) standpoint, and see the event unfolding in his mind's eye from the viewpoint in which it was originally experienced. This is called the first perceptual position. Alternatively a person might remember the event from a dissociated (exocentric) perspective - either from the point of view of another actor in the scene (second position), or from an abstract, disembodied point of view (third position). For example, a person trying to convince someone in an argument might say: "I can feel that it is right" (first position, K) or "You can tell that it is right" (second position, A) or "It can be seen that it is right" (third position, V). The representation systems and perceptual position are logically orthogonal - there being nine possible combinations in this example.

Using the essays written by the subjects as part of the post-experiment information that we collected, we counted the number of V, A, K predicates and references used as a proportion of the total number of sentences written by each subject. Similarly, we classified each sentence as belonging to either the first, second or third perceptual position. Hence variables were constructed that attempted to measure the extent of dominance with respect to representation system and perceptual position for each subject in the experiment, and these were included as explanatory variables in a statistical (regression) analysis of the data with the reported degree of presence taken as the dependent variable.

Since the VR system we were using presented the participant mainly with visual information, we expected - if the NLP hypothesis were useful - that visual dominance would be positively correlated with reported presence, and auditory dominance negatively correlated. The results were rather startling - even though the regression analysis was not statistically secure (the dependent variable being a measurement on an ordinal scale) the explanatory power of the model was very high indeed, with a multiple squared correlation coefficient of 0.99, and with a very high level of fit (better than 1% significance). The regression model resulted in the following conclusions:

(a) That independently of whether or not the subject has a virtual body, the higher the proportion of visual predicates and references used, the greater the sense of presence, and the higher the proportion of auditory predicates and references the lower the sense of presence.

(b) For those with a virtual body, the higher the proportion of kinesthetic references and predicates the higher the sense of presence. For those without a virtual body, the higher the sense of kinesthetic terms the lower the sense of presence.

(c) The level of presence increases with first perceptual position (P1) up to the mean level of P1, and then decreases. (The model was quadratic in P1). This is the same for each group, except that the rate of change is steeper for those in the control group.

The analysis and results are reported in (Slater and Usoh 1993a 1994a). It is result (b) that is most interesting in the present discussion. It indicates a relationship between kinesthetic dominance, the VB and reported degree of presence. The K system is the system of the body - it is very strongly related with proprioception as discussed in Section 9.1. This result gave us a clue that there is a relationship between the VB, proprioception and presence.

The experiment described here was only a pilot, and it was unsatisfactory from the point of view of direction of causality. We could not say that representation systems were a causal factor in presence, since the data used for measuring these was obtained after the VR experience. It could have been said that experience itself was a causal factor determining the representation systems used when writing about it. Therefore, we carried out a further major study, with 24 subjects, where we used a questionnaire to assess dominant representation systems and perceptual position well before the VR experience. This study, where each participant did have a VB, resulted again in a model with very strong explanatory power for the representation systems, but no significant effect was found for perceptual position. Again, the higher the visual dominance the greater the degree of presence, the higher the auditory dominance, the lower the degree of presence, and also (this time since all had the same VB) the higher the kinesthetic dominance, the higher the degree of presence. The experiment and results are discussed fully in (Slater, Usoh and Steed 1994c).

This experiment used a more comprehensive measurement of presence based on:

(a) The subject's sense of "being there" - a direct attempt to record the overall psychological state with respect to an environment;

(b) The extent to which, while immersed in the VE, it becomes more "real or present" than everyday reality;

(c) The "locality", that is the extent to which the VE is thought of as a "place" that was visited rather than just as a set of images.

This last is similar to the idea of Barfield and Weghorst who write that "... presence in a virtual environment necessitates a belief that the participant no longer inhabits the physical space but now occupies the computer generated virtual environment as a 'place'" (op. cit., p702). Each of these was measured on a seven point scale, and the overall score for an individual was the number of highest scores (6 or 7) out of three.

Especially interesting in this experiment is that we programmed the virtual left arm and hand to mirror the movements of the corresponding right hand limbs. The idea was to see the extent to which subjects would match their real left hand with the virtual one. Four out of the 24 subjects exhibited this matching behavior. These four subjects had a significantly higher score on the K representation system than the other subjects (in fact by more than double). We speculate that these subjects had a desire to match the proprioceptive with the sensory data. They saw their virtual left hand move, and the only way to achieve the matching was for them to move their real left hand in conjunction.

These four subjects must have had a very high degree of identification with their virtual bodies. In our first pilot experiment, where the virtual left arm was in a fixed position, some of the subjects wrote about their confusion or perhaps lack of identification with the VB. Strange effects were observed, and recorded:

• One subject on noticing the fixed virtual left arm began to move her real left arm very rapidly, in a manner indicating panic.
• Another wrote "I thought there was really something wrong with my [left] arm";

- Others talked of their virtual bodies being - "a dead weight", a useless thing", "nothing to do with me".

Such remarks were reminiscent of Sack's patients who lost the proprioceptive sense in some of their limbs. This suggests that the lack of a normal relationship between the proprioceptive system and the behavior of the VB could be very important factor in people's acceptance of and responses to immersive virtual environments.

9.3.3. Presence Summary

In this section we have examined the concept of presence in a VE, and in particular the relationship between the physical body, virtual body and presence. There are three aspects to the relationship that we have discussed so far. The first is that proprioception provides a sense of the physical body and its activities, leading to a mental body model. Presence is likely to be enhanced the more that this mental body model behaviorally matches the virtual body representation in the VE. Since the participant is only aware of this VB through the sensory (mainly visual) data supplied by the immersive system, presence requires that proprioceptive data be continually overlaid with consistent virtual sensory data. The second, is that evidence suggests that, other things being equal, a virtual body will, in any case, enhance the sense of presence. Third, the body is the repository of the sensory apparatus, which in turn leads to the fundamental representation systems based on the senses (visual, auditory and kinesthetic). The representation systems are a powerful factor in explaining people's reported sense of presence. In particular, this is true for people who are dominant on the kinesthetic representation system - that is, those for whom proprioceptive data (how they "feel") is an important explicit and verbalized component of their mental processing.

The unique feature of modern virtual reality systems is that they are general purpose presence transforming machines. Systems and applications have existed for many years that provide a high degree of presence: flight simulators are an obvious example. However, such systems always provide a very high sense of presence within a particular and fixed environment. A flight simulator can, for example, never be used to provide a sense of presence within a supermarket. An IVE system, can, however, be used to provide a sense of presence in an airplane cockpit, and also in a supermarket: it is only a question of the database and interaction model used. Obviously, since a flight simulator is specialized to airplanes it is typically much more successful than a virtual reality system for its particular application domain: but at the great cost always associated with very special purpose systems. The choice between an IVE and a traditional simulator then becomes a question of economics.

Steuer has gone as far as taking presence as the defining feature of VR: "A virtual reality is defined as a real or simulated environment in which a perceiver experiences telepresence" (Steuer 1992). We are tempted to extend this definition to include the importance of the VB:

> A virtual reality is a real or simulated reality in which the self has a (suspension of dis-) belief that he or she is in an environment other than that which his/her real body is located. Self perceives sensory information correlated with proprioceptively valid feedback about the behaviour and state of his/her body in that environment.

We have concentrated here on presence as the central phenomenon of virtual reality, and have examined its relationship to the body and VB. In the next section we show how we have exploited these relationships in the construction of interactive techniques.

9.4. Body Centred Interaction

9.4.1. Motivation and Concepts

In the first pilot experiment on presence discussed in Section 9.3, we observed that some subjects found it exceedingly difficult to move around the VE using a navigation metaphor based on hand gesture pointing. For example, the following are reports from their essays written after the experience:

> "Sometimes [I had] a desperate need to actually walk when virtually walking, there does seem to be a conflict between what the eyes see and the body feels - e.g. my feet appear to be floating but I can feel my feet on the ground."

> "Trying to separate virtual and physical movement: constantly being aware - my initial response was to make the physical move then forcing myself to use the mouse instead... The amount of concentration I had to use was something I remember particularly. Moving around with the mouse, forwards and backwards - and with the helmet turning around - it was difficult to reconcile the two ways of moving."

This illustrates in the negative the central idea of the BCI paradigm: interaction techniques should be constructed so that there is a match between sensory data ("what the eyes see") and proprioceptive feedback ("what the body feels"). The typical approach is to either overload almost all forms of interaction onto a set of hand gestures or manipulations (Vaananen and Bohm 1993; Brooks et. al. 1990) or to use inappropriate methodology taken from screen based interfaces, such as menus and icons. We are reminded of a famous passage written by Marx:

> K. Marx:
> "Men make their own history, but they do not make it just as they please; they do not make it under circumstances chosen by themselves, but under circumstances directly encountered, given and transmitted from the past. The tradition of all the dead

generations weighs like a nightmare on the brain of the living. And just when they seem engaged in revolutionising themselves and things, in creating something that has never yet existed ... they anxiously conjure up the spirits of the past to their service and borrow from them names, battle cries and costumes ..."[3]

Virtual Reality must, on the contrary, invent its own new ways of thinking, appropriate and native to the new technology.

Body Centered Interaction involves a number of components:

(a) Inference about the state of the body from limited information

One of the concepts of the BCI approach is the construction of an abstract (device independent) control model that defines the mapping between physical tracking capabilities and the associations with virtual body dynamics. For example, consider two extremes - a full body suit that tracks the position of all the major limbs of the body, compared to a six degrees of freedom 3D mouse held in one hand. It is assumed in both cases that there is a HMD that tracks the position and orientation of the head. Now in the former case, there is a relatively straightforward mapping between the tracking information and the position and orientation of the virtual body and its limbs. In the latter case, only the head position and orientation and the position and orientation of one hand is known. Hence in this case, the position and orientation of the VB as a whole is a matter for inference. The objective is to construct a consistent inferential model for this mapping. The discussion in Section 9.2.3 illustrates a primitive example of this.

(b) Body centered feedback

Interaction requires feedback about the state of the VB, and its relationship to the environment. This involves the generation of real-time shadows and reflections, that include the VB (as well as shadows of objects generally). It also involves the use of a graphics viewing model that simulates and stimulates peripheral vision, in spite of the relatively small field of view actually provided by the visual display devices.

In previous work (Chrysanthou and Slater 1992) we have constructed an algorithm for dynamic shadows in the context of polygonal scenes illuminated with local lighting. Shadows are well-known to be important in understanding spatial relationships (Puerta 1989). The shadow of the person's own VB would be an exciting method for feedback in this context. Mirrors and reflections are an obvious extension of this work.

Today's HMDs typically provide a reduced field of view compared to the average human FOV. Hence, unlike the situation in everyday reality, the participant is typically not always aware of the state of his virtual body, or of events that would normally be signalled by peripheral vision. We have developed a graphics viewing pipeline that does simulate peripheral vision, and have shown experimentally that it is possible to stimulate the behavior associated with peripheral vision in spite of the relatively small FOV of HMDs (Slater and Usoh 1993b).

---

[3] K. Marx, The Eighteenth Brumaire of Louis Napoleon, in Marx and Engels, *Selected Works in One Volume*, Lawrence and Wishart Ltd, 1968.

We are currently developing implementations of both the rapid shadow and peripheral vision models on the VR system.

(c) Magical and Mundane Interaction

Interaction is the ability of the participant to move through and change the world, that is, navigation and manipulation. This falls into two further categories, which we call *mundane* and *magical*. Mundane interaction is that which attempts to faithfully reproduce a corresponding interaction in everyday reality. For example, the process of picking up an object, or driving an automobile. Magical interaction involves actions that are not possible in everyday reality - such as a person flying by his or her own volition, walking through walls, tele-portation - that is moving instantaneously from place to place, psycho-kinesis - that is, action on an object at a distance, and other similar examples. Table 9.1 classifies these types of interaction.

Table 9.1. Magical and Mundane Interactions

Interaction	Examples	Manipulation Examples	Navigation Examples
Mundane Reproduction of interactions from the world of everyday reality.	picking something up; walking; driving an automobile.	object selection and placement; transformations, deformations.	walking; driving or flying a vehicle; space walks.
Magical Production of interactions that are only imaginable in everyday reality.	flying by own volition; tele-portation; psycho-kinesis.	scaling the environment; psycho-kinesis	flying under own volition; teleportation

To the extent that a VR system is to be used as a simulation of everyday reality, for example, for the purposes of training, it is necessary for the actions that a person makes in the VE to be intuitively associated with the corresponding actions that they would need to take in everyday reality. It is also possible for magical interaction to be accomplished in an intuitive way, involving the marshalling of mental models for activities on the part of the participant that even though achieving magical effects, can seem to be accomplished naturally. We have found that interactions based directly on the use of the person's VB seem to satisfy this criterion. The following sections consider examples from both categories: mundane - walking, climbing and descending steps and ladders; magical - scaling the environment and remote object selection.

9.4.2. Walking: The Virtual Treadmill

A standard solution for navigation in IVEs is to make use of the hand-held pointing device. VPL used the DataGlove (Fisher 1986; Foley 1987) with which a hand gesture would initiate movement, and the direction of movement would be controlled by the pointing direction. Velocity was controlled as part of the gesture: for example the smaller the angle between thumb and first finger the greater the velocity.

DIVISION's ProVision system typically employs a 3D mouse (though it supports gloves as well). Here the direction of movement is determined by gaze, and movement is caused when the user presses a button on the mouse. There are two speeds of travel controlled by a combination of button presses. Other methods of navigation are discussed in (Brooks et al. 1992; Fairchild et al. 1993; Iwata and Matsuda 1992; Mackinlay et. al. 1990; Robinett and Holloway 1992; Song and Norman 1993).

In the experiments discussed above we adjusted the ProVision's standard interface, and based direction of movement on the pointing direction of the 3D mouse. This disassociation of gaze and direction of movement gives the participant an extra degree of freedom in exploring the VE.

We mentioned above the difficulty that some subjects have using a pointing device for navigation. In some contexts such an approach might be natural, for example in a simulated space walk - but then the normal methods of moving around, such as taking one or two small steps would need to be disabled with perhaps the participant seated in a chair. The pointing method would be the only method for movement over large or small distances, so that the conflict mentioned by the subjects could not occur.

Brooks noted that "Physical motion powerfully aids the illusion of presence, and actual walking enables one to feel kinesthetically how large spaces are..." (Brooks 1992). As part of the Building Walkthrough project at the University of North Carolina, a steerable treadmill was constructed, that allowed users to actually experience walking through virtual buildings and building sites. The Virtual Treadmill is a similar idea, but implemented only in software, and without the restrictions necessitated by a real treadmill where the user cannot step off from it in order to really walk a few steps.

The idea of the Virtual Treadmill is straightforward - whenever participants carry out the activity of walking on the spot, that is standing in one place but with leg motions similar to walking, the system moves them forward in the virtual space, with direction of movement governed by gaze. This is achieved by passing all HMD data through a pattern recognizer filter which is able to distinguish head movements characteristic of such "walking on the spot" behavior from any other behavior at all. Therefore, virtual ground is covered in this technique by almost really walking, or by taking one or two actual physical steps: each case involving whole body movements similar to those of walking in everyday reality. Contrast this with the usual method used in VR, which is sometimes moving by actually walking, and other times using a pointing hand gesture. In the new method there is no use made at all of the hand-held pointing device. This can be reserved solely for other forms of interaction such as object manipulation.

Two studies with users were carried out regarding the influence of the Virtual Treadmill on navigation and presence. In each study there were 16 subjects divided into experimental and control groups - the experimental group were "walkers" - they used the Virtual Treadmill idea, and the controls were "pointers" - they used the hand gesture with the 3D mouse as usual. A full report of the first study is given in (Slater, Steed and Usoh 1993c). We concentrate here only on the results relating to presence. The task of both groups was to navigate through a room containing many obstacles, pick up an object, take it out into a corridor, and then locate and enter another room at the far side of the corridor. The objective was to place the object on a chair in that room. This chair was reachable only by crossing a chasm over a precipice. The control group first carried out this task as "pointers", answered a questionnaire, and then repeated the experiment as "walkers", and completed a second questionnaire. The experimental group did this in the opposite order. At the end of the first part of the experiment, each group had experienced only one type of navigation technique, only "walking" or "pointing". After the second part of the experiment, each person had experienced both types. Three control group subjects were not included in the comparative part of the study because the walking technique did not work for them at all. Overall though, the pattern recognizer correctly predicted behavior, that is it distinguished between walking on the spot and other activities with a success rate of between 85% and 95%.

Table 9.2 shows the results of this experiment in regard to subjective reporting on presence. There is no difference in presence between the two groups immediately after the end of Part I of the experiment, that is after each subject had experienced one method of walking. However, in the comparison after Part II, amongst those who had a preference, the walking method led to a higher subjective sense of presence. However, comparisons such as these are suspect, since it cannot be known whether the experience of the first session influenced the results of the second session.

In the second study the scenario was slightly different. The task was to pick up an object located in a corridor, take it into a room and place it on a particular chair. The chair was placed in such a way that the subjects had to cross a chasm over another room about 20 feet below, in order to reach it. They could get to the chair either by going out of their way to walk around a wide ledge around the edges of the room, or by directly moving the shorter distance across the chasm. This was a simple virtual version of the famous visual cliff experiment by E.J. Gibson (Gibson and Walk 1960). All subjects were watched by an observer, who in particular recorded whether or not they moved to the chair by walking around the ledge at the side of the room, or by walking directly across the precipice. In the event, only four subjects out of the sixteen (two from each group) walked across the precipice.

The main conclusion from the statistical analysis was that for the "walkers", the greater their association with the VB the higher the presence score, whereas for the "pointers" there was no correlation between VB association and the presence score. Other statistically significant factors were:

(a) path taken to the chair: a path directly over the precipice was associated with lower presence. This is as would be expected, and is useful in corroborating the veracity of the presence score.
(b) degree of nausea: a higher level of reported nausea was associated with a higher degree of presence. This same result has been found in each of our studies. We speculate that the sense of motion in

VR is a cause of both simulator sickness and an influence on presence (McCauley and Sharkey 1993). Finding nausea and presence associated would therefore be expected, even though there may not be a direct causal link between them. There is the further point that presence is concerned with the effect of the environment on the individual. A person who experiences nausea as a result of the VR has certainly been influenced by it!

Table 9.2. Subjective Reporting on Presence

Being there			**Real or present**			**Seeing/visiting**		
Please rate your sense of being there in the computer generated world...			To what extent were there times during the experience when the computer generated world became the "reality" for you, and you almost forgot about the "real world" outside?			When you think back about your experience, do you think of the computer generated world more as something that you saw, or more as somewhere that you visited?		
In the computer generated world I had a sense of "being there"...			*There were times during the experience when the computer generated world became more real or present for me compared to the "real world"...*			*The computer generated world seems to me to be more like...*		
1. not at all			1. at no time			1. something that I saw		
...			...			...		
7. very much			7. almost all of the time			7. somewhere that I visited		
Group	**Mean**	**Median**		**Mean**	**Median**		**Mean**	**Median**
Exp.	6	6		5	5		5	5
Control	5	5		4	3		5	4
Part II comparison: **prefer**: walking: 6 same: 5 mouse: 2 TOTAL:13			**Part II comparison:** **prefer**: walking: 7 same: 5 mouse: 1 TOTAL:13			**Part II comparison:** **prefer**: walking: 7 same: 6 mouse: 0 TOTAL:13		

These results were obtained from a logistic regression analysis, that is, counting the number of 6 or 7 scores across the three presence questions and using this count out of three as the dependent variable. Here the dependent variable is binomially distributed, with expected value related by the logistic function to a linear combination of independent and explanatory variables (Cox 1970).

An alternative analysis of the same data was carried out, where the three presence scores were combined into one overall score using a principal components analysis. A statistically significant normal regression model was obtained, with qualitatively similar results to the first analysis. The overall regression was significant at 5% with a multiple squared correlation coefficient of 0.81. Here though, instead of path to the chair being significant, a variable representing the comparison between vertigo experienced in the virtual world with what might have been experienced in the real world in a similar situation, was significant instead. Subjects were asked to rate their reaction to the visual cliff regarding the extent to which it was the same or different to what they would have expected it to be in real life. In the analysis a higher degree of presence was associated with the comparison resulting in a "same as real life". Loomis suggests that one objective way of assessing presence is the degree to which reactions are the same in virtual as in real environments (Loomis 1992b). Again this lends support to the measure of presence used actually bearing a strong relationship to the phenomenon of presence.

This experiment, in including the degree of subjective association with the virtual body, allowed for a more sophisticated analysis. The central thesis of the BCI paradigm, that presence is likely to be enhanced with interaction techniques that attempt to match proprioception and sensory data, especially that regarding the VB, seems to be supported - since only for the "walkers" was there a positive correlation between VB association and presence. This experiment is reported in (Slater, Steed and Usoh 1994b).

9.4.3. Steps and Ladders

The Virtual Treadmill has easy adaptation to other forms of navigation beside walking at ground level. Applications such as architectural walkthrough, or training for fire fighting, require participants to walk up steps or climb and descend ladders. Again, it is certainly possible to use a hand gesture, or allow participants to fly, and in some applications this would be acceptable if a degree of realism in these activities were not required. In the fire fighting example though, trainees would typically be required to carry objects (buckets, hoses, etc.) while climbing steps or ladders, so that the use of hand based gestures for navigation would not be suitable. Also, in a real fire fighting situation, the fire fighters do expend energy in moving through the scenario, and here what may be thought of as a disadvantage of the Virtual Treadmill - it certainly requires more energy to perform than pressing a button or making a hand gesture - becomes an advantage in terms of realism.

At the time of writing we have adapted the Virtual Treadmill to steps and ladders in a straightforward manner. When the process monitoring collision detection notifies the system of a collision between the VB and the bottom or top rung of a staircase or ladder, subsequent walking on the spot motions will move the participant up or down as appropriate. We do not currently support walking backwards down steps (this is never a good idea in reality). For ladders, we extend the whole body gesture so that while the hand is above the head and the person is moving on a ladder, they will climb up the ladder, and while the person's hand is below their head, they will move down the ladder.

Figures 9.1, 9.2 and 9.3 (see Color Section) show exterior views of a VB as it is climbing or descending steps and ladders, in one case holding a bucket.

9.4.4. Scaling the Environment

Scaling the environment as a whole is useful in applications where an overview of the entire scene is required, or alternatively when details need to be enlarged. This could be accomplished by defined hand gestures, or by menus and sliders. The BCI approach, however, requires the participant to carry out a whole body gesture which is semantically appropriate for the activity. Scaling the environment up is equivalent to shrinking the participant's VB. This can be accomplished by the person pushing down on his or her head with his hand and flexing the knees to lower the head, in an attempt to become smaller. Corresponding with this activity, the VB will become smaller, and the world will appear to grow larger, while the hand remains on top of the head. Shrinking the world is equivalent to growing the body. This can be accomplished with a placement of the hand under the chin, in a gesture of pushing upwards which grows the VB, and correspondingly the world appears to shrink.

This technique also supports magical navigation. Isaac Asimov's *Fantastic Voyage* can be accomplished in VR by shrinking the body to a tiny size in relation to the environment, so that the participant can move through what would in reality be microscopic spaces. (In the famous book, a doctor entered into the blood stream of a patient). Another application, would be to grow the body to a very large size, so that one small step would take the participant across to the other side of the environment. VR allows us to become microscopic creatures, or giants. The BCI paradigm tries to accomplish these magical techniques in an intuitive manner.

9.4.5. Body Centered Interaction Summary

The BCI paradigm therefore attempts to match sensory and proprioceptive data. An aspect of this is that it uses whole body gestures rather than limited hand based gestures or screen based interfaces in order to accomplish interactions. The goal is always to provide a gesture which corresponds in a semantic sense to the type of interaction. Hence walking is carried out by "almost walking", shrinking the body is accomplished by pushing down on the head. Other examples are easy to construct - for example selection of a distant object might be carried out by stretching the hand as far as possible away from the body. When the VR system detects such an event, it will grow the arm in the direction of pointing. Obviously, the kind of gestures possible are limited by the body tracking data available: the more of the body that is tracked, the more sophisticated the can gestures be. However, even with just the HMD tracker and glove or hand-held 3D mouse, quite a large number of different, intuitively appealing whole body gestures can be defined.

9.5. Communications

So far we have concentrated on a single isolated self and body within the VE. In this section we briefly consider the implications of the BCI paradigm for people communicating in a shared VE. In this context the body becomes a social as well as a personal object. The body is not only a private representation of self, and a means for interaction, but also a medium of communication with others. Others are represented to self through their bodies and the relationship of the body of others to that of self is extremely significant personally, socially, and culturally. In a recent book on the sociology of the body, Anthony Synnot discusses this aspect of the physical body:

> Anthony Synnot (Synnot 1993):
> "The body social is many things: the prime symbol of self, but also of the society; it is something we have, yet also what we are; it is both subject and object at the same time; it is individual and personal, as unique as a fingerprint or odour-plume, yet it is also common to all humanity ... The body is both an individual creation, physically and phenomenologically, and a cultural product; it is personal, and also state property."

Virtual bodies play a vital role in shared environments. The MultiG project at the Swedish Institute of Computer Science (Fahlen 1992; 1993) has constructed a distributed VE where participants at physically different locations take part in, for example, joint virtual meetings. People become aware of each other in the VE through a complex function of their aura ("a space that can be seen as the enabler of interactions with other objects"), focus (a "space within which the object directs its attention") and nimbus (a space "where the object projects some aspect of its presence to be perceived by other objects"). Participants are represented by a simple VB model (a block with eyes) which is nevertheless quite powerful in representing the presence of another being.

The body in MultiG is a static entity, with no limbs. However, in meetings body posture by itself can indicate the real events which are taking place, as opposed to the superficial events at the level of verbal discussion. Body posture can be conveyed with very little information - for example, in Figure 9.4a, the person depicted does not have to say anything for the observer to know what is being expressed.

Synnot shows that the face is the most powerful social symbol of self. Again, in meetings, where facial expression contradicts verbal agreement - which is likely to be more important? In Figure 9.4b we know that something is profoundly wrong in spite of the overt verbal agreement.

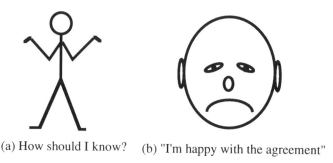

(a) How should I know?   (b) "I'm happy with the agreement"

Figure 9.4. Body Posture and Facial Expression.

Support for this kind of "body centered interaction" requires a different form of tracking technology. Rather than monitoring the body from the outside, using electromagnetic sensors such as the Polhemus, the body can be monitored from the "inside", using electrical recordings of the activity of the individual muscles or nerves, and electroencephalographic (EEG) recordings of potentials from the surface of the skull overlaying the motor cortex. There have been some applications of such biofeedback technology in VR (Lusted, Knapp and Lloyd 1992; 1993). Such work offers great promise for a different kind of sensor and tracking technology, more in tune with the requirements of BCI.

9.6. Conclusions

In this chapter we have concentrated on the role of the physical and virtual body in VR. The virtual body plays a primary role in immersive virtual environments:-

- it is the representation of self;
- it is likely to be a factor in increasing presence;
- it is the foundation of a model for interaction, body centered interaction;
- it is a medium of communication with others in shared environments;
- it may lead to a theory of Virtual Reality, through understanding of the relationship between the physical body, the virtual body, proprioception and presence.

The essence of Virtual Reality is that we (individual, group, simultaneously, asynchronously) are transported bodily to a computer generated environment. We recognize our own habitation there, through our body becoming an object in that environment. We recognize the habitation of others through the representation of their own bodies. This way of thinking can result in quite revolutionary forms of virtual communication. For example in asynchronous communication, suppose a person (X) wishes to leave a message for someone else (Y) who will enter the environment at some time after X has left. A traditional way of thinking would be to leave a written or perhaps auditory message. The VB, however, allows

X to leave a copy of his or her VB there in the environment to interact with Y, to perhaps act out a scenario depicting the required information (for example, in a training application). It is these new ways of thinking that must be adopted if VR is to fulfil its potential.

Acknowledgements

The research described in this paper is funded by the UK Science and Engineering Research Council (SERC), and Department of Trade and Industry, through grant CTA/2 of the London Parallel Applications Centre. Thanks to Anthony Steed for his continued help with the experiments described in this paper. The Virtual Treadmill is the subject of a patent application in the UK and other countries.

References

Barfield W, Weghorst S (1993) The Sense of Presence Within Virtual Environments: A Conceptual Framework, in *Human-Computer Interaction:Software and Hardware Interfaces*, Vol B, edited by G. Salvendy and M. Smith, Elsevier Publisher, pp.699-704.

Brooks FP Jr, Ouh-Young Ming, Batter J (1990) Project Grope - haptic displays for scientific visualization, *Computer Graphics* 24(4) pp.177-185.

Brooks FP et. al. (1992) *Final Technical Report: Walkthrough Project, Six Generations of Building Walkthroughs*, Department of Computer Science, University of North Carolina, Chapel Hill, N.C. pp.27599-3175.

Chrysanthou G, Slater M (1992) Dynamic Changes to Scenes Represented as BSP Trees, Eurographics 92, *Computer Graphics Forum*, 11(3), ed. A. Kilgour and L. Kjelldahl, pp.321-332.

Cox DR (1970) *Analysis of Binary Data*, London: Menthuen.

Dilts R., Grinder J, Bandler R, DeLozier J, Cameran-Bandler L (1979) *Neuro-Linguistic Programming I*, Meta Publications.

Ellis SR (1991) Nature and Origin of Virtual Environments: A Bibliographic Essay, *Computing Systems in Engineering*, 2(4), pp.321-347.

Fahlen L (1992). The MultiG Telepresence System, *Proceedings of the 4th Multi-G Workshop*, Stockholm-Kista, May 1992.

Fahlen L (1993) Virtual Reality and the MultG Project, *Virtual Reality International 93, Proceedings of the Third Annual Conference on Virtual Reality*, Meckler, London, 78-86.

Fairchild KM, Beng Hai Lee, Loo J, Ng H, Serra L (1993) The Heaven and Earth Virtual Reality: Designing Applications for Novice Users, *Proc. IEEE Virtual Reality Annual International Symposium (VRAIS)*, September 18-22, Seattle, Washington, pp.47-53.

Fisher S (1982) Viewpoint Dependent Imaging: An Interactive Stereoscopic Display, *Proceedings SPIE* 367, pp.41-45.

Fisher, S, McGreevy M, Humphries J, Robinett W (1986) Virtual Environment Display System, *Proc. ACM 1986 Workshop on 3D Interactive Graphics*, Chapel Hill, North Carolina, October pp.23-24.

Fisher S (1986) Telepresence master glove controller for dexterous robotic end-effectors, *SPIE Intelligent Robots and Computer Vision.*

Foley JD (1987) Interfaces For Advanced Computing, Scientific American, 257(4), October, pp.126-135.

Gibson EJ, Walk RD (1960) The "visual cliff", *Scientific American*, 202, 64-71.

Held RM, Durlach NI (1992) Telepresence, *Presence: Teleoperators and Virtual Environments*, 1, winter 1992, MIT Press, pp.109-112.

Heeter C (1992) Being There: The Subjective Experience of Presence, Telepresence, *Presence: Teleoperators and Virtual Environments,* 1(2), spring 1992, MIT Press, 262-271.

IwataH, Matsuda K (1992) Haptic Walkthrough Simulator: Its Design and Application to Studies on Cognitive Map, *Proc. Second International Conference on Artificial Reality and Tele-existence, ICAT 92*, pp.185-192.

Kalawsky R (1993) *The Science of Virtual Reality and Virtual Environments: A Technical, Scientific and Engineering Reference on Virtual Environments*, Addison-Wesley Publishing Company.

Loomis JM (1992a) Distal Attribution and Presence, Telepresence, *Presence: Teleoperators and Virtual Environments*, 1, winter 1992, MIT Press, , pp.113-119.

Loomis JM (1992b) Presence and Distal Attribution: Phenomenology, determinants, and assessment, *SPIE 1666 Human Vision, Visual Processing and Digital Display III,* 590-594.

Lusted HS, Knapp RB, Lloyd A (1992) Biosignal Processing in Virtual Reality, presented at the *3rd Annual Virtual Reality Conference,* San Jose, CA, 25th Sept. 1992.

Lusted HS, Knapp RB, Lloyd A (1993) Applications for Biosignal Processing in Virtual Reality, VR 93, Virtual Reality International, *Proceedings of the third annual conference on Virtual Reality*, London, pp134-137. Meckler.

Mackinlay JD, Card SK, Robertson GG (1990) Rapid Controlled Movement Through a Virtual 3D Workspace, *Computer Graphics (SIGGRAPH)* 24(4), , pp.171-176.

McCauley ME, Sharkey TJ (1993) Cybersickness: Perception of Self-motion in Virtual Environments, *Presence: Teleoperators and Virtual Environments*, 1(3), , pp.311-318.

Puerta, AM (1989) The power of shadows: shadow stereopsis. *Journal of the Optical Society of America,* Feb. 1989, 6, ,pp.309 - 311.

Robinett, W, Holloway R (1992) Implementation of Flying, Scaling and Grabbing in Virtual Worlds, *ACM Symposium on Interactive 3D Graphics*, Cambridge MA.

Sacks O (1985) *The Man Who Mistook His Wife for a Hat,* Picador.

SIGGRAPH 89, Panel Proceedings (1989) Virtual Environments and Interactivity: Windows to the Future, *Computer Graphics* 23(5), pp.7-38.

SIGGRAPH 90, Panel Proceedings (1990) Special Session, Hip, Hype and Hope - The Three Faces of Virtual Worlds.

Sheridan TB (1992) Musings on Telepresence and Virtual Presence, Telepresence, *Presence: Teleoperators and Virtual Environments*, 1, winter 1992, MIT Press, pp.120-126.

Slater M, Usoh M (1992) *An Experimental Exploration of Presence in Virtual Environments*, Department of Computer Science, QMW University of London.

Slater M, Usoh M (1993a) Presence in Immersive Virtual Environments, *Proceedings of the IEEE Conference - Virtual Reality Annual International Symposium*, IEEE Neural Networks Council, Seattle, WA (September, 1993), pp.90-96.

Slater M, Usoh M (1993b) Simulating Peripheral Vision in Immersive Virtual Environments, *Computers and Graphics*, November 1993.

Slater M, Usoh M (1994a) Representation Systems, Perceptual Position and Presence in Virtual Environments, Telepresence, *Presence: Teleoperators and Virtual Environments*, 2(3), Summer 1994 (in press).

Slater M., Steed A, Usoh M (1993c) The Virtual Treadmill: A Naturalistic Metaphor for Navigation in Immersive Virtual Environments, *First Eurographics Workshop on Virtual Reality*, ed. by M. Goebel, pp.71-86.

Slater M, Usoh M, Steed A (1994b) *Steps and Ladders in Virtual Reality*, Department of Computer Science, QMW University of London, submitted for publication.

Slater M, Usoh M, Steed A (1994c) *Depth of Presence in Virtual Environments*, QMW University of London, submitted for publication.

Song D, Norman M (1993) Nonlinear Interactive Motion Control Techniques for Virtual Space Navigation, *IEEE Virtual Reality Annual International Symposium* (VRAIS), September 18-22, Seattle, Washington, pp.111-117.

Steuer J (1992) Defining Virtual Reality: Dimensions Determining Telepresence, *Journal of Communication* 42(4), pp.73-93.

Sutherland IE (1965) The Ultimate Display, *Proceedings of the IFIPS Conference*, 2, pp.506-508.

Sutherland IE (1968) Head-Mounted Three-Dimensional Display, *Proceedings of the Fall Joint Computer Conference*, 33, pp.757-764.

Synnott A (1993) *The Body Social: Symbolism, Self and Society*, Routledge: London and New York.

Teitel MA (1990) The Eyephone, a Head Mounted Stereo Display, *SPIE*, 1256 Stereoscopic Displays and Applications.

Vaananen K, Bohm K (1993) Gesture Driven Interaction as a Human Factor in Virtual Environments - an approach with Neural Networks, in R.A. Earnshaw and M.A. Gigante (eds) *Virtual Reality Systems*, Academic Press, pp.93-106.

Zeltzer D (1992) Autonomy, Interaction and Presence, Telepresence, *Presence: Teleoperators and Virtual Environments*, 1, winter 1992, MIT Press, pp.127-132.

10

Manipulation and Exploration of Virtual Objects

Massimo Bergamasco
ARTS Lab, Scuola Superiore S. Anna, Pisa, Italy

10.1. Introduction

Recent developments of virtual environments (VE) applications have enhanced the problem of user's interaction with virtual entities. This paper deals with the research aspects associated with the control of manipulative and exploratory procedures of virtual objects. The terms manipulation and exploration of objects are used here with the same meaning they have in the real world. The objective of the research described in this paper is the development of software and hardware means that will allow the user to interact with virtual objects in a realistic, natural way, as he/she performs with real objects in the real world.

Manipulation procedures consist in grasping objects and moving them among the fingers according to sequences of movements that provide a finite displacement of the grasped object with respect to the palm. Let us imagine, for example, how the hand grasps a pencil from the table and re-arranges it by means of finger movements in order to reach the writing position.

Exploration procedures consist of controlled hand movements on the surface of objects; these movements are performed in order to extract information about specific features of the object, such as geometric shape, texture, hardness, temperature conditions, etc. It has been recognized that each feature requires specific patterns of hand movements in order to be extracted (Lederman et al. 1990).

Then the realistic control of the above procedures in VE implies that the man-machine interface system be capable of recording the movements of the human hand (fingers movements and gross movements of the hand) and also of replicating, on the human hand,

Artificial Life and and Virtual Reality Edited by Nadia Magnenat Thalmann and Daniel Thalmann
© 1994 John Wiley and Sons Ltd

virtual forces and contact conditions occurring when contact is detected between the virtual hand and the virtual object. Therefore hand movement recording and contact-force replication represent the two main functionalities of the interface system. At present, although several examples of tracking systems and glove-like advanced interfaces are available for hand and finger movements recording, the design of force and tactile feedback systems still presents methodological as well as technological problems (Bergamasco et al. 1991).

Another critical research issue in the framework of manipulation and exploration of virtual objects is represented by the modeling of the behavior of the virtual hand and virtual objects when relative contact occurs in VE.

These topics have represented the research activity on haptic interfaces development carried out so far at the ARTS Lab of the Scuola Superiore S. Anna.

10.2. Manipulation and Exploration of Virtual Objects

The user operating into an immersive VE usually wears head-mounted displays, sensorized gloves and possesses tracking systems on the metacarpus of the hand. At present, especially for commercial applications, grasping procedures of virtual objects consist of simple pointing and graphical hooking phases performed by the virtual hand with respect to the virtual object. However, according to this procedure, the only useful information to the purpose of grasping a virtual object is that obtained by the tracking sensor of the hand that is used, from the functional point of view, purely as a 3D mouse. The availability of a sensorized glove is completely useless or, at least, not fully exploited, according to whether the movements of the fingers are not considered at all or only used for recognizing a gesture - for example the transition between open fingers and closed fingers configurations - correspondent to the "grasping" meaning.

Realistic grasping procedures in VE means that the behavior of the virtual object, possessing specific physical properties, depends on the actions exerted on its surfaces by the virtual hand and, in the case, also by other virtual objects. The basis of a realistic grasping behavior is then the introduction of physically based modeling for the virtual object of interest. Graphical hooking tricks are avoided at the expense of increased modeling complexity and computational power requirements. The realistic modeling and the consequent graphical representation of the virtual object behavior when contact - or collisions - occur on its surface are then the starting point for the development of manipulative and explorative procedures of virtual objects.

The definition of realistic interactive procedures must be analyzed also from the point of view of the interface system to be developed.

When the user controls the manipulative procedure in VE, he/she has nothing in his/her real hands. The control of the procedure is performed by means of visual feedback. If we consider a realistic graphical representation of the VE, when the virtual hand is moved towards the virtual object, the pre-shaping movements of the fingers, that open in approaching the virtual object, bring some virtual fingers to be graphically covered by the virtual object, or it can happens that the visible virtual fingers cover the contact areas with the object. In these situations, in which the user cannot directly see the contact areas, how is it possible to notify the user of the incipient contact between the virtual fingers and the virtual object? This question is mainly related to the functional control that the user must perform and not to the graphical representation of the contact that can be easily solved by avoiding graphical interpenetration between the virtual fingers and the surface of the virtual object.

The answer to the above question is represented by the introduction of a force feedback system acting on the fingers of the user's hand. The role of the hand force feedback (HFF) system is that of blocking the flexion (closure) movements of the fingers as soon as contact between the virtual hand and the surface of the virtual object is detected. In this way the user perceives the sensation of being in contact with the virtual object.

Two considerations must be pointed out at this time of the presentation. The first is related to the fact that, although the HFF system is introduced, the interpenetration between the virtual hand (mainly the palmar surface of the fingers) and the surface of the virtual object cannot be avoided. In fact, there will always be a time delay, however short it could be, between the instant of time in which contact is detected by the modeling software and the time in which the HFF applies forces to the user's fingers. During this short time delay, since there is nothing among the fingers of the real hand, the human hand still goes on closing and interpenetration occurs. As explained later, interpenetration volumes for each contact area are exploited in order to have a simplified modeling of the normal contact force.

The second consideration deals with the different kind of forces that a general force feedback system should replicate to the user. These forces depend on the specific operation the user is doing and can largely vary both in terms of point of application, magnitude and also direction. For example, the forces involved during manipulative operations can be different from those arising during exploration procedures. In certain cases, in order to give a realistic sensation to the user, it is necessary to replicate the sensation of the weight of the virtual object, while for other operations, such as pushing tasks of virtual objects, the external forces to be applied to the human hand are completely different in terms of magnitude and direction. A presentation of the analysis of the range of forces to be replicated during manipulative and explorative procedures in VE has been given in (Bergamasco 1992). The results of this analysis show that the design of force feedback systems should start by having a knowledge of the forces that must be replicated for the specific operation the user is required to control in the VE. Once the spectrum of ideal forces is known, the ultimate design of the force feedback system must be addressed by optimizing the spectrum of obtainable forces. This is done by accurately studying the kinematics of the force feedback system (Allotta and Bergamasco 1994). In the case the force feedback system is located on the human limbs, constraints on the mobility of these limbs should be taken into account in order to allow the user to perform the manipulative or explorative procedure in a true natural way. Then design solutions and actuators/sensors technologies can affect the typology of the forces that can be replicated.

The solution we have identified for the development of force feedback systems allowing the user to control manipulative and exploratory procedures in VE is based on the following assumption: the replication of the spectrum of obtainable forces is shared among different force feedback systems. Each of these systems possesses specific performances in terms of point of application, magnitude and direction of the forces to be replicated. This solution is shown in Figure 10.1.

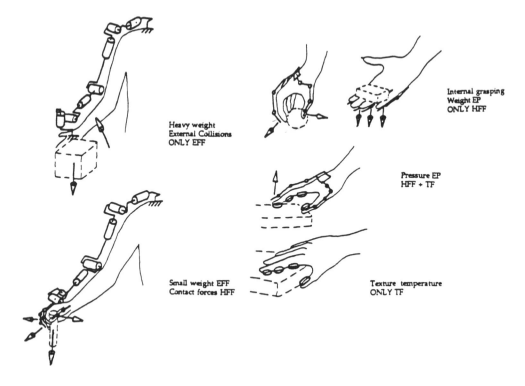

Figure 10.1. The distribution of the spectrum of reproducible forces among the different force feedback system. EFF: external force feedback systems; HFF: hand force feedback system; TF: tactile feedback system.

High magnitude external forces, such as collisions acting on the arm or on the hand or the weight of "heavy" virtual objects, are replicated by an external force feedback (EFF) system (Figure 10.1a). As it will be shown in the following sections, the EFF we have developed consists of a seven degrees of freedom (DOF) arm exoskeleton.

In the case of grasping operations, when the weight of the virtual object is large EFF is still controlled, while contact forces on the fingers are replicated by the hand force feedback (HFF) system (Figure 10.1b).

By decreasing the dimensions of the grasped virtual object, or when low magnitude external forces must be replicated to the fingers, only the HFF system is active (Figure 10.1c).

Especially for exploratory procedures, such as those procedures aiming at recognizing the hardness of a virtual object, HFF is considered; its action, producing forces in correspondence of the contact areas of the fingers, can be integrated with the replication of local geometrical features of the object that are generated by the tactile feedback (TF) system (Figure 10.1d).

Other kinds of object features, such as surface texture or temperature, can be replicated by means of the TF system (Figure 10.1e).

10.3. Modeling of a Realistic Grasping Procedure in VE

As outlined in the previous section, a realistic control of manipulation procedures in VE cannot be obtained without physically based modeling and faithful 3D graphical representation of the virtual hand and virtual object behaviors.

The modeling process for grasping procedures we have developed is divided in three phases (Bergamasco et al. 1994b):

1. determination of the contact geometry (contact areas) between the virtual hand and the virtual object;
2. modeling of the contact forces for each contact group;
3. determination of the object behavior inside the grasp (object stability and consequent slippage of the object); behavior in the case of pushing operations.

The first phase is aimed at determining the contact areas between the virtual hand and the virtual object. The developed algorithm involves the construction of a purposely designed grid of control points that can be considered as attached to the palmar side of the virtual hand during the manipulation procedure. The grid is composed of several groups G_i (with i = 1,..., 17) contact points P_{ij}. The groups G_i covers each phalanx on the fingers and thumb and also two regions of the palm; in total we have 17 groups. The points P_{ij} belonging to the same group G_i are arranged according to an orthogonal array of (5x7) elements (see Figure 10.2).

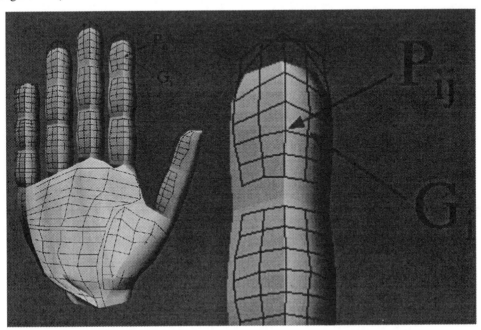

Figure 10.2. Map of the points on the palmar surface of the virtual hand.

The approach we have followed for the definition of the collision detection algorithm exploits two different steps. The first step referees to the condition in which the virtual object does not belong to the augmented virtual hand workspace. The term virtual hand workspace means the volume reachable by the fingers during manipulation and it is located towards the palmar side of the hand. During this first step tests on the distance between a gross control point (g.c.p.), located in the centre of the virtual hand metacarpus, and each surface of the object is calculated. As soon as the calculated distance becomes lower than a determined threshold (correspondent of the maximum dimension of the augmented hand workspace), the collision detection control is shifted to a different control algorithm that takes into account the distance between each of the control points P_{ij} defined above and each surface of the virtual object. At present we are working with virtual objects possessing simple geometry, such as spheres, cylinders and cubes, which surfaces can be easily analytically described. However work is in progress for the definition of the collision detection algorithms also for virtual objects of complex geometry. The introduction of a large number of control points, although introduces a large computational expense, possesses the advantage of geometrically characterizing the contact areas of the hand where contact occurs. This fact is a fundamental requirement for the control of HFF systems.

Each contact area is the set of points P_{ij} , belonging to a contact group G_i , which distance to the object surface has been detected as negative. Once contact areas have been calculated, the second phase of the process generates the contact forces correspondent to each of those areas. At present, both virtual object and virtual hand are considered as "rigid" objects: thus an interpenetration volume can be defined for each contact area. We assume that the normal contact force be proportional to the interpenetration volume. A representation of contact areas on the surface of the virtual hand and the normal forces calculated for each contact area are shown in Figure 10.3 (see Color Section).

The figure represents the result of a real experiment carried out (see Figure 10.4, Color Section) by utilizing a glove-like advanced interface system realized in our laboratory and called ARTS Glove which is capable of recording the movements of all the degrees of freedom of the human hand. The ARTS Glove is shown in Figure 10.5 (see Color Section). Gross motion of the hand are tracked by a Polhemus sensor, while the modeling and the graphical software are running on a Silicon Graphics 440-VGXT workstation. Representation rate of 30 frames/second has been obtained and good control in real-time conditions has been achieved.

The final phase of the modeling process refers to the determination of the behavior of the virtual object based on the exerted forces acting on it during the manipulative or explorative procedure. The first step in this phase is that of calculating the friction forces for each contact area. This task can be done only after having verified the relative movement of each contact group with respect to the object surface. The importance of this phase is fundamental for the control of the manipulative procedure. In fact, in the case the user wishes to grasp the virtual object, the wrench system exerted by the virtual fingers on the object must equilibrate, in every configuration of the hand, the virtual weight or other external wrenches acting on the object. Only after having verified this condition is it possible to represent the virtual object moving inside the grasp performed by the virtual fingers. No graphical hooking is done but, on the contrary, the behavior of the object is based on the result of this modeling (physically-based) process. Details of the algorithm utilized for the object stability inside the grasp and its successive behavior determination are beyond the scope of this paper and can be found in (Bergamasco et al. 1994b). The approach followed for grasping stability determination can be referred to the one described by (Kerr and Roth 1986); the modeling of the dynamic behavior of the object has followed the procedure described in (Baraff 1992). Preliminary experiments on grasping and manipulation procedures of virtual objects have been performed with the same hardware described above (and then without the utilization of a HFF system) by considering point contact without friction type for each contact area.

10.4. External Force Feedback Systems

In Section 10.2 the modalities of force replication according to the different operations (grasping, manipulation, exploration, pushing) to be controlled in VE have been presented. As schematically depicted in Fig. 10.1, it is assumed that collisions against the objects of the virtual environment as well as the weight of "heavy" virtual objects are replicated by an external force feedback (EFF) system. Among the different topologies of Force Feedback systems, or force replicating devices (FRDs) as outlined in (Allotta and Bergamasco 1994), developed so far for the replication of the forces to the human arm, we have addressed the design and realization of an arm exoskeleton (Bergamasco et al. 1994a). The arm exoskeleton is a mechanical structure wrapping up the whole arm of the user. The mechanical structure possesses seven degrees of freedom correspondent to the joints of the human arm from shoulder to the wrist, and allows natural mobility to the human arm. At present a version of the exoskeleton with 5 DOF (from shoulder joints to prono-supination joint of the forearm) (see Figure 10.6, Color Section) has been tested during tasks of interaction with the VE (see Figure 10.7, Color Section).

Joint rotation sensors and actuators are integrated in each joint; the arm exoskeleton structure follows the movements of the human arm and the information obtained from the joint rotation sensors are used to drive the correspondent movements of the virtual arm in VE. Once contact is detected in the VE the joint actuators are controlled in order to apply the desired contact forces at the level of the human hand. The control of the joint actuators is performed by considering, for each configuration of the arm, also additional torques devoted to implement the gravity compensation of the mechanical structure. In this way, the human operator does not have to counterbalance the weight of the links' structures during the movement of his/her arm.

Experiments have been carried out dealing with the exploration of geometrical features of the virtual environment as well as in the recognition of the shape of large (not seizable) virtual objects. The user, without exploiting visual feedback information, has demonstrated the feasibility of virtual object shape recognition tasks carried out by exploiting the only force information replicated, at the level of his/her hand, by the arm exoskeleton. Several collision functions have been tested and, at present, the tuning of the whole system, comprehensive not only of the mechanical structure of the exoskeleton, but also of its transputer-based controller and communication links with the graphical workstation, are in progress.

10.5. Hand Force Feedback Systems

The replication of contact forces at the finger level is performed by a hand force feedback (HFF) system consisting of a set of mechanical exoskeleton structures covering the fingers of the human hand. Each exoskeleton is capable of recording the movement of each joint of the finger and, at the same time, exerting forces in correspondence of the central part of the palmar surface of each phalanx. A picture of a prototypical HFF system developed in our laboratory is shown in Figure 10.8. The phalanxes of each fingers are attached to the links of the exoskeleton structure by means of purposely designed mechanical particulars; this particulars are connected to a glove which facilitates the wearing operation of the whole system.

The design of the HFF has considered the analysis of the set of forces to be replicated on each finger during manipulative and exploratory procedures in VE (Bergamasco 1992). Constraints due to present available actuator technologies (in particular the ratio power/volume and power/weight are disadvantageous with respect to the requirements of integration on a system that must be located on the human hand) and required ultimate mobility of the human hand have driven the kinematic solution. In particular we have assumed that the HFF be capable of exerting on the phalanxes forces possessing the following characteristics:

- line of action: normal to the longitudinal axis and belonging to the sagittal plane of the finger;
- direction: capable of producing an extension movement of the finger;
- magnitude: limited to the mechanical performances of the actuators.

The characteristics of the forces replicated by the HFF we have developed are illustrated in Figure 10.9.

At present the assembly phase of the HFF system for the whole hand (three fingers, little finger excluded, and the thumb) is in progress. Tests on the mechanical performances, in terms of effective applied forces to the phalanxes during both static and dynamic conditions, and on the control of the system have been addressed with the test equipment shown in Figure 10.10 (see Color Section).

10.6. Tactile Feedback Systems

The presence of a tactile feedback (TF) system reveals fundamental in order to integrate, in the advanced interface component, the functionality of rendering to the user information about local features of the virtual object. The term "local features" refers to different classes of object properties achievable from exploration tasks performed by the human hand. We can roughly classify local object features according on whether the contact between the hand and the virtual object is characterized by static or dynamic components.

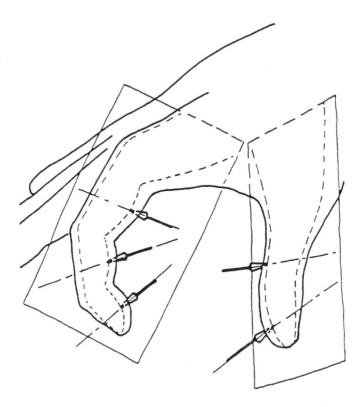

Figure 10.9. Representation of the active forces reproduced on the fingers by the HFF system.

In the framework of static contact conditions the extracted local features to be considered are those related to the local geometry of the object, such as the determination of a plane surface or the presence of an edge or of a vertex on the surface; temperature conditions of the object surface can be also considered as a feature extracted by static contact.

Relative movement between the virtual finger and the virtual object surface is exploited, as it happens in most cases of real exploratory procedures, for extracting other types of information from the object surface. Practical examples are those exploratory procedures aimed at recognizing the texture of the object surface or the presence of regions with different hardness.

The approach we have followed in our laboratory for the development of tactile feedback systems is not related to the design and realization of tactile effectors but, on the contrary, to the study of the rendering software modules generating the appropriate inputs to ideal tactile effectors. Appropriate input functions can be considered both in terms of indentation profiles for local geometry and texture reproduction as well as in terms of temperature or heat flow profiles for the replication of temperature conditions. This methodology is justified by the present lack of precise information about the effective requirements and specifications for the design of tactile feedback systems and also of reliable microfabrication technology for their hardware implementation. The modeling of the above mentioned input functions has been conceived in two steps: the first deals with the complete modeling of the physical phenomenon, which requires heavy computational load, and a second phase aimed at obtaining a similar modeling of the physical phenomenon but with reduced complexity and real-time performances. The software modules obtained as the output of the second phase will be implemented for practical experiments.

10.7. Conclusions

The approach followed in our laboratory dealing with the development of software and hardware components dedicated to the implementation of man-machine interfaces utilized for the interaction with VE has been presented. The objective of the described research approach is the capability, for the human operator, to control manipulative and exploratory procedures of virtual objects in a realistic, natural way.

Two primary aspects of manipulation and exploration processes in VE have been described: a) the definition of the roles of external force, hand force and tactile feedback systems that represent the main components of the man-machine interface system for the control of the interaction process, and b) the modeling of the grasping procedures, including both the determination of contact areas and contact forces on the virtual hand and virtual object as well as the physically-based modeling of the virtual object.

The description of the different components of the interface system developed in our laboratory has been presented. The work carried out until now is aimed at obtaining a complete haptic interface system in the near future: the ultimate goal of our research is in fact the realization of tools allowing the user to recognize virtual object features with the same modalities he/she performs in a real environment. We believe that research efforts devoted to this objective can open a wide spectrum of future applications for VE technologies; in fact, the control of manipulation of virtual objects can be considered as a primary need for interaction processes with VE in the next future.

Acknowledgements

The work described in this chapter has been carried out under the contracts EP 5363 GLAD-IN-ART and ESPRIT Basic Research 6358 SCATIS with the European Union. The author wishes to thank Silicon Graphics S.p.A. for the collaboration.

References

Allotta B, Bergamasco M (1994) The Range of Wrenches that can be Exterted by a Force Replication Device, submitted to the *International Workshop on Robot and Human Communication ROMAN'94,* Nagoya, Japan.

Baraff D (1992) Rigid Body Simulation, *Lecture Note for the SIGGRAPH '92 Course on "A Introduction to Physically Based Modeling,"* Chicago.

Bergamasco M., De Micheli DM, Parrini G, Salsedo F, Scattareggia Marchese S (1991) Design considerations for glove-like advanced interfaces, *Proc. of the International Conference on Advanced Robotics '91* ICAR, Pisa, Italy.

Bergamasco M (1992) Design of Hand Force Feedback Systems for Glove-like Advanced Interfaces, *Proc. of International Workshop on Robot and Human Communication ROMAN'92,* Tokyo, Japan.

Bergamasco M., Allotta B Bosio L Ferretti L, Parrini G Prisco GM, Salsedo F Sartini G (1994a) An Arm Exoskeleton System for Teleoperation and Virtual Environments Applications," accepted to the *IEEE International Conference on Robotics and Automation,* San Diego, CA.

Bergamasco M., Degl'Innocenti P, Rigucci G Bucciarelli D (1994b) Grasping and Moving Objects in Virtual Environments: a Preliminary Approach Towards a Realistic Behaviour, submitted to the *International Workshop on Robot and Human Communication ROMAN'94,* Nagoya, Japan.

Kerr J, Roth B (1986) Analysis of Multifinger Hands," *Intern. J. Robotics Research,* Vol.4, No.4.

Lederman SJ Klaztky R (1990) *Haptic Exploration and Object Representation, Vision and Action: the Control of Grasping,* Melvyn A. Goodale (Ed.), Ablex Publishing Corporation, Norwood, New Jersey.

11

Fundamentals of Auditory Virtual Environment

Hilmar Lehnert
Lehrstuhl fuer allgemeine Elektrotechnik und Akustik, Ruhr-Universitaet Bochum

11.1. Introduction

Virtual environment refers to a technology which is capable of shifting a subject into a different environment without physically moving him/her. To this end the inputs into the subject's sensory organs are manipulated in such a way, that the perceived environment is associated with the desired virtual environment and not with the physical one. The manipulation process is controlled by a computer model that is based on the physical description of the virtual environment. Consequently, the technology is able to create almost arbitrarily perceived environments. Although mainly based in the domain of computer graphics, virtual environment is by its nature a multi-modal technology. Suitable treatment of the non-visual modalities such as auditory, tactile/thermal and force-feedback perception is vital for the vast majority of virtual environment applications.

In this chapter some fundamentals of auditory virtual environments are presented. Most of the results are from SCATIS, an ESPRIT basic research project, which is funded by the European Union. The objective of SCATIS (Spatially Coordinated Auditory/Tactile Interactive Scenario) is to tackle fundamental psychophysical problems of auditive, tactile, and multi-modal virtual environments.

Artificial Life and and Virtual Reality Edited by Nadia Magnenat Thalmann and Daniel Thalmann
© 1994 John Wiley and Sons Ltd

11.2. Psychophysical Fundamentals

Before discussing the methods of application, and where and how the auditory modality has to be treated, it might be useful to survey some psychophysical fundamentals of hearing.

From a physiological point of view, the auditory system can be divided into four main parts: the external ear (torso, shoulders, head and pinnae), the middle ear (eardrum, ossicular chain), the inner ear (cochlea), and the nervous system with the brain. The external ear includes all acoustically relevant parts of the body. As will be explained later, the external ear is of paramount importance for spatial hearing. The middle ear is mainly an impedance transformer that connects the inner ear to the sound field. In the inner ear mechanical vibrations are converted into nerve spikes, which are processed by the nervous system.

11.2.1. Spatial Hearing

It is an every-day experience that humans can localize three-dimensionally sound sources in space. Three-dimensional localization of vision can be explained very easily: the two sensors are both two-dimensional and the third dimension is coded into the lateral disparity of the pictures. Here, the auditory system is very different, since the sensors are small compared to the wavelength, and therefore they are spatially zero-dimensional. Extracting spatial positions from only two sound signals is not unlike creating three-dimensional pictures with only two available pixels. In the following, this phenomenon is briefly explained. For a comprehensive review see Blauert (1983).

When a sound wave impinges on a human's head pronounced diffraction effects occur. These diffraction effects are dependent on the direction of incidence. As a consequence the resulting sound pressure signals at the ear drums are also functions of the direction of incidence and not only of the sound pressure signals of the incident sound wave. To be more precise, the external ear is a linear, direction dependent filter. Sound arriving from a specific direction of incidence is filtered according to this direction. Thus spatial information is coded into temporal and spectral information in the sound pressure signals in the eardrums. The brain is able to recognize these spectral and temporal patterns and to recover the spatial information. With respect to the three dimensions of space in spherical coordinates, the main mechanism for sound source localization can be separately identified for each coordinate .

(a) azimuth
Azimuth (left/right) perception is mainly based on interaural differences, that is to say the differences between the signals at the two eardrums. Azimuth can be perceived more accurately than the other coordinates. The minimum localization blurr is better than 1 degree.

(b) elevation
Elevation (front/back/up/down) perception is mainly based on monaural cues. They depend on whether the elevation angle specific frequency bands (so-called directional bands) are amplified or attenuated. Elevation perception is less accurate than azimuth perception. The best elevation accuracy is about 5 degrees (noise signals).

(c) distance

The mechanisms for distance perception in hearing are still under investigation. It was widely believed that the level of a (known) sound source was the main cue for distance judgment. However, recent investigations (Nielson 1991) have shown that if only level cues are provided distance perception is relatively poor. The human auditory system probably uses cues from the environment e.g. by analyzing reflection patterns. Accordingly, the accuracy of distance judgment depends largely on environmental conditions.

11.2.2. Listening in Reflective Environments

The acoustical environment has a significant impact not only on distance perception but also on a variety of other perceptual attributes. In fact being in an anechoic chamber where "no" acoustical environment is present is a rather unnatural and sometimes even unpleasant experience. Each acoustic space creates its own specific auditory image. Moreover, this auditory image, commonly referred to as auditory spatial impression (Reichardt et al. 1978) is a property of the environment and not of the sound signal it is excited by. A church sounds different from a living room or from a manufacturing plant, no matter whether the spaces are excited by speech, music, or noise. The perceptual attributes of auditory environment are manifold. Room acoustics have developed a large number of subjective parameters to describe attributes of auditory spatial impression, for example reverberance and spaciousness (see e.g. Lehnert 1993b)

With respect to virtual environment applications, it seems important to note that in any natural environment the listener acquires an auditory sense of immersion. Due to the reflective surfaces sound field components arrive from all directions of incidence. The listener is surrounded by sound and feels present in a natural sound field. There is a large difference between the auditory perception of being inside an environment and listening to a reproduction with conventional reproduction techniques such as intensity stereo, since the spatial reflection pattern that reaches the listener is that of the reproduction space and not that of the recording space. A more detailed discussion of this topic can be found in Lehnert (1992a).

11.2.3. Auditory Perception in Virtual Environments

In the previous sections, two important perception attributes provided by the human auditory system were discussed: sound source localization and spatial impression. These skills are both largely signal independent. Accordingly, these properties are a true function of the acoustic environment and a virtual environment generator should be able to create these perceptual attributes on the basis of the environment data. Besides these environment related perceptions, there are other abilities of the auditory system, which may be useful for virtual environment applications. These abilities depend on the sound signals provided, and so they are a function of both the environment and the input signals. First of all, sound sources can be identified, for example in a group of speakers, or a specific speaker can be identified by his voice. Furthermore, as icons are used to code an abstract function by means of a small picture, EARCONS can be used to present auditorily various kinds of message to a subject in a virtual space. If more than one sound source is active simultaneously, attention can be focused on a specific source at will, provided the sources are spatially separated (so-called cocktail party effect).

In nearly every situation listeners are surrounded by background sounds like fans, traffic, people talking, birds singing, wind blowing etc. These background sounds are used to monitor ongoing activities and to sense the presence of other people. The total absence of any background sounds is perceived to be very unnatural. The frequently observed "being under water"-feeling when being exposed to a virtual environment is most likely caused by the lack of any consistent auditive background scenario.

11.3. Physical Fundamentals

In this section some fundamentals of room acoustics will be surveyed very briefly. For a more detailed description, the reader may refer to a number of textbooks (e.g. Beranek 1962; Kuttruff 1973; Cremer and Müller 1978; Barron 1993). Sound waves in air can be described by a simple differential equation

$$\frac{\partial^2 p}{\partial r^2} = c^{-2} \frac{\partial^2 p}{\partial t^2} \qquad (11.1)$$

where the second spatial derivative of the sound pressure, p, is proportional the second temporal derivative of p. The proportional factor is the inverse square of the speed of sound, c.

Reflective surfaces represent the boundary conditions for which this differential equation has to be solved. Unfortunately, analytic solutions can only be obtained for very few geometric cases. In principal, numerical solutions are possible using for example a BEM (boundary-element method) after spatially quantizing the boundary condition. However, due to the large range of wavelengths in consideration (2 cm - 20 m), the required computational effort is extremely high. Approximations have to be used to obtain results for practical applications.

The most common approximation is that of geometric acoustics. In geometric acoustics a special solution of the wave equation is used: the sound ray. A wave front can be split into a number of sound rays. These sound rays can be individually traced. When hitting a surface, the rays are reflected according to the reflection law. The reflected sound field component is again a sound ray and the angle of emittance equals the angle of incidence.

This solution is valid as long as the wavelength of the sound is small in comparison to the linear dimensions of the surfaces, and large in comparison to the roughness and curvature of the surfaces. Looking again at the large range of wavelengths, the conditions for the application of geometric acoustics are practically never fulfilled. However, the results obtained by this approximation have proved to be surprisingly good. One possible explanation for this behavior is the following.

The geometric model treats the specular reflections correctly, but neglects diffuse reflections. A main difference between a diffuse and a specular reflection is that the former spreads the reflected sound energy over a wide solid angle range whereas the latter covers only a very small solid angle for the specular reflection. Accordingly, the energy density of a specularly reflected sound wave is much higher than that of a diffusely reflected one, even if the total reflected energy is the same. Therefore specular reflections are likely to have more significant effects on the perception than diffuse reflections have.

Provided that the conditions for the use of geometric acoustics are fulfilled, the mirror image principle may be used as shown in Figure 11.1.

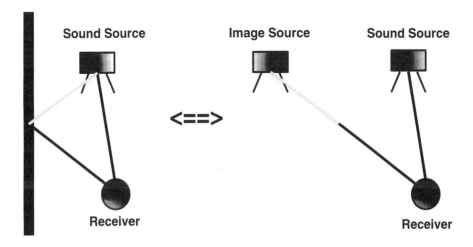

Figure 11.1. Mirror image principle.

A reflection can be modeled by mirroring the sound source at the plane of the reflecting surface. The resulting secondary sound source maintains the spatial (direction of incidence) and temporal (distance) properties of the reflection. The spectral properties can be modelled by filtering the signal of the emitted signal with a filter representing the reflection properties of the surface. In the case of a rigid surface, the secondary sound source emits the same signal as the primary source. The directivity of the sound source can be modeled in an analogous manner.

11.4. Computer Modeling

As already stated in the introduction, virtual environments are created by manipulating the input to the sensory organs according to a computer model of the virtual world. The most common way to do this is to calculate the relevant physical quantities at the position of the respective sensory organs, which would occur if the subject were in the virtual space. In the case of the auditory modality this means that the sound pressure signals at the subject's eardrums have to be calculated.

Computer models for auditory virtual environment are usually split into two stages. In the sound field modeling stage, the sound field components are calculated at the position of the receiver (with the receiver being absent). In the second stage, called auralization, these sound field components are made audible. This separation into two stages is used since the first stage is independent from the signal of the sound sources. Only in the second stage are the input signals processed and only the second stage needs access to the input signals.

The interface between the two stages is provided by the so-called spatial map of secondary sound sources (Lehnert and Blauert 1989). As described above, the secondary sources represent reflections in the environment.

11.4.1. Sound Field Modeling

The input into the sound field model is the physical description of the environment. The description has to include all parameters that would influence the sound field in the corresponding real environment. These parameters are

- geometrical and reflection properties of surrounding surfaces,
- position, orientation, and directional characteristics of the sound source(s),
- position, orientation, and directional characteristics of the receiver, and
- transmission properties of the propagation medium.

It should be noted that the reflection properties and the directivities have to be described as a complex function of frequency. These properties are heavily frequency dependent and do not only affect the energy but also the phase of the corresponding sound wave.

The task of the sound field modeling program is to calculate all reflections or mirror image sources in the environment for a given set of data. This task is similar to that of a visual rendering program common in the fields of computer graphics. Accordingly, the methods used for both domains are related. Since the graphical rendering methods are widely known, acoustics and optics are briefly compared in the following to identify common features and main differences.

One of the main differences is certainly the propagation speed in air. The propagation of light is so fast (3.108 m/s) that for every change in the environment, the stationary solution is immediately reached and, consequently, only the stationary solution is of interest. This is not the case in acoustics, since the speed of sound in air is only 344 m/s. Therefore smooth transients between two states are easily perceivable. Moreover, the transient events contain much information and the transition between two steady states needs to be modeled very accurately. Furthermore, most sound signals of interest are never stationary. The variations occur much faster than the time needed to establish a stationary sound field and therefore a stationary state is never reached at all.

Another major difference between optics and acoustics is a consequence of the different bandwidths of the modalities. The wavelength in consideration is in the order of some 100 nanometers in optics and ranges from 2 cm to 20 m in acoustics. In optics the predominating type of reflection is the diffuse reflection. In acoustics the linear dimensions of objects are always in the same order of magnitude as the wavelength and most reflections are neither specular nor diffuse but something inbetween.

For example, Figure 11.2 shows the reflection pattern of a 2 m x 2 m square rigid surface at 1 kHz for 45 degree incidence. Strong diffraction and diffusion effects can be observed.

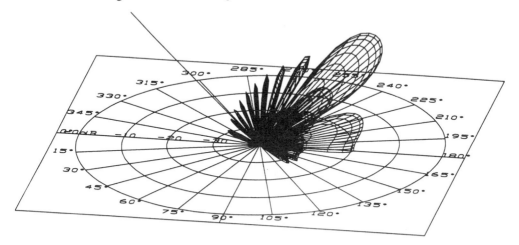

Figure 11.2. Calculated reflection pattern of a square surface of 2 m edge length for an 1 kHz sound wave at 45 degrees incident.

Specular reflections can be calculated using ray- tracing or the mirror image method. A detailed description of the algorithms, different dialects and their advantages and disadvantages can be found in Lehnert and Blauert (1992b) and Lehnert (1993b). The main difference between optical and acoustical raytracing is that in acoustics only one receiving point usually located in the center of the subject's head, needs to be considered. The generation of the two eardrum signals will be performed in the next stage. Another difference is that the order of reflection is much higher for acoustical ray-tracing. Comparing the average distance between two reflections (mean free path length) to the reverberation time results in a required order of about 50 to 100. Since the computation times for tracing such high orders are extremely high, simplifications are used to create adequate late reflections and reverberation.

A suitable method for rendering diffuse reflections in optics is the so-called radiosity algorithm (Goral et al. 1984). Due to the large difference in propagation speed between light and sound, this method cannot be applied in acoustics without significant modifications. A possible adaptation was described by Lewers (1993), where a network of surface nodes was constructed. These nodes exchange energy according to the form factors between the surfaces. The energy transfers are delayed according to the travel time. Point in time, angle of emittance and spectrum of the energy transfer are controlled by a statistical process, which is based on the results of a preceding raytracing procedure.

11.4.2. Auralization

The task of the auralization is to make the result of the sound field model audible. This result is the spatial map of secondary sound source, where each of the secondary sound sources emits a signal which is a filtered version of the signal from the primary source. For a single secondary source of, for example, second order the auralization can be performed using the structure of an "auralization unit" as shown in Figure 11.3.

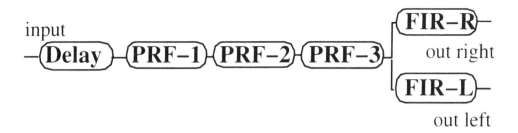

Figure 11.3. Structure of an auralization unit for a second order reflection.

First, the signal is delayed according to the distance between the secondary source and the receiver. Then three different pre-filters (PRF1 - PRF2) are used to create the spectral modifications of the secondary source with respect to the primary source. PRF1 models the directivity and PRF2 and PRF3 the reflections properties of the surfaces where the sound ray was reflected. Finally, spatial imaging is done by filtering the ear with the so-called head related impulse response (e.g. Moller 1992). These impulse responses describe the diffraction effect around the subjects head. They are measured by inserting miniature microphones into the ear canals of a subject and measuring the sound pressure spectrum when being exposed to a sound wave arriving from a specific direction of incidence. For each direction a set of impulse responses is stored. If equalized properly these impulse responses facilitate to create an auditory event at any desired location in the perceptive space. Figure 11.4 shows such a measured transfer function for a randomly selected direction of incidence of 30 degree azimuth and 30 degree elevation. At low frequencies the magnitude of the transfer functions is about unity (0 dB) since the head becomes almost acoustically transparent there. In the mid range, the signal at the left ear becomes significantly amplified with respect to the signal at the right one. In the range between 5 kHz and 10 kHz both transfer functions show pronounced dips which, are mainly important for elevation perception.

To be able to listen into the virtual environments, the outputs of all auralization units are simply added up and reproduced over headphones. Headphone reproduction offers two advantages: it is independent from the reproduction environment and it enables independent control over both ear signals.

For non real-time systems this structure needs to be implemented only once and all secondary sources can be processed subsequently. In this case it is even sufficient to use an unit impulse as the input signal. The result of the simulation procedure is the so-called binaural room impulse response, which is the pair of sound pressure signals at the ear drums, when the source is excited by an impulse. Since the sound field in a closed space is a linear system, the ear signals for arbitrary input signals can be calculated by simply convoluting the binaural room impulse response with the input signal.

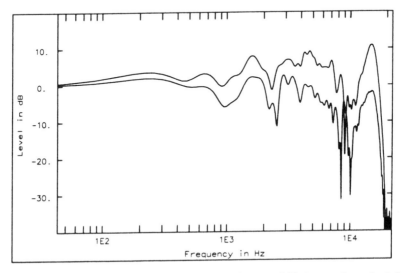

Figure 11.4. Head related transfer function for sound incidence of 30 degrees from the left and 30 degrees from above measured on a typical subject.

11.5. Real-Time Implementation

If the virtual environment is to be interactive, two requirements in the generating system must be fulfilled: Firstly, the delay between an action of the subject and the corresponding change in the sound pressure signals displayed to the subject must be below the perceptual threshold. This delay is commonly referred to as time lag. Secondly, the number of display updates per time interval must be so high that all movements are perceived as being continuous and smooth. The number of updates per time interval is commonly called frame rate. These two physical quantities correspond to the perceptual attributes "responsiveness" and "smoothness" (Appino et al. 1991). Required maximum time lag and minimum frame rate are presently not known for the auditory domain and it is one of the objectives of SCATIS to investigate this problem. It is expected that both values lie in the range of some ten milliseconds to about 100 milliseconds. Therefore, high requirements arise for both software and hardware components of the virtual environment generator. The consequence for the sound field model is that tracing for reflection with a order higher than two or three is not feasible. Thus, only the very early reflections can be traced in real time (Lehnert and

Blauert 1991). The later reflections and the reverberation have to be computed by a parametric reverberation algorithm (e.g. Schroeder 1962).

These simplifications may not significantly degrade the quality of the simulation, since with increasing order the number of reflections increases and the energy of a single reflection decreases. The higher order reflections are not perceived individually and the auditory relevance of a single reflection is very low. A statistical approach which is able to correctly mimic the frequency dependent energy decay over time and which is able to reproduce some spatial properties of the reverberation seems feasible. Regarding the auralization, the structure of a single auralization unit as shown in Figure 11.3 can still be applied. However, the computational requirement of a single unit is larger than 106 multiply-accumulate-add-operations per second and so suitable specialized hardware must be developed for this purpose and multiple auralization units have to be used in parallel. The implementation currently under development in SCATIS will use the following approach (Durlach et al. 1994). The six degrees of freedom of the subject's head will be tracked using a commercial device based on a magnetic field principle. The sound field model will be executed on a multi- purpose workstation. Benchmarks have shown, that reflections up to the second order can be traced in geometries with simple or moderate complexity. Auralization will be performed by a specially developed auralization processor. This processor consists of a free programmable network of DSP (digital signal processor) chips, digital signal inputs and outputs, and digital summation modules. The device will operate at a sampling rate of 44.1 kHz with a minimum quantization of 16 bits. It is intended to realize at least 32 independent auralization units.

11.6. Conclusion

For a large number of virtual environment applications suitable treatment of the auditory modality is unavoidable. If properly implemented, auditory perception attributes such as sound source localization and identification, spatial impression and auditive background scenarios will contribute significantly to the feeling of immersion in the virtual space. Auditory virtual environment generators are commonly separated into two parts: a sound field model and an auralization processor. The sound field model performs a rendering procedure similar to those in computer graphics and visual virtual environment. Algorithms like ray-tracing, image method, and radiosity are used to calculate the spatial, temporal and spectral properties of the sound field at the listener's position. The auralization processor enables listening into the virtual sound field by coding the results of the sound field model into the source signals.

Temporal properties are implemented by delaying signals, spectral properties by monaural filtering and spatial properties by binaural filtering with the so-called head related transfer function. High performance special purpose hardware is required for this task.

There is still a large need for investigating into the psychophysics of virtual environment generators. The perceptual consequences of typical effects like time lag, frame rate, time-lag jitter and frame jitter are not well understood even for a single modality, let alone in a multi-modal environment. There is hope that the perceptual quality of virtual environments can be improved greatly if we get a better understanding of the way in which humans perceive their environment and how a sense of presence is established.

References

Appino et al. (1992) An architecture for Virtual Worlds, *Presence*, Vol.1, No.1, pp.1-17.

Barron M (1993) *Auditorium Acoustics and Architectural Design*, E and FN Spon, London, England.

Beranek L (1962) *Music, Acoustics and Architecture*, John Wiley and Sons, New York, USA.

Blauert J (1983) *Spatial Hearing, The Psychophysics of Human Sound Localization*, MIT Press, Cambridge.

Cremer L, Müller H A (1978) *Die wissenschaftlichen Grundlagen der Raumakustik* Vol. 1, Hirzel Verlag.

Durlach N, Kramer G, Lehnert H, Shinn-Cunningham B, Wenzel E (1994) Implementation of Virtual Auditory Displays, Book chapter in preparation, *Conference on Binaural and Spatial Hearing*, Dayton, Ohio, USA, Sept. 1993

Goral, Greenberg, Batteille (1984) Modeling the Interaction of Light between Diffuse Surfaces, *Proc. SIGGRAPH '84*, 213-222.

Kuttruff H (1973) *Room Acoustics*, Applied Science Publishers Ltd., Barking, Essex, England.

Lehnert H, Blauert J (1989) A Concept for Binaural Room-Simulation, *IEEE Workshop on Application of Signal Processing to Audio and Acoustics*, New Paltz N.Y, USA.

Lehnert H, Blauert J (1991) Virtual Auditory Environment, *Proceedings of the 5th international conference on advanced robotics IEEE-ICAR,* Vol. 1, pp.211- 216.

Lehnert H (1992a) Aspects of Auralistaion in Binaural Room-Simulation, *Proceedings of the 92nd AES Convention*, San Francisco, Preprint 3390 (G- 6).

Lehnert H, Blauert J (1992b) Principles of Binaural Room Simulation, *Applied Acoustics*, Vol.36, No.3-4, pp.259-291.

Lehnert H (1993a) Auditory Spatial Impression, *Proceedings of the 12th International AES Conference*, Copenhagen, Denmark, pp.40-46.

Lehnert H (1993b) Systematic errors of the ray- tracing algorithm, *Applied Acoustics,* Vol.38, No.2-4, pp.207- 221.

Lewers T (1993) A Combined Beam Tracing and Radiant Exchange Computer Model of Room Acoustics, *Applied Acoustics,* Vol.38, No.2-4, pp.161-178.

Moller H (1992) Binaural Technology - Fundamentals, *Applied Acoustics*, Vol.36, No.3-4, pp.171-218.

Nielsen SH (1991) *Distance Perception in Hearing*, Dissertation, Aalborg University Press, Denmark.

Reichhardt W Lehmann U (1978) Raumeindruck als Oberbegriff von Raeumlichkeit und Halligkeit, Erlaeuterung des Raumeindrucksmaaes R, *Acustica*, Vol.40, No.5, pp.277-290.

Schroeder MR (1962) Natural Sounding Artificial Reverberation, *J. Audio Eng. Soc.*, Vol.10, No.3, pp.219-223.

12

Using Three-Dimensional Hand-Gesture Recognition as a New 3D Input Technique

U. Bröckl-Fox, L. Kettner, A. Klingert, L. Kobbelt
Institut für Betriebs- und Dialogsysteme, Universität Karlsruhe, Germany

12.1. Introduction

With the emerging of vision systems as input devices for current workstations - mainly used for teleconferencing - we now have available means to base the human computer-interaction no longer only on human tactile actions and the computer's reactions. With these devices it is possible to steer human-computer interaction by means of the computer's contact-free observation of the user's actions. This is a promising approach, especially for fields where the human-computer interaction is traditionally difficult e.g. manipulating 3D views and 3D geometries in telerobotics, virtual environments and CAD systems. Contact-free observation is a stringent prerequisite for applications requiring more dynamical user actions such as simulations of sports or human movements in general. Here, devices attached to the body or to be touched would perturb the human biomechanics.

Current solutions for 3D interaction comprise software approaches such as the 3D metaphors described in (Nielson and Olsen 1986; Chen et al. 1988; Ware and Osborne 1990) or hardware based approaches, which means special 3D devices, such as SpaceBall, 6D-joystick, 6D-mouse, trackball and DataGlove (Foley et al. 1990). (Gallenbacher 1993; Felger 1992) prefer in their overviews and evaluations of existing 3D input techniques the DataGlove due to the fact that it is less time consuming than other input devices (about 58% in comparison to the mouse) and that it is preferred by the users. Besides mere time

Artificial Life and and Virtual Reality Edited by Nadia Magnenat Thalmann and Daniel Thalmann
© 1994 John Wiley and Sons Ltd

advantages, the DataGlove offers several other advantages: it allows the user to manipulate computer-generated objects as if they were real, and brings the 3D objects into the same coordinate system as the hand. It almost requires no user training to get good results.

But for those systems where 3D interaction is mostly required today (CAD systems, multibody system simulation, kinematics e.g.) the DataGlove has one crucial disadvantage: the hand equipped with the DataGlove is no longer free for other tasks such as typing, mouse selection and so on. Due to (Myers and Rosson 1992) 14% of currently developed applications use 3D graphics. Of these none is pure 3D. At least some choices, menu selections or options have to be entered by mouse or keyboard. Most applications constantly swap between 3D object space and the two-dimensional space of the graphical user interfaces. For such applications a DataGlove is more likely to be a handicap than an advantage.

A better approach was described by (Krueger 1981): He propounded to extend his camera based system, used to record finger and hand movements in 2D, into a 3D system using multiple cameras.

Besides the advantage of glove-free hands, vision offers another, decisive one: with the elaborate vision algorithms for optical character recognition (Mori et al. 1992), or fingerprint identification or pattern recognition in general, we have at hand a well investigated theoretical base to construct user interfaces based on hand and face gesture recognition.

We will present a technique that follows Krueger's idea, but we will avoid using several cameras by a mirror construction in order to keep monetary and computational efforts low. Then we will give an outline of an efficient camera calibration algorithm. 3D hand-gesture recognition and its integration into a graphical user interface is discussed next. We will review the approaches to determine the 3D position and orientation of the user's hand. The chapter concludes with a summary and an outlook on our future work.

12.2. Using Mirrors to Get Several Views

An overall view of a workstation using the 3D gesture system is shown in Figure 12.1a. The user interacts in 3D space by moving his hand into the *"mirror-box"*. The mirror-box is sized approximately the same as a usual mouse pad and gives the user certainty about the work space in which he is allowed to interact. Two mirrors are arranged in an approximate angle of 45 degrees to the front plane (see Figure 12.1b). Therefore the three views of the scene intersect almost rectangular.

Using two mirrors instead of a single mirror results in three independent virtual views of the scene. This offers several advantages: first of all, the problem of hidden finger tips, caused for example by the hand itself or by other fingers within a single view, can be solved by analyzing an additional view. Secondly, and more importantly, the three views enable us to use a very simple algorithm to define interactively a 3D orientation: a linear mapping from the three images of the hands depicted in the three different views and the 3D manifold of all possible orientations can be established.

(a)

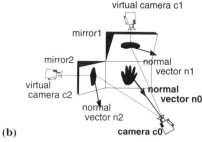

(b)

Figure 12.1. (a) Workstation using 3D gesture system (b) Two mirror system

12.3.   Retrieving 3D Information

Any virtual view observes features with three-dimensional world coordinates in the scene, but reduced to two dimensions in picture space. Therefore, one virtual view reduces the degree of freedom for the observed feature to one: the world coordinates can reside in a straight line of sight only. Two independent views of a scene give us two crossing lines. Their intersection point is the wanted 3D world coordinate. Hence stereo vision is sufficient, therefore this technique is called *reverse stereo algorithm*. The three different views from the mirror-box can easily be handled with a weighted least-square fit for all three lines of sight. The weights are determined from the exactness of the feature detection. This allows robust continuation despite partially hidden features.

A calibration process is used to determine all parameters for each virtual view, that are necessary for calculating the line of sight from a given two-dimensional coordinate in picture space. A calibration object is placed in the view volume with known world coordinates and correlated to its observed picture space coordinates. The literature on this subject reflects different techniques with reference to the set of view parameters and the type of calibration object. Our approach is a combination of the perspective transformation matrix and the two-plane method as stated in (Tsai 1986). If we know the intersection points of the line of sight with two different planes in world coordinates, we will have a two-point parametrization for the line.

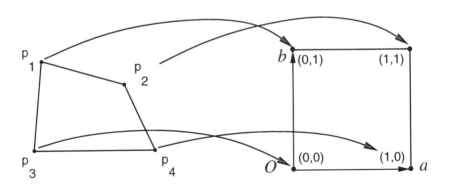

Figure 12.2. Transforming picture space into parameter space.

To analyze the effect of perspective transformation, consider a planar rectangle spread out by two vectors a and b with origin O, establishing a linear parametrization in the induced plane, as depicted in Figure 12.2 on the right hand. Depicted on the left hand is the rectangle projected into picture space, now with a projective parametrization and vanishing points. The inverse perspective transformation as depicted in Figure 12.2 can be written with projective geometry in homogeneous coordinates:

$$p \mapsto A\,p = \begin{pmatrix} a_{00} & a_{01} & a_{02} \\ a_{10} & a_{11} & a_{02} \\ a_{20} & a_{21} & 1 \end{pmatrix} \begin{pmatrix} p_x \\ p_y \\ 1 \end{pmatrix} = \begin{pmatrix} v\,\lambda \\ v\,\mu \\ v \end{pmatrix} \tag{12.1}$$

Each parameter point p known both in picture space and world space provides two linear equations for the matrix A after eliminating the third homogeneous component v. The four vertices of one rectangle exactly solve all eight unknown parameters of matrix A. Therefore we use two calibration rectangles positioned in different planes. Just to sum up - after the calibration process the two-dimensional coordinates of an observed feature point can be transformed with matrices B and C from two calibration rectangles into the two point form for the line of sight. Both matrices are composed of the corresponding matrix A and the application of the resulting linear parametrization λ and μ in world space to the world location of the rectangle: $\lambda a + \mu b + O$. Merging this method with the matrix technique (Sutherland 1974), the camera focus known in world coordinates can be used as the second calibration plane, because all straight lines are going through the focus, and no calculation needs to be done in this plane.

The absolute accuracy of this method is determined from calibration and feature extraction accuracy, whereas the relative accuracy is only limited by the feature extraction accuracy. The former reaches a standard deviation of 1.2 mm with 160 x 100 pixel resolution each virtual view.

12.4. Classification of Gestures

To use hand-gestures as a 3D input technique, we first have to determine *what* operation has to be performed: does the user want to translate, to pick or to rotate an object or the view? Here another advantage of vision systems helps us: its huge feature space that can be extracted even out of binary images. These features can be used for a classical pattern recognition algorithm that serves to distinguish among the different operations. This offers the user an event-driven dialog that is steered by simple and easy-to-remember hand-gestures.

12.4.1. Gesture Classes

The gesture recognition system is inserted into our 3D widget-set as a further possibility to steer the dialog flow, the traditional graphical user interface's push-button approach still remains to the user. The graphical user interface therefore is an efficient means to introduce and memorize the available hand-gestures. Furthermore it gives a visible feedback from the classification of the gestures showing the user's current dialog state. Figure 12.3 depicts the current implementation.

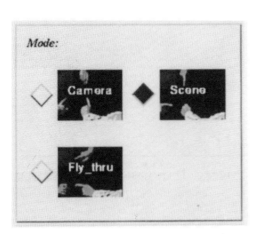
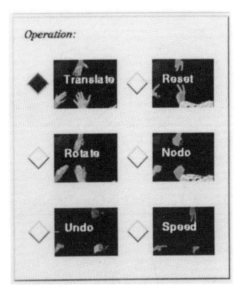

Figure 12.3. Control widgets for 3D interaction.

The illustration on the left shows the possible dialog modes: it is steered by the straddled forefinger pointing into different directions. Possible modes are *"Camera-in-hand"*, *"Scene-in-hand"* and *"Fly-through-scene"* having the same functionality as the metaphors described in (Ware and Osborne 1990). The 3D operations recognized by the system are shown in the right part of the widget. The *"Nodo"* operation has the same meaning as lifting the mouse in 2D graphical user interfaces, i.e. it enables the user to change the hand's position without performing any graphical actions and thus "walk" long distances through the 3D scene.

12.4.2. Classification Algorithm

There are mainly two methods of picture classification: one is using a neural network to examine all pixels of the input image and the other - the conventional geometric method - approximates a piece-wise linear discriminator to determine the corresponding gesture class out of a number of features that are extracted from the gesture's picture.

Prior experiences in (Bröckl-Fox and Hartenstein 1993) pointed out that the conventional geometric classification method (Rubine 1991) with its simple algorithm realizes recognition rates up to an acceptable 92%. In comparison with neural networks the geometric method shows a higher recognition speed and reliability. It allows the definition of a set of features that are characteristic to the different gesture classes.

The geometric classification method is based on the following mathematical background: We have three views and for each view k features, let be $n = 2k$ and $F=[f_1,...,f_n]$ the feature vector. The gesture classes $\Omega_1,...,\Omega_m$ are represented by their class weights $w_{i0},\cdots,w_{in}$, $(1 \leq i \leq m)$. Applying the following linear discriminant function h_j to the feature vector F and determining its maximum, we obtain the hand gesture's class $H(F)$:

$$h_j \quad = \quad w_{i0} + \sum_{k=1}^{n} w_{ik} \cdot f_k$$

$$H(F) \quad = \quad \left\{ j\colon \forall k\colon 1 \leq k, j \leq m\colon h_k(F) \leq h_j(F) \right\}$$

12.4.3. Features for Classification of Hand-Gestures

The following set of 2D features taken from the three 2D views are used to calculate the feature vector:

A: area of the hand
C: absolute curvature of contour
E: count of extreme points in radial coordinates
M: maximum / minimum distance from center of gravity to any point on the contour
B: area of bounding-box

D: length of bounding-box diagonal
L: length of contour
P: polar check i.e. number of cuts of equidistant circles round the center of
     gravity with the hand

All these features can be calculated efficiently from the *contour* of the hand, that is typically made up from $n = 200 ... 300$ pixels, in $O(n)$ steps, the contour itself also can be calculated in $O(n)$ time. On a SPARC-10 e.g. we need 28 m/s to classify a hand-gesture.

The discrimination power of the features chosen can be shown by some examples of piece-wise linear discriminators. As shown in figure 12.4a it is very easy to distinguish the gesture "translation" from the others because this gesture has a very large bounding-box area and contour length. To get a better differentiation between "rotation" and "translation" there are e.g. the features "polar check" and the absolute curvature C (Figure 12.4b). Clearly for a straddled hand the count of entrances and the curvature is higher than for a closed one.

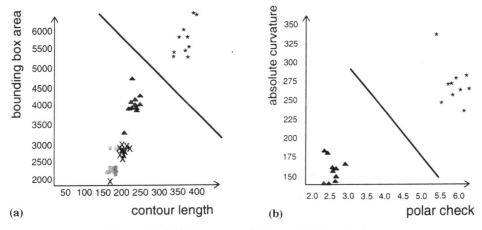

Figure 12.4. (a) Gesture translation   (b) Polar check.

These examples show that - even if we simply use piece-wise linear discriminators to classify the hand-gestures to distinguish among the most important 3D operation classes - a stable discrimination is possible.

12.4.4. Determining the Hand's Position and Orientation

Once we have classified the hand-gesture into a certain geometrical operation we have to obtain the data for that operation, namely the hand's position and orientation.

It is quite simple to get a clue of the 3D hand's position that changes properly with all movements of the hand. Calculate the 2D center of gravity from the first order moments (definition see (Duda and Hart 1973)) for two of the three views of the mirror-box and then apply the reverse stereo algorithm already described with these two 2D points as input results in a safe estimate of the 3D center of gravity of the hand.

The task to determine the hand's 3D orientation is somewhat more complicated. The approaches known for 3D orientation determination mostly try to determine the 33 orientation matrix by maximum likelihood estimates, probabilistic approaches, point-to-point correspondences and tensor product approximations.

We investigated the point-to-point correspondence approach using colored thimbles to mark the finger tips and tensor product approximations based on the zeroth to second order (2D-) moments of the three 2D images of the hand.

12.4.4.1.   Fingertip Observation

Our first approach, a point-to-point correspondence approach, was based on 24-bit color pictures. From these pictures 2D coordinates of three colored spheres, which are worn like thimbles and are used to mark the fingertips, were determined and the corresponding 3D coordinates are calculated by the reverse stereo algorithm already described. The implementation used the finger spheres in a universal metaphor that allowed rotations, translations and a scaling either of the 3D view or of the 3D geometries.

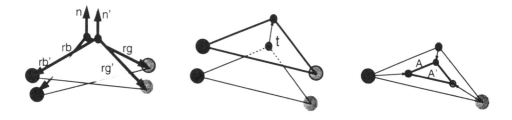

Figure 12.5. Metaphor for point-to-point correspondence approach.

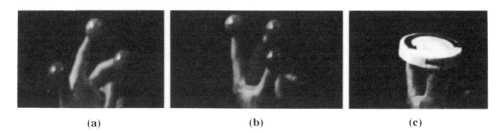

(a)   (b)   (c)

Figure 12.6. (a) Before rotation (b) After rotation (c) Dial knob.

Figure 12.5 shows an example of the *scene-in-hand metaphor*: the finger spheres are forming a triangle. This triangle can be turned about the normal vector like the dial knob in Figure 12.6c. Additionally, the change of the areas at the beginning and the end of a gesture represents a scale factor $s = A'/A$, and finally the relative change of the position of the forefinger-sphere represents a translation vector t.

The change of orientation i.e. the rotations induced by two subsequent triangle positions can be expressed in terms of the vectors rb and rg, the vectors from the red sphere to the green and blue spheres. The normal vector n of these can be found using cross product:

$n := rb \times rg$. From these three vectors an orthonormal basis B can be found in applying Graham-Schmidt orthogonalization (see (Lang 1984)) on them. Same can be done with the vectors rb' and rg' of the triangle's new position resulting in the orthonormal basis B'. The transformation matrix T to be applied on the view matrix then simply is $T := B'^T B$. If we want to use the *camera-in-hand metaphor* instead of the *scene-in-hand metaphor*, T can be calculated as follows: $T := B^T B'$.

Our intention was to try to detect the uncolored fingertips using a complex pattern analysis as it is done in (Grenander et al. 1991) and then continue as with the colored fingertips described above. Our experience with the color spheres has shown that even the simple task of finding the colored spheres is very dependent on the lighting around the mirror-box. So, in order to produce a stable user interface the system must be calibrated for all lighting situations, varying from full sunlight to weak candle light, taking all other color-influencing effects such as colors of furniture, into account. Since there is a much simpler approach we gave up any further investigations into that direction.

12.4.4.2. Moment Based Orientation Determination

Zeroth Order Moments - Area Based
This approach is based on the following observation: turning the hand around the horizontal or vertical axis of the 2D picture changes the area of the hand depicted. The relation area / angles is approximately linear in the cosine of $\alpha_{horizontal}$ and $\alpha_{vertical}$. We introduce the following variables:

$cos(x)$, $cos(y)$, $cos(z)$:	cosines of the rotations around the x,y,z-axis of the mirror-box' world coordinate system
$sin(x)$, $sin(y)$, $sin(z)$:	sines of the rotations around the x,y,z-axis of the mirror-box' world coordinate system
A_1, A_2, A_3:	observed areas of the rotated hand in the three images (in pixels)
S_1, S_2, S_3:	areas of the fully rotated hand in the three images (side view, in pixels)
F_1, F_2, F_3:	areas of the unrelated hand in the three images minus (front view minus side view, in pixels)

Summarizing for all three images the observation of area-change, we obtain the following nonlinear system of equations:

$$
\begin{aligned}
A_1 &= cos(y) \; sin(z) \; F_1 + S_1 \\
A_2 &= sin(x) \; sin(y) \; F_2 + S_2 \\
A_3 &= cos(x) \; cos(z) \; F_3 + S_3
\end{aligned}
\qquad (12.2)
$$

To solve this trigonometric nonlinear system we approximated the cosines and sines linearly setting $w' := 2w/\pi$, $cos(w) := 1 - w'$ and $sin(w) := w'$ for $w \in [0, \pi/2]$. This transforms (12.2) into:

$$
\begin{aligned}
A_1 &= (1-y') & (z') & & F_1 &+ S_1 \\
A_2 &= (x') & (y') & & F_2 &+ S_2 \\
A_3 &= (1-x') & (1-z') & & F_3 &+ S_3
\end{aligned}
\tag{12.3}
$$

This system has several solutions that are too complex to be noted here. Having x',y',z' at hand for two subsequent images and provided that the relative change for each angle is small ($\delta\alpha_{\{x,y,z\}} < \pi/4$) we can compute the relative change of the orientation.

The disadvantage of this method is that we have to have the S_1, S_2, S_3 and F_1, F_2, F_3 at hand for each user individually and - more obstructively - these areas must not change during interaction. But this is always the case if the user is not only rotating but also translating in the mirror-box: then S_i and F_i change because of the forearm enters or leaves the box.

Second Order Moments-Inertia Tensor based
We consider a binary image as a $(M \times N)$ matrix with the coefficient b_{ij} in $\{0,1\}$. Its 2D inertia tensor is defined as follows:

$$
J_{xx} = \sum_{i=1}^{M} \sum_{j=1}^{N} (j-\bar{x})^2 b_{ij}
$$

$$
J = \begin{pmatrix} J_{xx} & J_{xy} \\ J_{yx} & J_{yy} \end{pmatrix} \quad \text{with} \quad J_{yx} = J_{xy} = \sum_{i=1}^{M} \sum_{j=1}^{N} (i-\bar{y})(j-\bar{x}) b_{ij}
$$

$$
J_{yy} = \sum_{i=1}^{M} \sum_{j=1}^{N} (i-\bar{y})^2 b_{ij}
$$

where $(\bar{x}, \bar{y})$ is the image's center of gravity. Due to its symmetry, this matrix has two real eigenvalues

$$
\lambda_{1,2} = \frac{J_{xx} + J_{yy} \pm \sqrt{(J_{xx} - J_{yy})^2 + 4 J_{xy}^2}}{2}
$$

which are the minimum and maximum moment of inertia. The main axes of inertia are the corresponding eigenvectors. They can be determined by solving the linear equations $J - \lambda_i E_2 = 0$. Figure 12.7 depicts the motion of these eigenvectors for the three images of the hand in the mirror-box when the user's hand is rotated:

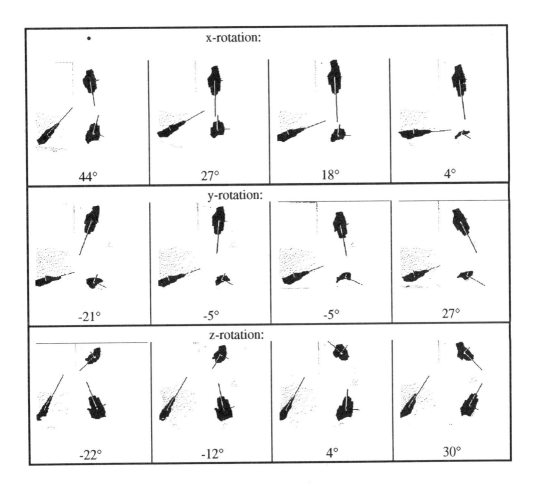

Figure 12.7. Rotations.

One can see that a rotation of the hand about the x-,y- or z-world-coordinate axis affects only the eigenvectors of the view that is normal to the rotation axis. The eigenvectors in the other views remain fairly unchanged if we only take those pairs of eigenvectors into account that are expressive. Expressive means that the moments of inertia of the eigenvectors differ relevantly, i.e. $\lambda_1 / \lambda_2 \in [2/3, 3/2]$.[1] Therefore, the angle of the eigenvector-system can be mapped directly onto the world-coordinate axis rotations as depicted in Figure 12.8.

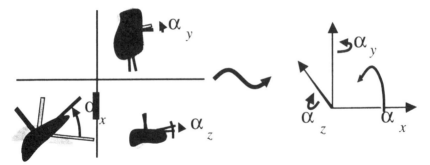

Figure 12.8. Mapping of the eigenvector system.

There is also a good geometric interpretation of this approach. Computing the main axis and moments of inertia is equivalent to approximating the user's hand to be a quadric. More precisely we approximate the orthogonal projections of the hand by an ellipse each. The main axes of these ellipses are then used to estimate the orientation of the hand. The moments $\lambda_{1,2}$ represent the reciprocal values of the main radii.

The main advantage of the quadric approach is the independence of the lighting and the actual area of the three projections. Thus, training the system for a specific user is no longer needed. Further, a 1:1 mapping of the rotation from the hand to the object is possible.

12.4.4.3. Rotation-invariant Feature Based Approach

The inertia tensor based orientation determination fails, if the hand's image is not expressive. This is the case if the hand forms e.g. a fist or any other object of approximately circular shape. Then an outstanding knuckle or finger causes unmeant rotations. For these cases we use a pattern matching approach that is based on rotation-invariant features defined as in (Lenz 1986).

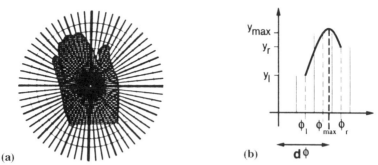

Figure 12.9. (a) Rotation-invariant feature (b) Quadratic interpolation of maximum correlation

An example of such a feature is shown in Figure 12.9a. Here, the pixels of the hand depicted are transformed into a radial coordinate system with its origin lying in the center of gravity of the hand. The angular coordinate space $[0, 2\pi]$ is quantized into n subintervals, so-called sectors. Then the grey-scales are summed up for each sector. We obtain a univariate function as shown in the upper right part of Figure 12.10, where the fingers can easily be identified from the local maxima of the function. It should be noted here that there are much more efficient and precise rotation-invariant features such as Zernike moments (Khotanzad and Hong 1988), but these are not as exemplifying as the sector-summation feature.

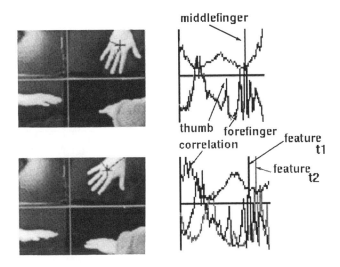

Figure 12.10. Example of a rotation-invariant feature

Things change when the hand is rotated. This situation is depicted in the lower part of Figure 12.10. We obtain two feature curves feature$_{t1}$ and feature$_{t2}$ whose shapes are nearly the same. The only difference is that feature$_{t2}$ is shifted along the ϕ-axis, the so-called *phase shift* d. This phase shift is exactly the rotation angle we are looking for. The phase shift is equal to the maximum cross-correlation of the two feature curves. The cross-correlations of the two features are plotted in Figure 12.10 on the top and bottom right respectively. In the upper right function plot the cross-correlation has its maximum at the right-most sector, i.e. for an angle of $2\pi = 0$ DEG, whereas in the lower right plot the maximum is at sector 4.

Using cross-correlation is a standard method for template matching since it can be determined efficiently by the discrete fast Fourier transform (DFFT) as follows:

$$C(i) = F^{-1} \{F\{\text{feature}_{t1}(i)\}F\{\text{feature}_{t2}(i^{mi})\}\}$$

Here, F denotes the DFFT, F^{-1} its inverse transform, and i^{mi} the mirrored angular coordinate. If we have n sectors, the time complexity for the cross-correlation is $O(n \log(n))$. Nevertheless, this approach becomes inefficient, if we want to enhance the angular resolution by increasing the number of sectors n. An angular resolution of, for instance, 0.1 requires 3600 sectors; too much for an application under real-time constraints.

Here a simple quadric interpolation of the cross-correlation function as shown in Figure 12.9b helps. Doing so, $d\phi$ can be calculated as $d\phi = \phi_{max} + \dfrac{\phi_1 - \phi_r}{-4\phi_{max} + 2\phi_1 + 2\phi_r}$ provided that $\phi_1 + \phi_r \neq 2\phi_{max}$; in these cases ϕ_{max} is the exact $d\phi$. A number of $n=64$ sectors has proven to be the best compromise between stability and efficiency. Table 12.1 lists the results in terms of stability and efficiency comparing the point-to-point approach (P2P), the inertia-tensor approach (IT) and the pattern recognition approach (PR). *Noise* stands for the rotations induced by the algorithms for a totally fixed, rigid (model-) hand, the *max. error* denotes the maximum error observed during our experiments. All values were measured with 128 x 96 pixel gray-scale images. The *times* were measured on a 50 Mhz Intel 486 processor.

Table 12.1. List of results in terms of stability and efficiency

approach	noise [DEG]	max. error [DEG]	time [m/s]
P2P	1.78	8.51	–
IT	0.48	4.85	127
PR	0.12	2.56	153

Comparing the results of IT and PR we find that we obtain a fourfold angular resolution at the cost of about 50% execution time.

12.5. Conclusion

We have successfully installed a new 3D input technique based on the recognition of the hand with a one camera system. Features of the hand depicted in three 2D views can be used to steer a complex 3D interaction sequence: both a sort of 3D operation as well as its geometrical data can be calculated from these features in a reliable way.
It is possible to determine 3D orientation and translation from a 128 x 96 pixel gray-scale image in such a manner that a 3D scene that is displayed on a 512 x 340 pixel window remains rigid if the hand is not moved.
    Seen from an economical point of view - provided that the workstation is already equipped with a vision system - we have a 3D interaction technique that is, in our opinions, superior to DataGlove systems at the initial cost of two mirrors and 0.5m² of black pasteboard. But even if we take the cost of a gray-scale camera (< $300) and frame-grabber card (< $175) into account we have a competitive 3D interaction system.
    The next step will be to compare this new method with existing 3D input media like the SpaceBall or DataGlove in terms of the required interaction times and user acceptance. We are also looking into extending the system to be two-handed in order to accomplish pick and place operations needed for telerobotics or molecular-modeling applications. Furthermore we are thinking of introducing the observation of the whole body using spherical or cylindrical mirrors that observe the entire room to obtain 18 degrees of freedom by applying the described algorithms onto the hands and the face. Finally, we plan to incorporate feedback into the mirror-box by means of airstream and/or heat radiator devices.

References

Bröckl-Fox U, Hartenstein K (1993) Gaphors: Combining Gestures and Metaphors in Order to Obtain a More Efficient 3D-Interface., *Proceedings of the IJCAI-93,* A one-day workshop LOOKING AT PEOPLE: Recognition and Interpretation of Human Action.

Chen MJ, Mountford J, Sellen A (1988) A Study in Interactive 3-D Rotation Using 2-D Control Devices. *ACM Transactions on Computer Graphics*, August, pp.121-129.

Duda RO, Hart PE (1973) *Pattern Classification and Scene Analysis* , Wiley and Sons.

Felger W (1992) How interactive visualization can benefit from multidimensional input devices, *Preprints zum Workshop: Visualisierung - Rolle von Echtzeit und Interaktivität,* GMD-HLRZ, W. Krüger, June.

Foley J, van Dam A, Feiner SK, Hughes JF (1990) *Computer Graphics-Principles and Practice* (2nd Ed.), Addison-Wesley Publishing Company.

Gallenbacher (1993) *Grafische Eingabe: Geräte, Methoden, Perspektiven, Evaluierung.* Master's thesis, TH Darmstadt, Fachbereich Graphisch Interaktive Systeme, *FRG,* 1993.

Grenander U, Chow Y, Keenan DM (1991) *Hands. A Pattern Theoretic Study of Biological Shapes.* Springer Verlag, Berlin, Heidelberg, New York, Tokyo.

Khotanzad A and Hong YH (1988) Rotation Invariant Pattern Recognition Using Zernike Moments, *ICPR* 1988, pp.326-328.

Krueger MW (1981) *Artificial Reality*, Addison-Wesley Publishing Company.

Lang S (1984) *Algebra*, Addison-Wesley Publishing Company.

Lenz R (1986) Rotation-Invariant Operators, *Proc. Int. Conf. on Pattern Recognition*, pp.1130-1132, 1986.

Mori S, Suen CY, Yamamoto Y (1992) Historical review of OCR research and development, *Proceedings of the IEEE*, July, pp.1029-1058,

Myers BA, Rosson MB (1992) *Survey on User Interface Programming.* Number RC 17624 (#77629) IBM Research Division.

Nielson GM, Olsen DR (1986) Direct Manipulation Techniques for 3D Objects Using 2D Locator Devices, *Proceedings of the 1986 Workshop on Interactive 3D Graphics*, Chapel Hill, October, pp.175-182.

Rubine D (1991) Specifying Gestures by Example, *Computer Graphics,* Vol. 25, No4.

Sutherland IE (1974) Three-Dimensional Data Input by Tablet, *Proceedings of the IEEE*, 62(4):453-461.

Tsai RY (1986) An Efficient and Accurate Camera Calibration Technique for 3D Machine Vision, *Computer Vision and Pattern Recognition*, IEEE, June, pp.364-374.

Ware C, Osborne S (1990) Exploration and Virtual Camera Control in Virtual Three Dimensional Environments, *ACM Transactions on Computer Graphics*, October, pp.175-183.

13

Realism in Virtual Reality

Peter Astheimer, Fan Dai, Martin Göbel, Rolf Kruse, Stefan Müller, Gabriel Zachmann
Fraunhofer-Institute for Computer Graphics (IGD)
Wilhelminenstr. 7, D-64283 Darmstadt, Germany

13.1. Introduction

Virtual Reality (VR) is known as a new dimension in man-machine communication that (up to now) combines real-time (3D) computer graphics and direct (mostly) intuitive interaction in 3D space.

It is our intention to develop virtual environments (VEs) that support human communication as accurate as possible although we are aware that the "ultimate illusion" is not achievable at all. We think that virtual environments must improve man machine communication as a first step, and as a second one should be used (like today's telephone) by "everyone" for human (-to-human) communication. Many developments in computer science and telecommunication (joint CAD, shared X, CSCW, ...) are well known examples for improving human communication.

Virtual environments should allow a better and faster understanding of even complex applications and provide means for intuitive operations and control. The car - as an example - is a very complex and highly integrated product consisting of numerous mechanical and electronic components. Driving as a result of interaction with a car is a process which is known by all people due to a common, easy-to-use, compact "user interface". The control of computer simulations using virtual environments is approaching this "comfort" in man-machine interaction.

The acceptance of virtual environments in industrial application, i.e. the use of virtual environments for product development, product presentation and process control is heavily dependent on key issues like:

Artificial Life and and Virtual Reality Edited by Nadia Magnenat Thalmann and Daniel Thalmann
© 1994 John Wiley and Sons Ltd

- the quality of presentation;
- the easiness of interaction and
- the correctness of behavior.

As many applications have an idea about the presentation quality which is achievable with today's animation systems, these requirements are set up also for virtual worlds. No architect, no designer would accept a computer generated representation of his design which looks (in the best case) more like a toy house than a building. A sense of realism has to be provided: starting with the building itself, nature as the environment, light situations depending on the seasons of a year and probably short term weather effects.

But presentation does not only effect the visual information provided by the machine. As virtual environments support multisensory man-machine communication, auditory and tactile information should also reflect a sufficient degree of realism to understand this information more easily. The state-of-the-art shows that auditory and tactile presentation is (at least) one step behind the visual presentation and that the synchronization of various presentation form is still an open problem in VE research.

Ease of interaction demands "standard" interaction or better communication techniques from human communication which have to be applied and understood by the machine. Gestures and speech are key components if applied in a combined and synchronized manner. Pointing on a virtual object with the index finger, saying "this thing is what I want to have" should be enough information for the machine to perform a corresponding operation within the virtual environment.

Finally, the simulations provided by the machine, the rules, the laws, the behavior of the world should somehow correspond to our human experience to use our common sense for understanding what is going on. Artificial rules or the inversion of physical laws has to be explained in detail to the user - common knowledge on the other hand provides the basis for efficient user interfaces.

A key feature of VR technologies is immersion. By this term we define the feeling of a VR user, that his virtual environment is real. More precisely, we define immersion analogously to Turing's definition of (artificial) intelligence: if the user cannot tell, which reality is "real", and which one is "virtual", then the computer generated one is immersive. A high degree of immersion is equivalent to a realistic virtual environment. Several conditions must be met to achieve this: the most important seems to be small feedback lag; second is a wide field-of-view. Displays should also be stereoscopic, which is usually the case with head-mounted displays. A low display resolution seems to be less significant.

In this chapter we want to present the state-of-the-art in providing realism in virtual environments. Techniques will be discussed to increase visual and auditory presentation. The behavior of virtual worlds -a further demand on realism - is introduced and interaction techniques are explained with regard to intuitive understanding. Finally, we explain some applications in virtual environments which aim for a high degree of realism. As a conclusion we try to point out that realism (or a realistic impression) is subjective and heavily dependent on the user himself.

13.2. Simulation of Visual Reality

For rendering 3D scenes, there are mainly three techniques used, which are very well developed: raytracing, scan conversion and volume rendering. Although the use of parallel computing architectures improved rendering speed of ray tracing and volume rendering techniques enormously within the last years, the real-time requirements of Virtual Reality can only be satisfied by the scan conversion method exploiting special graphics hardware.

Nowadays, we are restricted to using only polygons for modeling virtual environments, because these primitives can be rendered and shaded very fast by scan conversion hardware. Since the model complexity is always increasing by the user requirements, there are two challenging tasks for simulating visual appearance of polygonal models in a realistic manner: first, we have to improve the image quality; secondly, we have to increase rendering performance in order to get enough frames per second while handling complex data sets. In this chapter, several techniques for both tasks are described.

13.2.1. Improving Image Quality

Virtual environments are mainly modeled by a set of polygons, using standard CAD-systems. Apart from the pure geometrical description several material attributes have to be assigned to the surface descriptions, like surface colors and illumination properties. Some techniques for improving image quality are already supported by the computer graphics hardware (e.g., simple illumination schemes), while other techniques have to be used in a preprocess (e.g., radiosity simulation).

Hardware-shading
Relating to a camera definition (position and viewing direction of the observer), the model is projected onto the screen perspectively. Visibility detection algorithms are used to display surface obstructions in a correct manner. Based on virtual light sources in the scene (e.g. point light sources, directional lights or spot lights), the illumination of diffuse surfaces is simulated while rendering. Transparent, non-refracting materials and texture mapping facilities are supported by special graphical hardware. Textures especially are very important for improving visual realism. Scene complexity and surface details can be pretended by mapping scanned photographs onto object surfaces. Textures can also be used to display reflections (reflection mapping) and simulate atmospheric surroundings of virtual environments.

If the camera definition is connected to an input device, like a tracking system on top of a head-mounted display, up to 25 stereoscopic pictures per second can be computed of scenes defined by less than 20.000 textured polygons using the described hardware techniques. Even if these scenes look quite impressive, they still lack visual realism, because of missing shadows and non-physically based illumination models.

Shadow-algorithms
To improve the depth cues of rendered pictures, shadow algorithms have to be used. Several algorithms had been suggested by researchers to simulate shadows caused by objects

occluding a light source. As shadows of static objects (e.g. non-moving objects) appear in a view-independent way, they can be determined in a pre-process resulting in the generation of additional new shadow polygons. On the other hand, shadows of dynamic objects have to be computed in real-time by projecting the moving object onto important "working planes", like the floor or the top of a desk. This is a very important task for enabling user interaction. If an input device without any force feedback is used, the correct placement of objects in a virtual environment becomes a very complicated task. A good survey of shadow algorithms can be found in (Woo et al. 1990).

Shadow algorithms improve the visual realism of virtual environments, but the generated images still appear very synthetic. Therefore, more complex illumination models like the radiosity method have to be used.

Real radiosity and faked radiosity techniques

Radiosity can also be used as a pre-process in order to increase image quality for rendering virtual environments (see Cohen and Wallace 1993) for more details about radiosity algorithms). First, the object surfaces have to be subdivided into a set of patches and radiosity values are assigned to finite light sources. Then, the illumination exchange is simulated for mainly diffuse environments based on thermodynamic equations. Since diffuse reflections are view-independent, the results can be assigned to the scene description as vertex colors and interpolated in real-time by the graphics hardware.

As the radiosity technique increases the scene complexity by adding more patches to the scene, it seems to slow down the rendering performance. In fact, rendering becomes faster using this approach. Let us consider a test scene, where the floor is defined by a single quadrilateral, which is subdivided into 100 by 100 patches. The results of the radiosity pre-process are colors assigned to each patch vertex, that can be regarded as a texture defined by 101 by 101 color entries. Thus, the resulting texture can be mapped onto the original floor quadrilateral without loosing any rendering performance by improving image quality. Since the illumination is precomputed, rendering becomes even faster than rendering the original data set by using hardware shading facilities for each frame.

Having a closer look at illumination precomputation, one can notice that hardware shading becomes unnecessary in most cases. Using hardware shading facilities means, that the illumination is computed for each frame. Precomputing the illumination at the polygon vertices adopting the concept of virtual light sources would lead to the same result and speed up the rendering process. This so-called faked radiosity algorithm can be easily extended by using shadow rays between the virtual light sources and the polygon vertices in order to take into account shadow situations. Using this strategy implies again the subdivision of surface polygons into smaller patches, in order to enable displaying high illumination gradients and discontinuities by using linear color interpolation mechanisms (Gouraud-shading).

Radiosity techniques had been improved to simulate light exchange also in non-diffuse environments (e.g. light passing from a non-diffuse light source over mirrors and materials with more complex reflection functions). Unfortunately, we are restricted to the display of diffuse patches by the scan conversion method. For displaying more complex surface properties, ray tracing algorithms have to be used, which are up to now not able to satisfy the real-time requirements of VR, as mentioned earlier.

Radiosity in dynamic scenes

Although the radiosity method proved to increase visual realism, it is not very often used in modern VR systems. One of the reasons is, that the radiosity module requires some topological information about the scene model, which are very difficult to achieve from some CAD-systems. Sometimes a pipeline of interactive programs has to be used, in order to ensure the data consistency needed by the radiosity module (Baum et al. 1991).

But, the main reason for the radiosity refusal is its restricted usage for static environments. Any interaction with the scene geometry or its materials would result in an expensive time recalculation of the radiosity simulation. This leads to the common phrase: Radiosity scenes are like museums, you may look around, but do not touch anything!

Several algorithms have been investigated in order to overcome this problem. The main idea is, that interacting with any object of the scene tends to be local and affects only small parts of the illumination process. Therefore, information can be reused which is already provided by the radiosity pre-process and coherences of the scene are exploited, in order to identify small parts affected by the change. These algorithms proved to be very fast, but they still need longer than the rendering frame rate. Therefore, the radiosity update has to be computed incrementally and independently of the rendering loop (e.g., the user grabs an object of a virtual environment and the shadow disappears step by step while the user is able to continue navigating through the scene). An example for this algorithm is displayed in Figure 13.1 (see Color Section) (Müller and Schöffel 1994).

13.2.2. Increasing Rendering Performance

Using object hierarchies is one of the most beneficial tools available for managing database complexity for the purpose of improving display performance (Strauss and Carey 1992). Neighboring objects are grouped recursively to composite objects. For example a village consists of some houses and trees while each tree is defined by a list of polygons. These object hierarchies are defined by the user himself or supported by the system using spatial information of the scene. Bounding volumes are assigned to each tree node surrounding all objects of the related subtree.

In this section, some algorithms are described, how object hierarchies can be exploited to speed up the rendering process. The main idea of object hierarchies is to provide a scene structure in order to reduce global database search, if only small parts of a scene need to be evaluated by any software module. Thus, the described algorithms can easily be extended to speed up other VR modules (e.g. collision detection, acoustical rendering, etc.).

Viewing culling and hierarchy traversal

For rendering the scene, its descriptive hierarchy (scene graph) is traversed. If the bounding volume of a composite object is totally outside of the viewing frustum, the underlying subtree is no longer considered by the traversal. If the bounding volume is totally inside the viewing frustum, all underlying objects have to be rendered and the according bounding volumes do not need to be tested.

If the virtual camera is placed in a room or a floor of a building, only local environments have to be considered for rendering. This is realized by adding switch nodes or portal nodes to the hierarchy. If the user passes through a portal object (e.g., a door or a window) or leaves the bounding volume of a switch node subtree, the next database is loaded and displayed.

Level-of-detail

Another very important feature of hierarchical scene description is the usage of level-of-detail nodes. For example, a complex model of an automobile may have door handles, side- and rear-view mirrors, license plates, and other small details. A short distance away, these features may no longer be visible, even though the car itself is still a visually significant element of the scene. In a hierarchy, several more or less detailed representations of an object have to be modeled by the user. By traversing the object hierarchy, the rendering system chooses the proper subtree dependent on observer's distance, view angle and movement criteria.

Apart from modeling level-of-detail representations by the user, they can be automatically determined by the system (Astheimer and Pöche 1994; Pöche 1994). A straightforward approach for a level-of-detail is the substitution of the object with its bounding box. This obvious solution is immediately rejected when observing the jerky transition between the box and the object. In our tool we provide a set of algorithms which operate on points, edges, angles, face areas or normals or a combination of these.

When changing the viewpoint it may be necessary to switch from one level-of-detail immediately to another one. This transition between two different object representations can be of constant type (one level permanently selected), switch type (one level substitutes another) or fade type (within a given number of image frames the new level will fade from transparent to opaque while the current will fade from opaque to transparent).

The generation of multiple levels-of-detail of objects can be controlled either to match a given quality (shape, appearance) or a given quantity (number of points, faces). All available techniques in this tool provide quality control to meet application demands in interior design and architecture. Because the visual results of applied techniques are not always predictable the generation is an interactive process.

In 1993 we have imported and prepared some dozen models for VR. Figure 13.2 (see Color Section) shows several computed levels-of-detail of the bust of Beethoven. The complexity decreases from approximately 2500 faces (large main window) to approximately 100 faces (small window lower right).

Rendering caches and multiprocessing

Traversing the scene graph costs valuable CPU time by dereferencing complex data structures. The output of the traversing module is a display list - a very flat data structure which only includes rendering commands that can be passed to the rendering hardware with a minimum of CPU cost. Rendering static environments, this data remains constant for further rendering steps. Therefore, caches can be attached to static subtrees after their first traversal containing the computed display list. Rendering caches help to speed up the rendering performance in a drastic way for static environments. If a subtree becomes dynamic after changing one of its including object, all cache entries normally become invalid.

To speed up rendering for mainly dynamic environments, multiprocessor systems can be used. A producer process can run on a single processor traversing the hierarchy and culling the bounding volumes against the viewing frustum. The computed display list is passed by a second processor to the rendering hardware. For stereoscopic rendering two consumers are needed.

The simulations changing the transformation matrices or the shape of some objects in the hierarchy are often independent tasks and can also run on parallel processors. In interactive or immersive systems the input or navigation devices can also be controlled by several processors.

13.3. Simulation of Acoustic Reality

A virtual reality application ideally immerses humans totally in pseudo-real or imaginary virtual worlds. This is theoretically achieved by stimulating all human senses (see, hear, touch, taste, smell) and by immediate responses to user actions. Today's software and hardware technology is far from the realization of such an idealized, utopic system. The graphics part of VR systems - the generation and display of multiple image frames per second - is well understood and existing systems generally satisfy our needs.

In contrast to device development for the rest of our senses, audio hardware and basic software is readily available (Astheimer 1993a, 1993b): Midi-equipment and workstation audio for sound generation and effects, filter processors and 3D-audio cards for spatial audio. Although there is no ideal, general purpose device or device combination for VR, the available range of products can be utilized to do something. Two categories of sound in VR can be identified.

Simulation of real world acoustics: based on our experiences in everyday life the physical behavior of sound can be modeled (Astheimer 1993d). This comprises sound generation, e.g. caused by object collision, sound propagation and auralization (See Figure 13.3, Color Section). Although this cannot be processed today to its full extent in real-time, this approach has the big advantage, that no training for the user is required to recognize conveyed information. Immersive user interfaces can be used to evaluate the simulation results.

Sound at the user interface: sound can be applied to support the user in his current task or to provide information about invisible proceedings. Such sonification techniques have been primarily applied in 2D desktop interfaces and non-immersive systems (Kramer 1994), while virtual reality techniques now open the door to complex 3D interactive worlds. The application of everyday sounds with implicit meanings/analogies can reduce or avoid the training effort otherwise required to understand abstract information codings (Cohen 1993).

Acoustic simulations which consider sound propagation in an environment are based on the assumptions of the theory of geometrical room acoustics (Kuttruff 1973). The theory justifies results when the dimensions of the enclosure are large compared to the wavelength of the sound, when the frequency of the sound is above 1 kHz and when all objects possess specular reflecting material. These assumptions hold true for most situations, even for outside simulations of buildings, cities or landscapes (air turbulence and wind has to be considered).

The acoustic rendering pipeline comprises two stages, a simulation pass and an auralization pass (Astheimer 1993c).

In the first stage (simulation) the acoustic world model, which consists of geometrically defined objects with acoustic attributes, receiver and sound sources, is interpreted to calculate the propagation of a finite energy pulse. Detectors collect the time-dependent direct, reflected, diffracted and refracted energy at a certain position in form of the impulse response (like an image rendered in computer graphics).

The impulse responses for multiple detectors (e.g. a 3D grid) can be computed in the same computational pass. One impulse response ideally has to be computed for each involved frequency or octavo, because the material absorption depends on frequency and angle of incidence. For simplification typically only one frequency of about 1 kHz is used. Also diffraction, refraction and interference effects are mostly neglected.

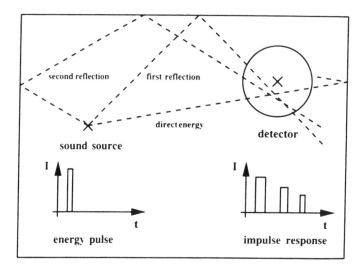

Figure 13.4. Principle of particle tracing.

Acoustic rendering algorithms are of two types: image source algorithms compute the mirror images of virtual sound sources every time a reflection is detected. This is very easy for rectangular rooms and can be performed in real-time (Allen and Berkley 1979).

For arbitrary environments each virtual source has to be checked, whether it is visible or not (Borish 1984). Because the ratio between visible and invisible virtual sources is very small, the straightforward version of this algorithm is not very effective (computationally) (Vorländer 1989).

Ray tracing algorithms trace the propagation of sound particles or rays in a scene model, where receiver volumes detect passing particles (Figure 13.4) (Krokstad et al. 1968; Vorländer 1988). Here the same problems as in visual ray tracing are encountered: the calculation of the intersection of a ray with the nearest object is very expensive and requires a structured object database for speed-up. Both image source and particle tracing algorithms can produce identical results (Vorländer 1989).

The acoustic rendering algorithms are too complex to be processed with full precision in real-time for arbitrary environments. There are two real-time approaches, which attempt to preserve and reproduce the aural key effects. One approach applies the renderer in a precomputational phase to compute a 2D or 3D grid of impulse responses, which is evaluated by the next stage. Sound sources can not be moved (same as in radiosity lighting). The other approach is confined to the computation of some early reflections and estimates the late diffuse contribution to the reverberation by statistical means (Lehnert et al. 1992) .

13.4. Simulation of Behavior

The behavior of the objects is very important for the realism of the virtual environment. Our real world is dynamic. Things change over time according to physical laws. Humans recognize not only the form, color and sound, but also these changes. Additionally, manipulation of virtual objects is only realistic, if these objects respond correctly to the user's actions.

Recently, first approaches are known showing the possibilities of integrating dynamic objects into virtual worlds (e.g. Astheimer and Dai (1993). Generally, there are two ways to do that: off-line and integrated simulation of dynamics. The relatively simple way is to generate an animation off-line and then present it with existing VR techniques. This way, the user can navigate in the dynamic scene to get a better feeling of what is moving there. To have partial control of the scene, motions can be defined as actions of individual objects, which are invoked by e.g. hitting a virtual control button.

The off-line approach allows to process even very complex dynamic scenes, because the resulting purely geometrical transformations are supported very well by graphics hardware. The disadvantages of the off-line approach are, that no interactions between the motion parts and no interactive intervention of the dynamic process is possible.

To have control of the motions and/or to interact with the objects with dynamic behavior, simulations have to be integrated into the VR-systems. This requires an advanced model of the virtual world, and a concept of manipulating this model. A purely geometrical and graphical model of the virtual world is not able to respond to the user's actions. Therefore, the model must contain physical characteristics of the objects.

We need a physically-based modeling approach. Based on such a model, simulations provide not only the lighting effects, but also dynamic behavior of the objects. Physical states of the virtual worlds and the user inputs are evaluated together. Motions are generated on-line using physical and heuristic rules.

Modeling
Physically-based modeling is the technique of modeling dynamic scenes for animation based on the simulation of physical behaviors. This is a relatively new research area, but with a lot of usable results (Eurographics 1993; Badler et al. 1991; Witkin and Kass 1991). Simulation of dynamics using laws of physics is not new at all. But to apply it to interactive computer graphics is a challenging work. Especially for virtual environment

applications, there is a high demand on photo-realism, animation speed and interactivity simultaneously.

Conceptually, a virtual world can be considered a set of objects, which interact with each other. In addition to the geometrical and graphical attributes, physical properties are to be specified. Different rules and methods are needed for different kinds of objects to simulate their behavior. This requires, for a heterogeneous, complex scene, the classification of objects according to their physical characteristics, e.g. in: rigid body, deformable solids, and fluid. We know, that most objects are rather hybrid composed. Mechanical systems are structured, consisting of several parts connected by links. The human body is articulated, with parts like muscle, tissues and the skeleton. Therefore, a hierarchical, layered object data structure is highly recommended.

For each class of objects, the same, or similar rules of motion (and/or other changes) are applicable. We call them global rules.

There are active objects too. They cause changes in the world according to the relations between all objects. For active objects like human, animals, autonomous machines, special rules are necessary. These are object-class dependent and often different even for objects of the same type. For example, the behavior of machines are programmed by the human and can be always simulated, but the behavior of a human is only partly determined, so that object-specific heuristic rules and/or explicit descriptions are often needed for the simulation of active objects.

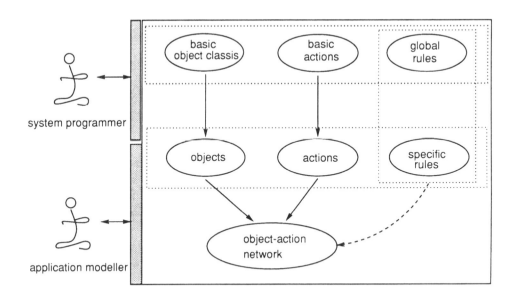

Figure 13.5. Modeling objects and actions.

An object can perform different actions, not simultaneously, but each once according to the actual situation. That means, which action is to be performed and when this happens are controlled by the evaluation of objects information. An action is invoked by checking some relevant data and will be executed until a specified goal is reached. This evaluation and activation mechanism can be described using "sensors" and "conditions". Sensors register different information e.g. geometry, position, state of individual objects and of the whole scene. They provide the conditions with concrete values. Conditions have a Boolean value and control the actions. Each action is associated with a condition, which can be of course composed of more than one "sub-conditions".

Furthermore, the objects are interrelated with each other. These relations are either interactions or physical connections. Interactions between objects can be represented by the sensors and actions. As a result, the objects and actions build a network. This object-action-network (O-A-N) describes the contents (objects) and behavior (actions) of the virtual world (Dai 1994).

The Users
Users of a virtual environment system interact with the virtual world via the input and output devices. For the model, they are nothing else than a kind of active objects. The special characteristics of these objects is, that they are not controlled by the program, but fully by the users. There is no need to model the behavior of the users, just register it via the input devices and control the virtual objects representing the users.

Using new input devices like DataGlove and tracking systems, we are able to get the basic motions of the users like: move limbs, move fingers, speak, etc. These directly cause transformations of the graphical objects representing the users or users' hands. The more difficult job is to interpret these basic actions into high-level actions and to execute these actions.

We can distinguish between two types of user actions:

* own actions like go, run, gestures, messages, and
* object manipulations: grasp and put, push or pull, lift, hit, etc.

Especially object manipulation requires the analysis of geometrical contacts, forces and material properties. Physically-based models meet this requirement very well.

Simulation
The higher hierarchy levels of an object-action-network describe more logical relations and dependencies, where on the lower, basic level there are mostly descriptions about temporal and spatial changes. The former is partly comparable with a procedural network. Therefore, the simulation of the virtual world based on the object-action-network runs in two steps: inference of the network and the rules to get the solution of the logical problem, and further, calculation of the state and spatial changes in the virtual world by applying the rules of physics (Figure 13.6).

The inference process is nothing else than the interpretation of the actions and conditions using logical rules, and the selection of physical (and heuristic) rules of motion, respectively selection of numerical problem solvers. Numerical problem solvers calculate the state changes in the virtual world as continuous functions of time. The basis for the calculation are the laws of motion known from physics.

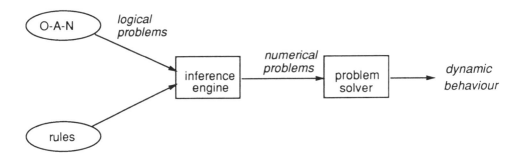

Figure 13.6. Simulation of behavior.

With the classification of objects into rigid, deformable solids and fluids on the lower physical level, or mechanical parts, animals, human, landscape etc., on the more functional level, corresponding rules and procedures can be implemented in a structured order.

The implementation of numerical problem solvers is discussed in various publications about physically-based modeling. The special aspect in our case is, that all things have to be interactive, so there is a high demand on efficiency.

13.5. Intuitive Interaction

There are two genuine different types of virtual environments:

- The virtual environment is actually a projection of some real environment.
- The virtual environment does not exist in any form. It might have existed in the past, or it might exist in the future.

In accordance with this distinction, interaction can be classified as to whether

- the user manipulates existing, real objects. Examples are: repair of a satellite by means of another spacecraft armed with tools; steering of a car on ground which humans cannot enter (e.g., the moon, radioactively polluted terrain, etc.); exploration and modification of the structure of materials at atomic scale (Taylor et al. 1993).
- the user manipulates not existing objects. Examples might be: examination and modification of the interior design of a building which is still in planning; visualization of fabrication processes, such that deficiencies or dangers for human operators can be detected at an early stage; simulation of surgical operations (actually, flight simulators have probably been the first virtual environments).

In order to accomplish these interaction tasks, it is highly desirable to develop interaction techniques which are as intuitive as possible. Conventional interaction devices (keyboard, mouse, tablet, etc.) are not fit for natural interaction with most VR applications. One of the more intuitive ways is the "virtual trackball" or the "rolling trackball" (Kirk 1992, p. 51 ff), which both utilize the mouse.

The shortcoming of all of the above mentioned devices is their low input dimension (at most two). However, new devices like SpaceMouse, DataGlove, tracking systems, Cricket, etc., provide six or more dimensions. This allows highly efficient, natural interaction techniques; some of them are:

- Gesture recognition; usually, these are static gestures like "fist", "hitch-hike", etc., but there is also research going on to recognize dynamic gestures which consist of a continuous sequence of static gestures together with hand positions. Gestures can be defined as spheres in Rd (where d = 10 or d = 20, typically); then, they can be recognized by a simple point-in-sphere test. Another approach to gesture recognition is the use of back-propagation networks (perceptrons) (Väänänen and Böhm 1992). In both cases, a good glove calibration is essential; also, each user should have his own gesture definition data or neural network. Gestures are very well suited to trigger actions, like program exit, display of a menu, or one of the following actions.

- Navigation through virtual environments or steering of a real exploration device (e.g., the repair robot or the microscope needle). Some techniques are (see also Ware and Osborne 1990; Robinett and Holloway 1992; Felger et al. 1993):

  - point-and-fly: the user points in a certain direction with his navigation device (e.g., glove or cricket) and forms a certain gesture with his hand or presses a certain button at the cricket. The speed of the motion can be controlled by the user through the bend of the thumb or the pressure on the cricket button. This navigation technique seems to be the most widely used one. The idea of the point-and-fly navigation paradigm (Figure 13.7) is to steer a cart with a camera mounted on top; (a) without head tracking: the cart is moved by the "fly" gesture in the direction the user points; this includes translational and rotational movements; (b) with head tracking: the cart is moved only translational; the camera is mounted on a stand which in turn is moved by the head tracking relative to the cart. (Mackinlay 1990) have suggested a more sophisticated point-and-fly mode: the user points at the desired object and the VR system computes a "swerved" path which will place the user eventually in front of the object. Again, the speed can be controlled.
  - eyeball-in-hand: this paradigm is accomplished by connecting the viewpoint and the viewing direction directly to a tracking system which would track the position and orientation of the input device. This technique can be very suitable for close examination of single objects from different viewpoints.
  - scene-in-hand: this is the dual technique to the above one. The viewpoint is modified by the inverse transformations as with the eyeball-in-hand technique.

- 3D menus (Jacoby and Ellis 1992) are the straightforward extension of the well-known 2D menus to suit the full 3D approach of VR applications. Usually their appearance is triggered by a gesture or a button of some other interaction device. The user can then choose an item by pointing at the specific 3D button or by hitting the 3D button with the graphical echo of the device.

The modeling of objects simply by pressing or dragging at the surface of an object. The user can manipulate any facet, i.e., vertex, edge, or polygon. In order to achieve a realistic behavior, the manipulation should affect also the neighborhood (Bryson 1992). This influence might be determined by predefined weighting functions, or it might be based on the preservation of physical properties (e.g., volume, or surface), or on other constraints. Other representations like B-Spline surfaces, NURBS, or even CSG might be useful, or even necessary.

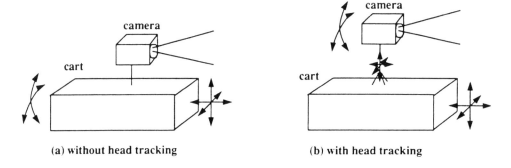

(a) without head tracking   (b) with head tracking

Figure 13.7. The point-and-fly navigation paradigm

Considering the above discussion, we think that a VR application should provide exact and reliable gesture recognition; however, experience has shown that VR systems should not be overloaded with gesture driven interaction (Riedel and Herrmann 1993). One gesture for flying forward, one for flying backward, one for moving objects, one for displaying menus, one for opening doors, and one for selecting objects seems far too much. The casual user will confuse the gestures, and the everyday user will find them not very natural. In fact, a set of gestures which trigger specific actions can be considered another type of (invisible) menu, which is no more realistic or natural than the common 2D menus known from X/Motif or the above mentioned 3D menus.

In order to reduce the number of gestures for interaction, other techniques have been developed, e.g.:

- In order to select an object, the user has to send out a "selector" along a ray.
- The user carries a permanent menu along (around the user's "virtual waist"); this menu contains several tools which can be selected with the glove; then, the assigned action can be made, e.g. an object can be moved, colors can be changed, etc. (Riedel and Herrmann 1993)

Other input devices like Cricket or SpaceMouse can provide similarly simple interaction sufficient for some VR applications. Yet, the glove is the most natural input device.

We think, that many interaction tasks should still become much more intuitive and efficient. If the user wants to move an object, he should be able to do this by just pushing or pulling it with his hand, just like he would do it in reality (well, in reality you might need considerable effort because of the object's weight). And if you want to model an object, the VR system should just let you press on or drag at the surface of the object like a potter would model his clay.

If interaction techniques should become more realistic, exact and real-time collision detection in complex scenes is needed; also, much more physically based behavior of objects is required than is currently available in most VR systems.

Our Potter (see Figure 13.8, Color Section) is a research application to investigate new intuitive modeling techniques like the ones mentioned above. The cube consists of a large triangle mesh (~5000 triangles); these can be modeled directly with the index finger of the hand.

An example assembly system (see Figure 13.9, Color Section) called Puzzle, has been built to investigate the efficiency of several input devices (glove, SpaceBall, dials, mouse); the glove came out on top significantly (Felger 1992). The user can grab objects and move them; an exact real-time collision detection prohibits mutual penetrations. When two fitting objects are very close together, a snapping mechanism "glues" these two together. The goal is to assemble all parts in one. This VR system also incorporates sound as audible feedback; specific sounds are played back when a collision occurs, when two objects snap together, and when the goal is reached.

13.6. Applications

With Virtual Design (Astheimer et al. 1993a, 1993b), the VR system implemented by the authors, a lot of different applications have been realized (Astheimer et al. 1994). Especially in the field of architecture and interior design, many models have been prepared and imported into the system. The models originally have been created from a number of furniture companies, others have been designed from architects or from ship construction.

In Figure 13.10 (see Color Section) an example from the field of architecture is shown, which was designed as an entrance pavilion of the park "Englischer Garten" in Munich. The challenging task for the architect Mr. Economides was to design a building which reflects the metamorphosis from the city to the park within the architecture. The back of the pavilion mainly consists of concrete (the face of the city), while the other part consists of organic elements representing the park. The virtual environment was modeled using the CAD system of Nemetschek.

As we can imagine, such concepts are very difficult to explain using standard presentation methods. In VR, the user is able to experience the design and concept by himself by walking through the virtual house and exploring the concept.

The model of the city of Darmstadt and Erfurt have been prepared and imported in our VR system. For the presentation of Darmstadt (see Figure 13.11, Color Section), a 2D polygonal model has been gained by applying image processing programs to land-register data. A fixed height was assigned to each building layout in order to automatically generate a 3D model and important building had been re-modeled using a CAD-system.

Photographs of building facades had been scanned and retouched (in order to get rid of disturbing picture elements like cars and people in front of the buildings) and mapped to the virtual model.

In Figure 13.12 (see Color Section) the VR presentation of an operation room of the hospital area of a ship is displayed. The department of the ship company Bloom & Voss, which generated this model, had to construct all kinds of pipes very close to the ceiling for the supply of water, electricity, air, etc. The construction of these pipes in a collision-free manner is a very complicated task for modern CAD systems. The entire model of a floor of this ship containing seven rooms have been integrated into our VR system. Using the immersive walk-through ability of VR, all pipes have been examined and several pipe collisions have been detected.

In interior design a broad range of models can be imported. These generated worlds can be interactively explored with available VR techniques, objects can be modified or manipulated. It does not matter which system was used to generate the data or from which application domain they are.

When exploring these worlds critical parts can be presented in a highly realistic fashion, so that they can be evaluated beforehand to avoid cost-intensive re-planning cycles. Alternatives can be tested to yield an optimal design. With VR interaction techniques it is possible to vary color or material of furniture pieces, to select and place different chairs from a series and vary facade details of buildings. Another important application is the evaluation of visual appearance to fit in a given landscape and acoustical noise pollution to meet human conditions.

13.7. Some Thoughts on Realism - One Step Further in VR

Basically, realism is concerned with the fidelity of rendering of "reality" into a particular representation. In VR this overall process can be divided into several information transformation processes. First, a part of the real world is modelled as the combination of abstract objects with certain extensions, positions, colors, behavior and other attributes. Then, in the second part, these abstract objects are, driven by algorithms, rendered into a representation. A user can perceive this representation through his senses and, as the third and final transformation process, use it to construct a mental model of the "reality" surrounding him.

In the field of VR, most research interest focuses on the second part of these processes. This includes understanding of the physical behavior of real world objects, finding mathematical models to describe these principles and investigating sophisticated algorithms and data structures to apply them to the abstract objects mentioned above. Demonstrating this approach to realism in VR, some basic concepts and major ideas have been described in the previous sections.

VR is communication

The upcoming section wants to extend the view to other, not necessarily new, goals in research on VR. The attempt is to point out, that an adequate approach to realism has to take into account all three representation steps as well as their interdependencies. It is assumed that the basic idea of VR is to mediate some information, i.e. in this case one view of reality, through a medium (virtual environments) to a recipient, who is willing to get this information.

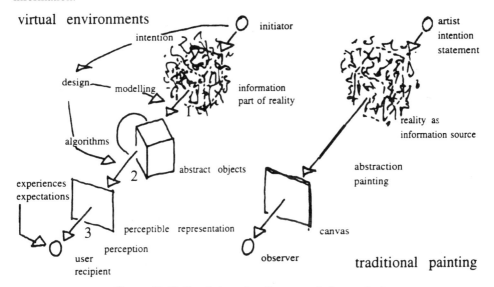

Figure 13.13. Rendering of reality - two design methods.

That suggests the understanding of VR as a kind of communication and comes to the conclusion that realism depends on the credibility of the representation to the user. To optimize the effectiveness of achieving this credibility one should pay attention to all phases of this communication process, i.e. the initial goals, the modeling, the options and restrictions of the medium and the abilities, experiences and expectations of the recipient, during creating and presenting virtual environments.

Influences on the result

As an example of the influence of modeling, consider a typical portrait by Archimboldo with its realistic rendering of fruits. However, seen just as still-life of fruit, the impression is not at all realistic due to modeling, i.e. the highly artificial arrangement of the fruit. On the other hand the tendency of people to perceive it as an even less realistic human face is an example for the influence of perception on realism.

Another example for the interdependencies between modeling, the perception of the user, and his realistic impression would be the modeling of an office with a workstation on the desk. For a computer scientist as a user, the modeling of the workstation has to be relatively detailed and accurate compared to the modeling of, e.g. the window frames, to create an harmonic impression, at least in the sense of this particular observer. Whereas an architect will not be interested in information about the type of the computer, but he instinctively will have a closer look on the construction details of the room. This illustrates the influence of the individual perception on the affect the representation has on the user.

Problems of controlling the result through design

The characteristic difficulty in designing a virtual environment is that the entire process has to be kept in mind, while not all three steps of it can be controlled to the same extent. Only the representation as abstract objects can be influenced directly, while the perceptible representation can be influenced only indirectly by choosing and modifying the algorithm that generates it. Finally the process of perception itself is beyond the control.

This creates a particular design situation compared to the design in other media. A traditional painting for example is created through working directly on the canvas. Once finished, it can be examined for a long time and therefore its information density can be very high. Regarded as the typical element of an animation is a dramaturgy over time. But in interactive real-time applications the single picture cannot be controlled totally in its impression, and there is no fixed path guiding the spectator from one point to the next. Other principles of designing and controlling the effect on the user have to be developed.

Lost in space or guided tours ?

Like in hypertext systems, the problem is to let the user act free, but at the same time ensure that he is not lost in space, overloaded with information, he never wanted, or just bored. Instead of restricting the users interaction possibilities, the principle of foresighted guidance can be borrowed from architecture.

One important principle to represent complex information in a certain communication context is abstraction. As a part of the design process it is applied to reduce data amounts, sharpen the message by confining it to one level and modulate the information hierarchy. Thus abstraction can be employed to guide the user during the exploration in VR.

The interrelation between modeling and rendering is illustrated when abstraction is used as an automated process during the VR session, like the "level-of-detail" algorithm does with geometry as described in section 13.2.2. However, abstraction does not apply only to modelling of the abstract objects, but to all forms of representations the user is confronted with, i.e. all effects included with the rendering of the abstract objects into a perceptible representation.

One possibility working in this direction is to generate sharp and diffuse scene regions or objects, focusing the interest in the message without losing the context. The technique supporting this "soft guiding" is introduced as "inexact rendering". The degree of abstraction itself might change on fixed conditions or continuously, furthermore it can depend on the distance to the observer, on the interests of the user, or the experiences the visitor of the virtual environment already made.

Synergy - exploration as an entire experience

So far we have concentrated on the entireness of the rendering-process as an important factor of realism. Another factor worth mentioning is the entireness of the experience in VR, stimulating multiple senses over a period of time. The ability of humans to remember and connect complex situations consisting of parallel events on different levels underlines the importance of tuning the single components mutually. A coherent outlook results in more realism than detailed geometric information, physical correctness, and so on.

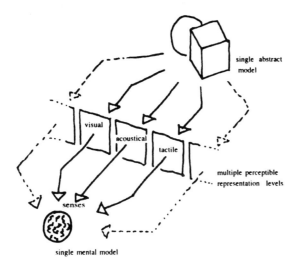

Figure 13.14. Entireness of representation.

The design of future virtual worlds should utilize all kinds of simulation simultaneously. A perfectly synchronized event on multiple levels can replace data intensive elements and reinforce the user's perception. Simple but effective, the animation of an object might reproduce the characteristic of it better than a fixed but more complex geometry. In addition, keeping in mind the limited bandwidth of human receptivity and the inability to reproduce a detailed picture, one should try to reduce the information to the necessary level, not only to get better computer performance, but more to prevent information overkill and concentrate on the statements the environment includes.

Outlook
The introduced aspects and techniques of design control, abstraction, reduction, guidance and entireness including their interrelations and interdependencies cannot only be employed to support the realistic impression of a virtual environment. They can also be used to communicate any kind of information, be it figurative or abstract.

The question before building virtual worlds including modeling, coloring, texturing, interaction etc. should be: what is the expression of this virtual environment and which conclusions from the exploration will be drawn? Furthermore, does it make sense to limit the possible expression to imitations of parts of the real world? Like any technical development the first step is to simulate existing objects, well-known situations and proved working processes. But after some time, new forms of applications, that we cannot imagine now and particular conventions for the design and the perception of virtual environments (e.g. giving up the principle of perspective), will be developed over time just like it happened with the rise of printing, but instead of taking centuries it will only take years. Not until this point will VR unleash its full power and step out of the shadow of realism.

References

*Akka R (1992) *Automatic software control of display parameters for stereoscopic graphics images.* Unpublished results.

Allen JB, Berkley DA (1979) Image method for efficiently simulating small-room acoustics, *Journal Acoustical Society of America*, April.

Astheimer P, Dai F (1993) Dynamic Objects in Virtual Worlds - Integrating Simulations in a Virtual Reality Toolkit, *Proceedings ESS '93,* the European Simulation Symposium, Delft, October 25 - 28, pp.299-304.

*Astheimer P, Felger W (1993) Virtuelle Realität in der Architektur, *Bau-Informatik*, Werner-Verlag, Düsseldorf, Heft 2, pp.54-58.

*Astheimer P, Göbel, M (1993) Integration akustischer Effekte und Simulationen in VR-Entwicklungsumgebungen, in: Warnecke, H.J., Bullinger, H.-J. (Hrsg.): *Virtual Reality '93*, Springer Verlag, Februar 1993, pp.187-208.

Astheimer P (1993a) Realtime Sonification to enhance the Human-Computer-Interaction in Virtual Worlds, in: *Fourth Eurographics Workshop on Visualization in Scientific Computing*, Abingdon, England.

Astheimer P (1993b) Sounds of Silence - How to animate Virtual Worlds with Sound, *Proceedings of ICAT/VET*, Houston, Texas.

Astheimer P (1993c) What you see is what you hear - Acoustics applied to Virtual Worlds, *IEEE Symposium on Research Frontiers in Virtual Reality*, San Jose, USA, October, pp.100-107.

Astheimer P (1993d) Acoustic Virtual Reality - Imitation of Real Worlds, Panel Acoustic Ecologies in Virtual Reality and Telepresence Applications, *Proceedings Virtual Reality Systems* Fall 1993, New York.

Astheimer P, Felger W, Müller S (1993a) Virtual Design - A Generic Virtual Reality System, in: Göbel M (Ed.): *1st Eurographics Workshop on Virtual Environments*, September 7th, Barcelona, Spain, pp.41-57.

Astheimer P, Felger, W., Müller, S (1993b) Virtual Design - A Generic VR System for Industrial Applications, *Computers & Graphics*, Pergamon Press, vol. 17, no. 6.

Astheimer P, Felger, W., Göbel M, Müller S, Ziegler R (1994) Industrielle Anwendungen der Virtuellen Realität - Beispiele, Erfahrungen, Probleme & Zukunftsperspektiven, *VR '94*, Stuttgart

Astheimer P, Pöche ML (1994) Level-of-Detail Generation and its Application in Virtual Reality, submitted to *VRST '94*, Singapore

Badler NI, Barsky BA, Zeltzer D (Eds.) (1991) *Making Them Move, Mechanics, Control, and Animation of Articulated Figures*, Morgan Kaufmann Publishers, Inc. San Mateo, California.

Borish, J (1984) Extension of the image model to arbitrary polyhedra, *Journal Acoustical Society of America*, June 1984

Baum DR, Mann S, Smith KP, Winget JM (1991) Making Radiosity Usable: Automatic Preprocessing and Meshing Techniques for the Generation of Accurate Radiosity Solutions, *Computer Graphics (Siggraph '91)*, vol. 25, no. 4, pp. 51-60

Bryson S (1992) Paradigms for the shaping of surfaces in a virtual environment, in: *Siggraph '92, 19th International Conference On Computer Graphics and Interaction Techniques*, Course Notes 9, pp. 13.1 - 13.10.

Cohen J (1993) Kirk Here:"Using Genre Sounds To Monitor Background Activity, *INTERCHI '93 Adjunct Proceedings*, Amsterdam, pp. 63 - 64

Cohen MF, Wallace JR (1993) *Radiosity and Realistic Image Synthesis*, Academic Press Professional.

Cruz-Neira C, Sandin DJ, DeFanti TA (1993) Surround-screen projection-based virtual reality: The design and implementation of the CAVE, *Proc. SIGGRAPH, Computer Graphics*, Vol. 27, pp. 135 - 142, Aug. 1993

Dai F (1994) Living Virtual Worlds - A Physically-Based Modelling Approach, submitted to *VRST '94*, to be held in Singapore, August 23-26, 1994.

*DeHaemer MJ, Zyda MJ (1993) Simplification of Objects Rendered by Polygonal Approximations, *Computers & Graphics*, vol. 15, no. 2, pp. 175 - 184.

*Encarnacao JL, Astheimer P, Felger W, Frühauf T, Göbel M, Müller S (1993) Graphics and Visualization: The Essential Features for the Classification of Systems, *Proceedings ICCG*, Bombay.

Eurographics (1993) *State of the Art Reports, Eurographics'93*, Barcelona.

*Feiner S, MacIntyre B, Seligmann D (1993) Knowledge-based augmented reality, *Communications of the ACM*, Vol.36, No7, pp.53 - 62.

Felger, W (1992) How interactive visualization can benefit from multidimensional input devices, In J R Alexander, editor, *Visual Data Interpretation Proc.*, SPIE 1668.

Felger, W, Fröhlich, T, Göbel, M (1993) Techniken zur Navigation durch Virtuelle Welten, In *Virtual Reality '93*, Anwendungen und Trends,Fraunhofer-IPA, -IAO, Springer, pp. 209 - 222.

*Funkhouser, TA, Sequin, CH (1993) Visualization of Complex Virtual Environments, *Computer Graphics*, pp. 247 - 254

*Falby JS, Zyda MJ, Pratt DR, Mackey RL (1993) NPSNET: Hierarchical Data Structures for Real-Time Three-Dimensional Visual Simulation, *Computers & Graphics*, vol. 17, No. 1, pp. 65 - 69

*Hofmann GR, Reichenberger K (1989) Realismus als eine Kategorie technischer Bildqualitaet ? - Ein Diskussionsbeitrag, in: M Paul (Hrsg.): *Proceedings GI - 19.Jahrestagung Muenchen*, Springer Verlag

Jacoby RH, Ellis SR (1992) Using virtual menus in a virtual environment, *ACM Computer Graphics, Siggraph '92*, Course Notes(9).

Kirk D (ed.) (1992) *Graphics Gems III*, Academic Press, Inc., San Diego, CA.

Kramer, G (Ed.) (1994) *Auditory Display: Sonification, Audification and Auditory Interfaces*, Addison Wesley.

Krokstad A, Ström S, Sörsdahl S (1968) Calculating the acoustical room response by the use of a ray tracing technique, *Journal Sound Vibrations*, No 8.

Kuttruff H (1973) *Room Acoustics*, Applied Science, London

Lehnert, H et al. (1992) *SCATIS - Spatially Coordinated Auditory/Tactile Interactive Scenario*, ESPRIT Basic Research Project #6358, Information Package.

*Lipton L (1992) *The CrystalEyes Handbook*, StereoGraphics Corp.

Mackinlay JD, Card SK, Robertson GG (1990) Rapid controlled movement through a virtual 3D workspace, *Proc. SIGGRAPH, Computer Graphics*, Vol. 24, pp.171 - 176.

Müller S, Schöffel F (1994) Fast Radiosity Repropagation For Interactive Virtual Environments Using A Shadow-Form-Factor-List, submitted to *SIGGRAPH 94*, Orlando, Florida.

Pöche ML (1994) *Konzeption und Realisierung von Level-of-Detail Techniken zur Reduzierung der Szenenkomplexität auf der Basis des Vis-A-Vis Rendering-Systems*, Diplomarbeit, TH Darmstadt, Februar 1994

*Rheingold H (1992) *Virtuelle Welten*, Rowohlt Verlag, Hamburg; Original edition: Virtual Reality, Summit Books/Simon & Schuster, New York 1991

Riedel O, Herrmann G (1993) Virusi: Virtual user interface - iconorientierte benutzerschnittstelle für vr-applikationen, in: *Virtual Reality '93*, Anwendungen und Trends, pp. 227 - 24. Fraunhofer-IPA, -IAO, Springer.

Robinett W, Holloway R (1992) Implementation of flying, scaling, and grabbing in virtual worlds, in: D. Zeltzer (ed.), *Computer Graphics (1992 Symposium on Interactive 3D Graphics)*, volume 25, pp. 189 - 192.

*Rossignac, J, Borrel, P (1993) Multi-resolution 3D approximation for rendering complex scenes, in: (Falcidieno B, Kunii TL, eds.) *Modeling in Computer Graphics*, Springer, pp. 455 - 465

*Schmitt FJM, Barsky BA, Du WH (1986) An Adaptive Subdivision Method for Surface-Fitting from Sampled Data, *Computer Graphics*, vol. 20, no. 4, pp. 179 - 188.

*Schaub M (1992) *Code_X - Multimediales Design*, DuMont, Köln.

*Schröder F, Roßbach P (1994) Managing the Complexity of Digital Terrain Models, to appear in: *Computers & Graphics*.

*Schroeder WJ, Zarge JA, Lorensen WE (1992) Decimation of Triangle Meshes, *Computer Graphics*, vol. 26, no. 2, pp.65-70.

*Southard DA (19..)Transformations for stereoscopic visual simulation, *Computers & Graphics*, Vol.16, No4, pp.401-410.

Strauss P.S., Carey R (1992) An Object-Oriented 3D Graphics Toolkit, *Proc. SIGGRAPH'92, Computer Graphics*, Vol.26, No2, July pp.341-349.

Takala T, Hahn J (1992) Sound Rendering, *Proc. SIGGRAPH'92, Computer Graphics*, Vol.26, No2, pp.211-219.

Taylor RM, Robinett W, Chi VL, Brooks FP, Wright WV, Williams RS, Snyder EJ (1993) The nanomanipulator: A virtual interface for a scanning tunneling microscope, *Proc. SIGGRAPH '93*, pp.127-134.

Väänänen K, Böhm K (1992) Gesture driven interaction as a human factor in virtual environments, *Proc. Virtual Reality Systems*, University of London.

Vorländer M (1988) Ein Strahlverfolgungsverfahren zur Berechnung von Schallfeldern in Räumen, *Acustica* 65

Vorländer M (1989) Simulation of the transient and steady-state sound propagation in rooms using a new combined ray-tracing/image-source algorithm, *Journal Acoustical Society of America*

Ware C, Osborne, S (1990) Exploration and virtual camera control in virtual three dimensional environments, in: R. Riesenfeld, C. Sequin (eds.), *Computer Graphics (1990 Symposium on Interactive 3D Graphics)*, Vol.24, pp.175-183.

Witkin A, Kass M (Eds.) (1991) An Introduction to Physically Based Modelling, *SIGGRAPH'91 course notes* C23.

Woo A, Poulin P, Fournier, A (1990) A Survey of Shadow Algorithms, *IEEE Computer Graphics and Applications*, Vol. 10, No. 6, pp.13-32.

---

* not referenced in this chapter

14

Shared Objects in Private Workspaces: Cooperative Work in Virtual Worlds

Gurminder Singh, Luis Serra
Institute of Systems Science, National University of Singapore, Kent Ridge, Singapore

14.1. Introduction

The majority of existing virtual worlds are single-user systems. Even though, compared with traditional systems these systems provide tremendous benefit to the user, their utility in the real world is quite limited. The reason for this is that these systems do not support collaboration among a group of users. We believe that networking coupled with highly interactive technology of virtual worlds will dominate the world of computers and information technology. It will not be enough to produce slick single-user, standalone virtual worlds. These systems will have to connect people, systems, information streams and technologies with one another. The information that is currently shared through file systems or through other "static" media will have to be exchanged through the network. This information has to reside "in the net" where it is easy to get at.

Developing virtual worlds that support collaboration among a group of users is a complex and time-consuming task. In order to develop such virtual worlds, the developer has to be proficient in network programming, object management, graphics programming, device handling, and user interface design. Even after gaining expertise in such diverse specializations, developing network-based virtual worlds takes a long time since network-based programs are inherently more difficult to program and debug than standalone

Artificial Life and and Virtual Reality Edited by Nadia Magnenat Thalmann and Daniel Thalmann
© 1994 John Wiley and Sons Ltd

programs. In view of all this, we have developed the BrickNet toolkit to enable the rapid and easy development of network-based virtual worlds.

BrickNet is designed for the creation of virtual worlds that operate on workstations connected over a network and share information with each other, forming a loosely coupled system (Ellis, et al. 1991). It enables graphical objects to be maintained, managed, and used efficiently, and permits objects to be shared by multiple virtual worlds or "clients". A client can connect to a "server" to request objects of its interest. These objects are deposited by other clients connected to the same server or another server on the network (see Figure 14.1). Depending on the availability and access rights of objects, the server satisfies client requests.

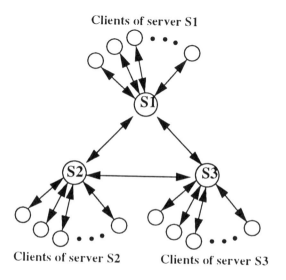

Figure 14.1. A BrickNet server handles several clients. servers communicate with one another to satisfy client requests.

BrickNet provides comprehensive support for graphical, behavioral and network modeling of virtual worlds. The basic philosophy of BrickNet is to provide the developer with a "virtual world shell" which the developer can customize by populating it with objects of interest, by modifying its behavioral properties, and by specifying the objects' network behavior.

Virtual worlds constructed using BrickNet are characterized as follows:

- Private Workspaces: In BrickNet virtual worlds, each user has his own workspace which is populated by shared and private objects. BrickNet virtual worlds are not restricted to sharing an identical set of objects. A virtual world manages its own set of objects, some or all of which may be shared with the other virtual worlds on the network.

- Object-Oriented Virtual Worlds: BrickNet virtual worlds are comprised of objects that embody their graphical, behavioral and network properties. These worlds are created in an interpretive, object-oriented environment which allows objects to be added, deleted and their attributes modified easily at runtime.
- Client-Server Configuration: A BrickNet server acts as an object request broker and communication server for its clients. Servers, distributed over a network, communicate with one another to provide a service to the client without its explicit knowledge of multiple servers or inter-server communication. The clients are unaware of the locale of the servers serving the client requests. Clients run asynchronously without having to wait for the data to arrive from the server.

BrickNet is aimed at collaborative design environments where a complete design task is distributed over several design nodes. Each node is responsible for a part of the design and shares its design objects with others to facilitate collaboration on the larger design task. BrickNet can also be used to construct multi-user games, groupware systems (Ellis et al. 1991), concurrent engineering systems (Reddy et al. 1993) and other asynchronous network-based interactive, graphical environments.

Using BrickNet, we have developed several complex applications. As a result, we have found that proper information sharing is vital to the success of network-based virtual worlds. Two key aspects of structuring complex network-based virtual worlds are:

- to ensure that the network does not bog down the application, and
- that when the application has greater need for computing resources, it should be able to defer processing of network messages.

BrickNet currently runs on a network of Silicon Graphics workstations. It has been implemented in the Starship (Loo 1991) and C programming languages. Starship is a general-purpose, interpretive, frame-based language. It provides both the object-oriented model and the frame model. The communication part of BrickNet has been implemented using UDP. Our I/O devices include one Virtual Research EYEGEN 3 HMD, one Virtual Research Flight Helmet, one pair of Crystal Eyes stereo glasses, one Ascension Bird, two Logitech 6D mouse, one ImmersionProbe, and one Beachtron 3D sound hardware.

This chapter provides an overview of BrickNet and gives examples of its use. For implementation details on BrickNet, see (Singh et al. 1994; Serra et al. 1993).

14.2. Related Work

Multi-user virtual worlds can be divided into two groups. In the first group we put all those systems in which the content (or the set of objects) of all virtual worlds is the same. Individual users may be looking at different parts of the virtual space but they all have the same objects loaded in their worlds. In the second group, we put those systems in which virtual worlds are not restricted to sharing an identical set of objects. The objects loaded in a virtual world may differ from the objects loaded in another virtual world.

Both VUE (Appino et al. 1992) and MR (Shaw et al. 1993) initially started as single user systems but have been extended to handle multi-user virtual worlds in which the content of the virtual worlds is largely the same. In multi-user VUE (Codella et al., 1992; Codella et al. 1993) multiple users share a single simulation (or virtual world content). Each user can have a different interface (or style) for the same simulation and see a small amount of state information from other users (e.g., each user can see other users' hands).

Multi-user MR allows multiple independent applications to communicate with one another through its Peer package (Shaw and Green 1993). The MR toolkit distributes the computation or simulation part of the virtual world as well as device handling. It supports the decoupled simulation model by dividing a virtual world into four components: presentation, interaction, geometric model, and computation. The computation component proceeds independent of the other system components and generates data for the geometric model component. The geometric component converts the data into a form amenable to output by the presentation component. The interaction component manages all input from the user and coordinates all output to the user. The MR toolkit allows for the distribution of these four components across workstations on a network. In this case, the data sharing facility of MR allows two processes to share the same data structure by one process producing data and the other consuming it. An MR application has a centralized process, called the master process, which collects device data from the device servers, and which dispatches the device and application data to any slave process which might need it. The Peer package allows a master process to communicate with other master processes on other machines. Each MR toolkit master process, or peer, maintains a list of other peers that it is connected to. Peers are connected pair-wise, and a peer may send a message to any or all other peers at once.

SIMNET (Calvin et al. 1993; Alluisi 1991) uses an object- and event-based approach to distributed, interactive virtual worlds for battlefield simulation and training. In SIMNET, virtual worlds consist of objects that interact with each other by broadcasting a series of events. An object initiating an event does not calculate which other objects might be affected by it. It is the receiving object's responsibility to determine whether the event is of its interest or not. To minimize communication processing and bandwidth requirements, objects transmit only changes in their behavior. Until an update is received, the new position of a remote (or a network-based) object is extrapolated from the states last reported by those objects. NPSNET (Zyda et al. 1992) uses many of the same networking concepts used in SIMNET. Despite differences in the implementation of the two systems and the other important contributions of the NPSNET research that make network-based virtual worlds affordable, they can be treated identically for our purposes. Like NPSNET, VERN (Blau et al. 1992) is also based on the networking technology of SIMNET. A distinguishing feature of VERN is its extensible object-oriented class hierarchy which abstracts communication and process control to the highest levels of the hierarchy.

DIVE (Carlsson and Hagsand 1993), (Fahlen et al. 1993) uses peer-to-peer communication to implement shared virtual worlds. A DIVE world consists of a set of objects to which DIVE processes can connect. DIVE processes connected to the same world are all identical in their content. If there are multiple DIVE worlds running on the network, a DIVE process can dynamically change worlds, but at any one time it can be a member of exactly one world.

VEOS (Bricken 1990) is an extendable, user-level framework for prototyping distributed VR applications. It facilitates coarse-grained parallelism by using heavyweight sequential processes, similar to UNIX processes. The VEOS application programmer's interface is provided by XLISP.

14.2.1. Relation to BrickNet

BrickNet allows multiple clients to exchange objects and object updates with one another through BrickNet servers. BrickNet clients (usually) differ in their content from each other. Clients connected to different BrickNet servers can share objects through their servers. A BrickNet client can be further distributed based on VUE, MR or other software organizations.

Unlike multi-user VUE, BrickNet does not force users to share a common object space, although such a scenario is possible to implement with BrickNet. Like multi-user VUE, SIMNET, NPSNET and VERN all focus on supporting multi-user-same-content applications, although their software organization and communication mechanisms are different. In the multi-user MR toolkit, applications (different content) can communicate device data and small amounts of application data with each other. MR does not provide any sophisticated mechanism to allow applications to exchange objects and object updates. In DIVE, all processes (or clients) connected to a world (or server) are identical, but they can change their worlds dynamically. Once a process connects to a new world, it loses contact with its old world and switches its content completely to that of the new world. In BrickNet, clients cannot dynamically change their server, but they can share information across servers.

OMA (OMG 1992; Moad 1992) provides an architecture that combines distributed processing with object-oriented computing to make it easier for developers to build cooperative-processing applications and to help make these applications more portable. From the architectural point of view, OMA's Object Services and Object Request Broker components are similar to BrickNet's object and update handling, but, as described in Sections 14.5 and 14.6, BrickNet's support for object management (in the WHEN_AVAILABLE and TIME_BASED modes) is more advanced than that of OMA's. In addition, BrickNet is geared towards supporting the special requirements of virtual worlds to which OMA does not pay any attention.

14.3. A Demonstration Scenario

To help understand the types of applications that BrickNet is aimed at, we describe a collaborative design environment which has been built using BrickNet. This environment is representative of design systems supported by BrickNet, although it has been simplified here for expository purposes. Our example environment consists of four clients connected to a BrickNet server (Figure 14.2). Two of these clients, named ChairClient and the LampClient, are running a furniture design application involving chairs and lamps, respectively. These clients share their objects with others with an EXCLUSIVE_UPDATE access restriction. That means other clients can down load the objects (the chairs and lamps) to look at them, but they cannot modify the original objects. The other clients, named KitchenClient and LivingRoomClient, use the objects designed by the ChairClient and LampClient in addition to their local objects.

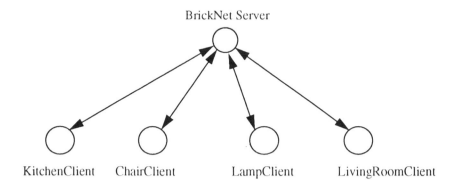

Figure 14.2. Architecture of the Collaborative Design Environment.

For the sake of brevity we describe how the KitchenClient is constructed and how it interacts and shares information with the other clients. The two main components of a BrickNet virtual world are the Person and World classes. In order to specify the "shell" within which the KitchenDesigner moves, the developer need only fill in the details for these two classes. This would be done as follows:

```
(KitchenDesigner SolidPerson){              %1
  :world (KitchenWorld World);              %2
  :navigation (a Walkthrough);              %3
  .hand:controller (Logitech6D class new);  %4
  .head:controller (HeadTracker class new); %5
  }
```

Line %1 says that KitchenDesigner is an instance of SolidPerson, which itself is a subclass of Solid (a generic class that stands for all objects with physical appearance). KitchenDesigner is contained in the KitchenWorld (line %2), and is set up to navigate using a particular mode called Walkthrough interaction mode (line %3). The same Person has a Hand attached to a Logitech6D input device (line %4). The Head is attached to a HeadTracker (line %5). Defaults are assumed for all attributes that are not explicitly defined. For example, by default, the head has two eyes, and the display mode is stereoscopic.

The KitchenWorld is defined as an instance of World (a container class) including a Cupboard and a Table at the specified locations. Each of the prototype objects used here would have been created previously, and initialized using a similar specification.

```
(KitchenWorld World){                                          %1
    include (Cupboard SolidCupboard) #vector[10.0 0.0 0.0];    %2
    include (Table SolidTable) #vector[10.0 0.0 10.0];     }   %3
```

Clients thus constructed connect to the BrickNet server when they are run. Once connected to the server, the clients can share their objects with other clients by depositing them with the server and can lease objects deposited by other clients from the server. In our example, the KitchenClient leases a DiningChair and a KitchenLamp designed by ChairClient and LampClient respectively. Figure 14.3 shows the configuration of the various clients in this example.

BrickNet enables the user to visualize the status of the current server-client configuration (see Figure 14.4, Color Section). Each client is represented by a node that displays the current activity in that virtual world. This is accomplished using "dynamic portals". These are a significant extension of the simple portal concept. A simple portal is a way of taking the user from one virtual world to another. Sometimes such portals give information (minimal at best) about where the user will end up if the portal is hit. Dynamic portals not only tell where the user will end up but also what is going on in the world where the user will end up. For example, a simple portal may show that the user will end up in a place which has medical instruments, but it does not tell whether the instruments are being assembled there or being used in an operating theater. Dynamic portals are somewhat similar to the picture-in-picture facility available in the latest televisions. Concurrently with video playback, these televisions can show the current program being shown on a selected channel, in a small window.

In our example environment, when the user hits the desired node, the user ends up in the virtual world represented by the dynamic portal on the node. This is accomplished by transferring that virtual world's contents over the net to the current user who can then select the objects of interest. These are then copied into the user's own virtual world (of course, whether an object can be copied or not, and the other permissions on the mode of copying, are controlled by the original owner of the object). Using this environment, the user can assemble network-based virtual worlds in a purely visual and interactive fashion.

When the user enters the ChairWorld and selects, for example the DiningChair, the ChairClient transfers the Starship program code that creates the chair object to the KitchenClient. When this code is executed by the KitchenClient, a shared chair object is created in the KitchenWorld. When the ChairDesigner modifies the chair object, the ChairClient sends updates to the BrickNet server, which then automatically forwards them to the KitchenClient. The ChairClient does not have to know which other clients have its chair object. The BrickNet server maintains this information and decides to forward updates to whichever client should get them.

The object updates are sent in the form of Starship code that the KitchenClient executes to effect the changes. This is possible due to the interpreted nature of Starship. The same updates are sent to other clients that have requested a copy of the chair object. Since the LampClient has not requested the chair object, it is not sent the updates. This filtering of messages is done by the BrickNet server.

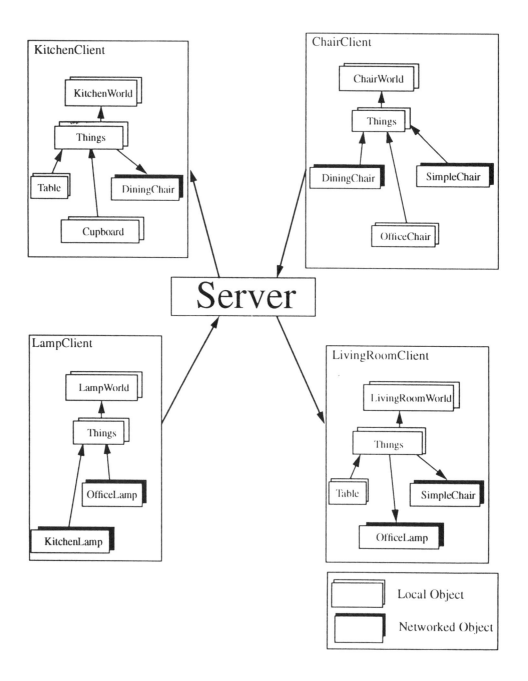

Figure 14.3. Networked configuration of multiple worlds.

14.4. Architecture of BrickNet

BrickNet supports the layered architecture for network-based virtual worlds shown in Figure 14.5. Before we describe the layers of this architecture, we briefly describe the concept of client and server in BrickNet.

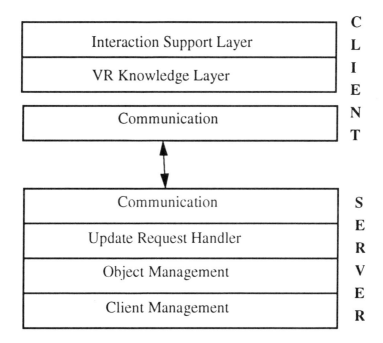

Figure 14.5. Architecture of BrickNet servers and clients

A server is designed to handle multiple clients in an asynchronous mode. A client executes autonomously and has a virtual world of its own that includes objects leased from a server. Clients may also use local objects that have no relation to the server or other clients. A client can deposit an object with the server and share it with other clients. Such sharing can be restricted in various ways. For example, an object might only be visible to other clients but not updatable by them; an object might only be updatable by its current owner; updates may or may not be sent to other clients who have leased out the object from the server.

A server can be seen as an object request broker and a communication manager. As an object request broker, it enables objects to be maintained, managed, and used efficiently. A server also permits objects to be shared by multiple clients. It keeps track of client requests for objects and object updates, and services these requests when possible. As a communication manager, a BrickNet server keeps track of clients' status (active or passive), their addresses and port information, and manages the sending and receiving of packets of information. In BrickNet, clients do not communicate directly with each other, they always go through servers to update each other.

BrickNet objects are network-based. In addition to client-specific messages, BrickNet objects understand a set of standard messages and react to them in standard ways. For example, consider that client A has deposited an object O that has been leased out by client B. Client A owns O and has EXCLUSIVE_UPDATE privilege on it. When client A destroys O, it is automatically removed from client B's environment. Client B does not have to write routines to handle such messages unless the client wants to change their standard behavior.

In the following section, the various layers of BrickNet clients and servers shown in Figure 14.5 are explained.

14.5. Client Layers

A BrickNet client consists of three layers; the interaction support layer, the VR knowledge layer and the communication layer (see Figure 14.5). The internal organization of these layers and their content is described in the rest of this section.

14.5.1. Interaction Support Layer

The interaction support layer is the user interface part of the virtual world. The user interacts with the virtual world through devices and interaction techniques that are part of this layer. For example, this layer decides how a virtual object is picked and moved.

From the developer's point of view, the interaction support layer frees them from the lowest level details of a VR application, thus enabling them to concentrate on the VR application proper. This is accomplished by providing a set of building blocks (each building block is called a brick) which manage windows, process graphics, manipulate input devices, measure time and performance, etc.

It is important to note that the interaction support layer may be further distributed based on, for example, VUE (Appino et al. 1992) or MR (Shaw et al. 1993) frameworks. In our case, we simply run device drivers as separate processes. The device data read by these drivers is collected by BrickNet clients when they need it.

14.5.2. VR Knowledge Layer

The knowledge layer manages objects that form the "content" of the virtual world. In a network-based virtual world, most of these objects are obtained from the server, and hence are network-based.

The knowledge layer organizes VR applications according to a metaphor that tries to be consistent with the way the user experiences the real world. This metaphor assumes that a person (the VR end user) is moving and interacting within a world populated by solid objects that are governed by a set of physical and environmental laws. Each of these components is represented by a class which is interconnected to the other classes by means of semantic network links such as is-part-of. Based on these classes, a VR application is constructed by first selecting the components of the world, assigning them behaviors, choosing a set of laws and then running the simulation loop.

The rest of this section explains how various BrickNet classes are used to put together virtual worlds and how these worlds communicate with servers to share objects and updates.

14.5.2.1. The Solid and World classes

We shall describe first the two main classes: Solid and World. Solid represents the common attributes of a 3D object, such as shape, behaviour, position and orientation in space, and the material and texture that give it appearance. In order to cater for different shapes and behaviours, Solid has a different subclass for each different solid object. For example, Person and Chair are both subclasses of Solid, the former having complex behaviours whilst the latter is inanimate. A distinction is made in BrickNet between the geometrical shape of a Solid, which is handled by a "geometry" object of the type described in the Interaction Support Layer (see Section 14.5.1), and the `complete' Solid, which includes additional attributes such as material, texture, position and orientation, and behavioural properties.

World is a container class that describes and keeps track of the entities that make a virtual world, such as the things in it (e.g. instances of Solid), the persons inhabiting the world and the laws governing the world (such as the force of gravity), etc.

The KitchenDesigner navigates through this KitchenWorld that contains a Kitchen with objects in it. KitchenDesigner, being a composite Solid, has two main components: one head and one hand. The head in turn contains a left eye and a right eye. This structure is hierarchical and natural to manipulate: moving and rotating the Person automatically moves and rotates the head and hand, and rotating the head automatically rotates its two eyes.

The KitchenWorld contains a list of objects which are instances of Solid. Each object can in turn be a composite object. For example, the lamp has a light attached to it, which behaves as a light source in the virtual world.

BrickNet worlds also have laws such as physical and environmental laws. A law determines the general behavior of the things in the world and the characteristics of the rendering of the virtual scene. An example of a PhysicalLaw is the force of gravity or the non-penetrating nature of things. The EnvironmentalLaw refers to the brightness of the ambient light in the world, the effect of fog, depth cues etc.

Input devices such as the Ascension Bird or Polhemus FastTrack may be attached to either the Head, the Hand or the Person. If a controller is attached to the Hand it controls the action of the Hand; if it is attached to the Head (usually a head-tracker) it interprets the head movements; and similarly the controller attached to the Person itself controls the movement of the person in the virtual space.

A Navigation technique is attached to the KitchenDesigner. This navigation determines how the user navigates through the virtual world, which also depends on the type of controllers attached. For example, a walk-through navigation allows the user to walk through the virtual world; a fly-through navigation enables the user to fly around the world, etc.

BrickNet provides visual tools to help the developer inspect the configuration of the application. Figure 14.6 (see Color Section) shows a snapshot of a typical inspection session.

14.5.2.2. Object and Update Management

A BrickNet client usually contains two types of objects: local and remote (or network-based). The local objects, as their names suggest, are local to the virtual world and not shared with other clients on the network. So the state and existence of such objects is not affected by the other clients on the network. Usually, local objects are used as background objects or as scratch objects. The network-based objects enable clients to share information with one another. Updates on the state of such an object are sent to all the clients who have the object and have expressed interest in updates on the object. In the rest of this section we will focus on network-based objects only.

BrickNet clients make requests for objects to the server in the "WHEN_AVAILABLE", "NOW" or "TIME_BASED" modes. Clients request objects in the WHEN_AVAILABLE mode if they are interested in the object, even though it may not be available when the request is made. The NOW mode is designed to ask for objects to be delivered right away when the request reaches the server. If the request cannot be satisfied when it is received, a failure message is sent to the client. In the TIME_BASED mode, the client can specify the amount of time within which it would like to receive the requested object. If the object cannot be delivered within the stated time, the server sends a failure message to the client. How the server handles requests for objects is explained in section 14.6.2.

Using the above modes of requesting objects, developers can implement efficient object usage strategies. For example, clients can anticipate their objects requirements based on user interaction and make requests for objects before they are actually needed. An example where this strategy works well is with walk-throughs in large multi-storied buildings. Imagine that the user has entered the elevator to go to the fifth floor of the building. As soon as the user chooses the floor number, the client can send requests for fifth floor objects. By the time, the user reaches the fifth floor the client may have received the fifth floor objects. In this type of an application, objects are loaded only when they are needed as opposed to simpler strategies where large numbers of objects are loaded in the environment even when they are not needed.

BrickNet allows clients to request objects from other servers. In this mode, called TRY_HARD, the original server checks with other BrickNet servers on the network for the availability of the requested object. If the requested object is available, it is sent to the original server which made the request, which in turn sends the object to the client who requested it. This server cannot distribute the received object to other servers as it does not own it. The ownership of the object still rests with the dispatcher server.

Just as a client can log pending object requests with a server, servers can also log pending object requests with each other. From this perspective, clients and servers are symmetrical. However, a client does not interact with other clients directly whereas a server does.

In BrickNet, objects are referenced through object names. To facilitate client operation, BrickNet allows clients to request objects by constructing object names using regular expressions. This enables clients to send one request for several objects.

The shared objects, leased by a client from other clients on the net, are updated when the client receives object updates from its server. When an update message arrives, it is first received by the client's communication layer. This layer stores the message until it is retrieved by the client for processing. In most cases, clients process network messages once each simulation cycle. But this behavior is modifiable by the programmer. For example, the client, if it needs more processing power for a short while, may decide to defer processing the network messages. In such cases, the communication layer retains the messages. Similarly, the client may decide to devote more time to processing network messages if it needs to do so. The programming of this behavior depends on the requirements of the application.

When an object is shared by multiple clients, it is possible to end up with an inconsistent object state if clients simultaneously try to update it. In order to prevent this, BrickNet uses the concept of current owner of an object. Only the current owner is allowed to update the object and have the updates sent to the other interested clients. When a client wants to update an object, it sends a request to the server asking for ownership of the object. If there is no current owner of the object, the server grants this permission. After having updated the object, the client is expected to give up the ownership of the object so that it can be transferred to whoever else wants it.

Sometimes there is a need to synchronize object states among clients. BrickNet provides a finer grain of synchronization than most other systems. When a BrickNet client, who owns an object, wants to ensure that other clients who have leased out the object are synchronized with it, it sends a sync message to the server. The server in turn checks with each client who has leased out the object. These clients then send a sync-acknowledgment to the server. The server, after it has received acknowledgments from all relevant clients, sends a sync-confirm message to the requesting client.

14.6. Server Layers

A BrickNet server consists of four layers: the client management layer, the update request handler layer, the object management layer and the communication layer. These layers are described in the following sub-sections.

14.6.1. Client Management Layer

The client management layer in the server is responsible for maintaining client-specific information. When a client is registered with the server, a new record for the client is created and managed by this layer. This record contains information about the client's ports for communication, its status (active or sleeping) and pending requests made by the client.

In order to ensure that all leased objects are updated in each client's world in BrickNet, the UPDATE_MESSAGE is used. When an object is modified by the owner client, the client sends the UPDATE_MESSAGE with modification data of the object to the server. Then the server distributes this message with the data to all the clients that have leased the object. Once a client receives the UPDATE_MESSAGE, it uses the data to update the object in its own world.

To reduce the network traffic, BrickNet provides QUENCHING and UNQUENCHING messages. A quenching message is one that is sent by a client to inform the server to stop sending certain messages for a given period of time. One situation where quenching messages can be used is when a client decides to stop collaborative work for a period of time and does not wish to be informed of any updates for all leased objects during the break. The client sends a quenching message to request that the server to stop sending any UPDATE_MESSAGE for the period of time. If the period of time is not specified then the server waits until it receives an unquenching message from the client before it resumes sending the client the UPDATE_MESSAGE.

In the case of UPDATE_MESSAGE, the action taken by the server when it receives an unquenching message for UPDATE_MESSAGE is fairly straightforward; the server sends an UPDATE_MESSAGE for all objects leased by the client. However, for some messages such as DELETE_MESSAGE, the task undertaken by the server when receiving the unquenching message may not be as simple. In this case of DELETE_MESSAGE, the server will have to check which leased objects of the client have been deleted before sending DELETE_MESSAGE for those deleted objects.

14.6.2. Object Management Layer

The object management layer keeps track of objects deposited by various clients and object access rights and updates. When a client makes a request for an object, this layer sends the object if access rights permit.

In the WHEN_AVAILABLE mode, if the requested object cannot be sent to the client immediately (because of non-availability of the object or its access right restrictions), the request is queued by the BrickNet server in a pending request queue. As soon as an object becomes available for distribution, BrickNet clears pending requests for the object. If an object is requested in the NOW mode, BrickNet sends the object as soon as it gets the request. However, if the object cannot be sent immediately, the request is not queued in the pending request queue. In the "TIME_BASED" mode, the client that makes the request specifies the length of time for which it is interested in the object. If the requested object can be delivered within the stated time slot, the server sends the object to the client. Otherwise, the request is removed from the pending queue.

If a client sends an object request in WHEN_AVAILABLE mode and uses a regular expression to construct the object name, the server first sends the objects that match the given regular expression and then places the request in the client's pending request queue. As and when other clients submit objects, the server matches the regular expression with the new object's name. If the match succeeds, the object is sent. However, the original request is not removed from the client's pending request queue.

14.6.3. Update Request Handler

The next layer, called the update request handler, manages clients' update requests. This layer ensures that clients have the correct permissions for updates. For example, if a client sends a position update for an object, this layer goes through the object database maintained by the object management layer and sends the update to other clients who may have expressed interest in such updates.

Clients, when they request objects, can choose to be updated or not after the requested objects have been sent. If a client asks for updates, all object updates are automatically sent by the server to the client whenever the object is updated by its current owner. These updates are received by the communication layer of the client and processed by the receiving client.

As explained in Section 14.6.1, clients can prevent update messages from being sent to them by servers for a limited duration.

14.6.4. Communication Layer

The communication layer in BrickNet servers implements the communication protocol to receive messages from, and to send messages to, clients. It manages communication with multiple, networked clients running on heterogeneous hardware. The communication layer is responsible for the security and reliability of communication between clients and the server.

BrickNet servers asynchronously communicate with multiple, networked clients running on heterogeneous hardware. This communication takes place by sending and receiving packets. Each packet has a sender id, a message type, length of the data and the data itself. The sender of a packet encodes this information using the BrickNet encoding scheme. When the packet arrives at its destination, the receiver decodes the packet and processes it.

14.7. Discussion and Conclusions

The BrickNet toolkit provides a rich set of functionalities geared towards expediting the creation of network-based virtual worlds. It eliminates the need to learn about low level graphics, device handling and network programming. This is achieved by providing higher level support for graphical, behavioral and network modeling of virtual worlds. Instead of asking the developer to start from scratch, as is the case with most other toolkits, BrickNet provides a "virtual world shell" which is customized by populating it with objects of interest, by modifying its behavioral properties, and by specifying the objects' network behavior. This makes it possible for the developer to create network-based virtual worlds quickly and easily.

In network-based virtual worlds, the distribution strategy followed can have a profound effect on the performance of virtual worlds. Here we discuss BrickNet's strategy in the light of some of the other possible distribution strategies.

In a client-server arrangement, where a server supports the communication and distribution needs of several clients, the server can become a bottleneck if it has to serve too many clients. An overloaded server can lead to delay in message routing and object requests being satisfied. The flip side of the client-server architecture is that since several functions (such as client management, shared-object management, update distribution, message routing, and error-recovery) are handled by the server, clients can focus on local interaction and graphical update as these are critical issues in virtual worlds. A common solution to the server overloading problem is to run servers on high-compute-performance machines and clients on high-graphics-performance machines. A more interesting solution has been followed in BrickNet by using a number of cooperating servers. A server in this type of configuration manages its own (smaller) set of clients and occasionally interacts with other servers to satisfy the requirements of its clients or other servers' requirements. This kind of setup has all the advantages of a client-server organization and at the same time it softens the impact of disadvantages. It is also more fail-safe; if a server crashes, only a subset of all the cooperating clients suffer. In the single server organization, if the server crashes, all clients are affected.

Another approach to solving the server bottleneck problem is to have clients directly manage communication with other clients. Here the functions of the server have to be supported by each client, making the clients heavier. Each client has to mediate communication with other clients and has to know who to communicate with and when. This can adversely affect the graphical update and interaction in the virtual world. The two significant advantages of this approach are that it is more fail-safe and the communication bottleneck is less likely to occur. In this approach, if a client crashes, it only affects those clients that have borrowed objects from or leased objects to the crashed client. Because each client manages its own communication and object sharing with other clients, the communication bottleneck is unlikely to occur, except in cases where the client load is highly uneven. Keeping in view that graphical update and smoothness in interaction are key requirements in virtual worlds, it is critical for the client to delegate as much communication and object management work as possible. This strategy, however, does not facilitate delegating work to the server.

In BrickNet, messages are sent only to clients who have the affected object and have expressed interest in receiving updates. This strategy is very different from broadcasting messages to all clients whether the messages are relevant or not. In this case, the clients receive the messages and discard the messages that they do not need. This approach leads to a significant amount of redundant network traffic and wasted processing time of the clients. The advantage of this approach is that it is easy to implement. In the BrickNet approach, where messages are filtered and sent only to relevant clients, there is minimal amount of network traffic and all messages received by the clients are useful.

There are other approaches to reducing network traffic. For example, SIMNET (Calvin et al. 1993) uses dead-reckoning algorithm to predict vehicle movement. So updates are sent less frequently than once every cycle. Once an update is to be sent, it is broadcast to all clients. In BrickNet, clients can decide how often to send updates, allowing dead-reckoning-like algorithms to be implemented. But updates are always sent to relevant clients only.

BrickNet pays special attention to the need for maintaining interactive response in network-based virtual worlds by separating graphical update from network messages. It executes the client's communication layer as a separate process which receives all the messages meant for the clients from the network and stores them until the client retrieves and processes them. This scheme allows the clients to defer processing network messages and devote all resources to supporting interaction when necessary. For example, instead of checking for network messages once each simulation cycle, the client can decide to check them every other cycle (or according to any other scheme). In this case, the perceived network latency would be larger but it would help solve the real-time graphical update problem. This capability has proved extremely useful in maintaining responsiveness of network-based virtual worlds.

BrickNet has been used to develop network-based virtual worlds in several areas, including design, planning, medicine and visualization. The two examples that are particularly interesting are the ship planning environment and the office design environment. The ship planning environment enables multiple users to load containers destined for different parts of the world in a ship. As containers are loaded in the ship, all users are updated about the addition of containers and their locations on the ship. In this case, the content of all virtual worlds is the same. As soon as any of the users makes an update, it is sent to all of the clients. The second environment, namely the network-based design environment, has been described in Section 14.2. Here each virtual world has different content depending on the object being designed. These applications have exercised a variety of the toolkit's capabilities, including smart object management, regular expression-based object naming and flexible object update strategy.

Experience with BrickNet has revealed several important aspects of its approach and design. Not surprisingly, the main positive aspect of the experience has been that it cuts down tremendously on the time and effort required for developing network-based virtual worlds. Since the toolkit is easy to learn, it does not take much time to start programming in the BrickNet framework.

We have found BrickNet to be suitable for implementing several types of network-based virtual worlds. BrickNet's object management strategy coupled with asynchronous communication leads to greater flexibility in designing virtual worlds. In one of our applications, we use BrickNet to implement a system to visualize different views of a network-based planning system. This flexibility is a direct consequence of BrickNet's ability to maintain, manage and use objects efficiently through its smart object management scheme.

References

Alluisi EA. (1991) The Development of Technology for Collective Training: SIMNET, A Case History, *Human Factors*, Vol.33, No.3, pp.343-362.

Appino PA, Lewis JB, Koved L, Ling DT, Rabenhorst DA, Codella, CF (1992). An Architecture for Virtual Worlds, *PRESENCE: Teleoperators and Virtual Environments*, Vol.1, No.1, pp.1-17.

Blau B, Hughes CE, Moshell JM, Lisle C (1992) Networked Virtual Environments, *Proc. 1992 Symp on Interactive 3D Graphics*, Cambridge, Massachusetts, 29 March - 1 April 1992, pp.157-160.

Bricken W (1990) *Virtual environment operating system: Preliminary functional architecture*, TR-HITL-M- 90-2, Human Interface Technology Lab, University of Washington, Seattle, 1990.

Calvin J, Dicken A, Gaines B, Metzger P, Miller D, Owen D (1993). The SIMNET Virtual World Architecture, *Proc. IEEE Virtual Reality Annual International Symposium (VRAIS'93)*, Sept. 18-22, 1993, Seattle, Washington, USA, pp.450-455.

Carlsson C Hagsand O (1993) DIVE - a Multi-User Virtual Reality System, *Proc. IEEE Virtual Reality Annual International Symposium (VRAIS'93)*, Sept. 18-22, 1993, Seattle, Washington, USA, pp.394-400.

Codella C, Jalili R, Koved L, Lewis BJ, Ling DT, Lipscomb JS, Rabenhorst DA, Wang CP, Norton A, Sweeney P, Turk G (1992), Interactive simulation in a multi-person virtual world, *Proc. ACM SIGCHI'92: Human Factors in Computing Systems,* ACM, New York, pp.329-334.

Codella C, Jalili R, Koved L, Lewis BJ (1993) A Toolkit for Developing Multi-User, Distributed Virtual Environments, *Proc. IEEE Virtual Reality Annual International Symposium (VRAIS'93),* Sept. 18-22, 1993, Seattle, Washington, USA, pp.401-407.

Ellis CA, Gibbs SJ, Rein GL (1991) Groupware: Some Issues and Experiences. Communications of ACM, Vol.34, No.1, pp.39-58.

Fahlen LE, Stahl O, Brown CG, Carlsson C (1993). A space-based model for user-interaction in shared synthetic environments, *Proc. ACM InterCHI'93*, Amsterdam, Holland, 24-29 April 1993, pp:43-48.

Loo PL (1991) *The Starship Manual* (Version 2.0), ISS TR#91-54-0, Institute of Systems Science, National University of Singapore, Kent Ridge, Singapore 0511.

Moad J (1992) Can the OMG Unite your Enterprise, *Datamation.* April 1992, pp.38-42.

OMG (1992) Object Services Architecture, *Object Management Group*, 492 Old Connecticut Path, Framingham, MA 01701, USA.

Serra L, Ng H, Fairchild K (1993) Building Virtual Realities with Bricks, Proc. 2nd International Conference "Interfaces to Real and Virtual Worlds", Montpelier, France, 22-26 March 1993, pp.101-109.

Shaw C, Green M, Liang J, Sun Y (1993) Decoupled Simulation in Virtual Reality with the MR Toolkit, *ACM Transactions on Information Systems*, 11(3), pp.287-317.

Shaw C, Green M (1993) The MR Toolkit Peers Package and Experiment, *Proc. IEEE Virtual Reality Annual International Symposium (VRAIS'93)*, Sept. 18-22, 1993, Seattle, Washington, USA, pp.463-469.

Singh G, Serra , Png W, Ng H (1994) BrickNet: A Software Toolkit for Network-Based Virtual Worlds, *PRESENCE: Teleoperators and Virtual Environments,* Vol.3, No.1, 1994, (to appear)

Reddy YVR, Srinivas K, Jagannathan V, Karinthi R (1993) Computer Support for Concurrent Engineering, *IEEE Computer*, 26(1):12-16

Zyda MJ, Pratt DR, Monahan JG, Wilson KP (1992) NPSNET: Constructing a 3D Virtual World, *Proc. 1992 Symposium on Interactive 3D Graphics,* 29 March - 1 April 1992, pp.147-156.